Tudor History

A Captivating Guide to the Tudors, the Wars of the Roses, the Six Wives of Henry VIII and the Life of Elizabeth I

Free Bonus from Captivating History (Available for a Limited time)

Hi History Lovers!

Now you have a chance to join our exclusive history list so you can get your first history ebook for free as well as discounts and a potential to get more history books for free! Simply visit the link below to join.

Captivatinghistory.com/ebook

Also, make sure to follow us on Facebook, Twitter and Youtube by searching for Captivating History.

Contents

Part 1: The Tudors

A Captivating Guide to the History of England from Henry VII to Elizabeth I

Introduction

Five Tudor monarchs sat on the throne of England and Ireland from 1485 to 1603. The family earned their royal rights through strategic planning and battlefield prowess, and kept them because of intellect, strength and sheer determination. The Tudors, one of England's most powerful and famous royal dynasties, knitted together a fragmented and small island nation that became one of the world's financial, colonial and technological superpowers. There is so much more to the story of these kings and queens than beheadings, political marriages and the reformation of the church – but those events remain some of the family's most enthralling moments.

Chapter 1 – The Tudors of Wales

The story of the Tudors begins in the late 12th century, when the family was neither powerful nor famous. In fact, the first Tudors were not even English, but Welsh. The Tudor dynasty traces its beginnings to Ednyfed Fychan, who was born sometime in the late 12th century. A servant of the localized North Welsh monarchy, Fychan made himself and his family indispensable to the Princes of the Kingdom of Gwynedd in Medieval Wales. Officially, he was the Court Seneschal: a soldier in charge of feasts, household ceremonies and occasional judgments within the community – essentially, a steward of the great house. Unofficially, he was the kingdom's most trusted diplomat, and ambassador to the English.

Fychan was intensely loyal to the Llywelyn monarchs of Gwynedd in Wales and was recognized as one of the kingdom's most valuable warriors. At a time when Wales and England were completely independent of one another, grievances and spontaneous land grabs were common and Wales in particular needed to be vigilant. When King John of England sent his own soldiers to conquer Welsh Llywelyn lands, Ednyfed successfully defended his country and took the heads of three English lords home to his ruler.

In thanks, Llywelyn had Ednyfed update his family coat of arms to include three helmeted heads. The Prince's loyal servant received lordships over the lands of Brynffanigl and Criccieth, and was also named Chief Justice of the realm. Ednyfed Fychan was a highly-valued man due to his defense of the kingdom and his work within it. In addition to his estates, titles and royal favors, the most telling gift was his status as a tax-free landowner. At a time when Llywelyn was consolidating the Northern Welsh kingdoms and establishing a system of feudalism throughout the land, tax-free status was only granted to royal family members, clergy and born nobility. Fychan's line of descent was granted the same land rights as the most noble courtier; this was his true entrance into the aristocracy.

To further embed himself and his progeny into the political fabric of the region, Ednyfed Fychan married Princess Gwenllian from South Wales. Through the marriage, Ednyfed became cousins with Llywelyn himself – thus beginning the march of his ancient family towards its own throne. Gwenllian gave birth to six sons, all of whom followed in their father's political footsteps by serving the Kingdom of Gwynedd. The Tudors were largely soldiers and diplomats whose work took them into the English kingdoms of East Anglia and Wessex regularly. The family became very well known in England, enjoying a noble reception at the courts of kings.

Ednyfed's grandson, Tudur Hen, was the first bearer of the famous Welsh name that would eventually be anglicized into "Tudor". Tudur Hen was the Lord of Penmynydd in Anglesey, North Wales. This stronghold was home to several generations of Tudors, including one of particular importance to the royal dynasty: Owain Tudur.

Owain ap Maredud ap Tudur was born between 1390 and 1400. By the 15th century, the Tudur given name had become a formal part of the family's surname, so that when Owain traveled to England he was called Owen Tudor. Owen was a credit to his forebears in every way, except that he used his political drive to the benefit of England instead of his ancestral Wales. Where his father had supported the

Welsh revolt against England, Owen Tudor instead sought his fortunes with the powerful oppressor of his homeland.

He ingratiated himself with Henry V, the contemporary English ruler from the house of Lancaster, and became as necessary to the English king as his ancestor had been to the Prince of Gwynedd. Many of the stories of Owen Tudor and King Henry V have fallen into legend, but early biographers claim that the former fought in the king's army and joined the royal retinue at court in 1415 as a royal steward. Tudor is said to have served the king's wife, Queen Catherine of Valois, by bringing her meals and tasting her dishes before she ate. Medieval royalty was always paranoid about being poisoned, so their most-trusted courtiers were required to eat from the royal plates in case the food had been tampered with. Tudor's role as the queen's taster belies his history with – and fierce loyalty for – the king and his family.

When Owen Tudor joined the royal court, Henry V was beginning a massive military campaign against the French. For nearly one hundred years, the House of Plantagenet—of which Henry V was a member—had fought the House of Valois for control of France. In the fall of 1415, Henry V's outnumbered army won a dramatic victory over the French at the Battle of Agincourt. Over the next several years, Henry would go on to conquer Normandy and its capital Rouen, one of the most prosperous cities in Europe. By August of 1419, his army was at the gates of Paris.

The French were in a precarious position. They had suffered significant military defeats, and the kingdom's noble families were preoccupied with intrigue and infighting. The Duke of Burgundy, a member of the Valois family, believed an alliance with the English was in the country's best interested. He persuaded King Charles VI and Queen Isabeau to sign the Treaty of Troyes, which proclaimed Henry V, rather than their own son Charles, and Henry's future sons as the rightful heirs to the French throne. To solidify Henry's claim, he was married to Charles and Isabeau's daughter, Catherine of Valois.

Henry and Catherine's son Henry was born in December 1421, but Henry V's good fortunes were at their end. In August 1422, he died suddenly in France, leaving England with an infant king. Before dying from apparent dysentery, Henry had named his brother, John, English regent until his son was old enough to rule independently. The nine-month-old King of England was also the grandchild and heir to the reigning King Charles VI of France through his mother Catherine of Valois, and through the Treaty of Troyes. With Charles VI's death in October 1422, Henry VI inherited France, as well as England, before his first birthday.

After Henry V's death, Owen Tudor remained in service to Henry VI and his regent. His proximity to the Crown gave him ample opportunity to draw the notice of Queen Catherine, who was nine years his junior. Despite his Welsh royal blood, Tudor was still considered a simple courtier in England. Until 1432, he was not even afforded the "Rights of an Englishman." Nevertheless, Tudor and Catherine became lovers. Whether they married or not is unknown, but they had three sons: Edmund, Jaspar and Edward. There was at least one daughter, Margaret, and perhaps others—few records regarding unmarried women were kept in the fifteenth century.

In mixing his blood with that of the French heiress, Owen Tudor solidified the standing of his children and their descendants as noble and royal. However, a law had been enacted to prevent the dowager queen from remarrying without the consent of the ruling king; Henry VI could not officially consent until he reached the age of sixteen. Therefore, when Catherine died young in 1437, Owen Tudor was arrested and jailed for breaking this law.

Two years later, Owen Tudor received a royal pardon and was given his lands and titles back by King Henry VI, who had reached the age of majority. He also was gifted an annual pension of forty pounds and remained a vital part of the English king's household until 1450. A decade later, he returned to Wales to fight in the Wars of the Roses on the side of the ruling Lancasters. At the Battle of Mortimer's Cross, Tudor was captured and brought before Edward of

York. Expecting merely to be taken hostage, Tudor realized moments before his beheading that he was going to die. His last words were rather romantic:

"That hede shalle ly on the stocke that wass wonte to ly on Quene Katheryns lappe. [sic]"

Chapter 2 – The Wars of the Roses

Owen Tudor could not have predicted that the war which took his life would, one day, make kings of his descendants. His two sons who lived to adulthood, Edmund and Jasper, were treated well by King Henry VI, their half-brother. Edmund, the elder brother, was made the first Earl of Richmond in 1452. But it was Edmund's marriage to twelve-year-old Margaret Beaufort in 1455 that would set the Tudors on the path to the crown.

In 1437, Henry VI reached age sixteen and assumed responsibility for England. He displayed a true desire for his role as monarch; however, his character and beliefs about the kingdom differed from his father's. Henry, like many kings before him, was burdened by the Hundred Years' War between England and France. During Henry VI's regency period, the English had lost traction in France. Instead of ramping up military efforts as was the advice of his council, the king wanted to foster a new era of peace between the nations.

The king was convinced that, in order to begin a time of peace with France, he should marry the niece of French King Charles VII,

Margaret of Anjou. The bride was fifteen years old when she married the thirty-four-year-old King of England in 1445. Though young, Margaret was focused and political. She made sure that her new husband followed through on his promise to transfer the French province of Maine back to the French crown.

The land transfer was a divisive issue among the English nobility, which had already grown fragmented during the childhood of their boy-king. But by 1450, a far more pressing issue had emerged: after five years of marriage, Henry VI still had no heir. To make matters worse, the king struggled with bouts of insanity. With a weak king and no obvious heir, several candidates for the throne began jockeying for power.

Two families—the Beauforts and the Yorks—could both trace their ancestry to Edward III, who had ruled England from 1327 to 1377. As members of the House of Plantagenet, both families held claim to the throne. Like Henry VI, the Beauforts belonged to the Lancastrian line, and aligned themselves with the king. Richard of York, however, saw in the king's illness an opportunity to expand his own power. In 1453, Margaret was finally pregnant, but Henry's instability prevented him from governing. Richard successfully maneuvered to make himself Lord Protector—essentially, the regent of England during Henry's incapacity.

Henry had sufficiently improved by 1455 to arrange a promising marriage for Edmund Tudor. Margaret Beaufort had previously been married at the age of 9 to John de la Pole, but this political pairing was annulled to allow for the match between Henry's Tudor half-brother and the daughter of his cousin and prominent ally: John Beaufort, 1st Duke of Somerset. Almost immediately after the marriage, Edmund Tudor departed for a diplomatic mission to Wales. The visit was successful until, back in England, the political strife between the Lancasters and the Yorks erupted into military conflict at the Battle of St. Albans. Richard of York claimed victory over the royal army, led by Margaret Beaufort's uncle Edward. King

Henry was captured, and Richard cemented his power as Lord Protector.

The War of the Roses had begun. For over thirty years, the Lancaster and York families battled each other for the throne of England. The name of the war is a poetic reference to the emblems of both parties: the red rose of the Lancasters and the white rose of the Yorks.

Edmund Tudor was an early casualty of the war. Soon after the Battle of St. Albans, Richard's son Edward York sent thousands of troops into Wales to assert his authority. Edmund was captured and imprisoned and died shortly thereafter of the bubonic plague. The same Edward of York would order Owen Tudor's beheading in 1460.

Upon Edmund's death, young Margaret Beaufort, Countess of Richmond and Derby, became a thirteen-year-old widow. Two months later, on January 28, 1457, she became the mother of the future Tudor king. The infant Henry was directly related to the Welsh royal houses through his paternal grandfather Owen Tudor, the French House of Valois through his paternal grandmother Catherine of Valois, and the English ruling Lancasters of the House of Plantagenet through his mother; in terms of bloodlines, Henry Tudor was a genuine candidate for the English throne.

Unlike his half-uncle Henry VI, Henry Tudor would be no boy-king. In the first three decades of his life, four other men claimed the throne. After a second battle at St. Albans—in which Edward of York, like his father before him, claimed victory—Henry VI fled to Scotland with Margaret, and Edward assumed the throne as Edward IV. In 1470, Margaret forged a secret alliance with two of Edward IV's main supporters, allowing her husband to regain his throne. But Henry's victory was short-lived; the following year, the king was captured by Yorkist soldiers and imprisoned in the Tower of London. He died there one month later, presumably murdered on the order of Edward IV, who had regained power.

Edward retained the throne until his death in 1483, when his son, Edward V, replaced him. The younger Edward was captured by the followers of Richard III, Edward IV's brother, and disappeared at the age of twelve. Despite the fact that both Edward and Richard were of the House of York, the latter decided to seize the throne for his own purposes, not that of the York cause.

Richard III installed himself as the King of England in 1483, but his grasp on the throne was uneasy. Henry Tudor, among thousands of others, had mourned not only the loss of his friend, Henry VI, but the loss of the Lancastrian line. After the death of Henry's son Edward of Westminster in 1471, the Lancaster family was without heirs, making a Yorkish king the only sensible option for England.

Unless, of course, there were one more option that had heretofore been overlooked: the legitimate claim of Henry Tudor. With no Lancaster to fight for, Henry let the idea of kingship ruminate in his brain for fourteen years, which he spent in the relative safety of Brittany. After the death of twelve-year-old Edward V, Tudor decided it was time to heed his mother's advice and pursue the throne for himself.

Tudor traveled westward, gathering an army as he did so. In his birth country, Tudor found immense support for his bid to the throne. Henry already possessed the Lancastrian bloodline necessary to challenge Richard of York, but he made his potential kingship even more enticing for the English when he promised to make a York woman his queen. When he met Richard III and the York soldiers on the battlefield at Bosworth Field, Henry had amassed 5,000 soldiers for his cause. In addition, his army was supplied by Brittany and France.

On the 22nd of August, 1485, the Tudor and York armies met between Leicester and Market Bosworth in England. The royal army outnumbered Tudor's by an estimated 3,000 soldiers, but Richard didn't count on the treason of two of his trusted men: Lord Stanley and his brother, Sir William Stanley. Perhaps he should have, since the former was married to none other than Margaret Beaufort, Henry Tudor's own mother. When the battle began, Lord Stanley remained inactive, while his brother joined directly with the opposing Tudor ranks.

Even so outnumbered, the Tudor army managed to out maneuver their opposition. Richard fought fiercely, gunning for his primary foe straight from the beginning of the battle. Before he could engage Henry with his sword, however, the Tudor army surrounded and killed the king.

With Richard dead, Henry Tudor proudly pronounced himself the King of England. True to his word, he married Elizabeth of York, thus joining the warring families of York and Lancaster together on the throne. The Battle of Bosworth Field was the final major battle of the Wars of the Roses. The triumph inspired a lengthy poem in praise of King Henry VII and those who helped his cause:

"Sir Perciuall Thriball, the other hight,
& noble Knight, & in his hart was true;
King Richards standard hee kept vpright
vntill both his leggs were hewen him froe;

the ground he wold neuer lett itt goe,
whilest the breath his brest ws within;
yett men pray ffor the Knights 2
that euer was soe true to their King.

then they moued to a mountaine on height,
with a lowde voice they cryed king HENERY,
the crowne of gold that was bright,
to the Lord stanley deliuered itt bee. [sic]"

To commemorate the end of three decades of civil war, King Henry VII created his new emblem: the Tudor rose, with red and white petals. It was the beginning of the infamous Tudor dynasty that would see England into the modern age.

Chapter 3 – Catherine of Valois, Mother of the Tudor Dynasty

Catherine of Valois was born to Charles VI, King of France, and Isabella of Bavaria in 1401 in Paris. She was educated at a convent outside of the capital city and provided with religious texts throughout her childhood. Daughter of a great monarchy, she was considered an important bargaining chip in European politics – particularly with regard to England.

While Catherine was still a child, her parents seriously considered betrothing her to the English Prince of Wales, Henry Plantagenet (Lancaster), but the English king died in 1413, before negotiations could be settled. Of his own volition, young Henry decided to pursue the marriage once more after he ascended the throne. Having never met Catherine, his interest in her was purely political and aimed at consolidating England with several English-occupied regions of France.

As the marriage talks continued, so too did Henry V's military campaigns in France. The English king recaptured Agincourt, a much-contested piece of land in the north-eastern part of modern France. Much was made of Henry's accomplishments abroad and all his successors would try to find similar glory for themselves, only to be disappointed. Once he had captured the region in the name of England in October of 1415, King Henry V put his energy into reaching a peaceful agreement with France that would be to his own benefit.

Charles VI of France eventually agreed to Henry's terms of peace, including that the English king would be named heir to the throne of France. In order for this incredible stipulation to make sense for the Valois family, Charles arranged for his daughter to marry Henry V and become the Queen of England. She did so in France on June 2, 1420, at the age of nineteen. Once the newlyweds arrived in England, King Henry started planning a lavish coronation ceremony for Catherine that took place in February of the next year.

Despite having achieved so much with France, Henry V went back to the mainland to push for even more land. He died from illness while abroad, leaving the English throne to his infant son who was less than a year old. Catherine of Valois was widowed at the age of 21 and given the relationship between herself, France and England; she probably expected to rule England as regent for her tiny son Henry VI. Such an arrangement would have made a lot of sense; Catherine was the boy's only remaining parent and she strengthened the ties between her son and the French throne. However, Henry V, after becoming very ill, had designated his brother, Humphrey of Lancaster, as Lord Protector over the child king. Henry V's other brother, John of Lancaster, was appointed Regent of France.

There are two possibilities when it comes to explaining why Henry VI's mother was overlooked as regent. The first is that Catherine was simply too French to be considered an appropriate regent over England. Though the two countries had reached an important agreement at that point, it was still possible that Catherine and her father, King Charles VI, might overturn the original treaty and make England a political annex of France.

The second reason is that Catherine's father was a known sufferer of mental illness. He displayed a number of symptoms of delusion, including the tendency to race from room to room insisting that enemies were pursuing him. He also forgot about the existence of his wife and children from time to time and believed that he was made of glass. This sickness ran in his family and would affect Henry VI, Catherine's own son. Perhaps, to Henry V, it was unwise to leave the two kingdoms in the hands of a family whose most remarkable virtue was that of madness. Catherine of Valois did not have any sort of mental illness herself, but it would have been an easy issue to bring up if she were given any sort of real power over King Henry VI.

So, upon the death of her husband the king, Catherine became the Dowager Queen of England. In title she was the most noble mother of the king but, in reality, Catherine struggled to find firm footing in a country that was not her own. She was still young, attractive, and of royal blood, so suitors were not in short supply. The man she chose, however, was something of a surprise. Catherine chose to marry the man who'd been one of her closest servants: Owen Tudor.

The two became grandparents to Henry Tudor, the man who would fight King Richard III for the crown of England and end the Wars of the Roses. Perhaps unknowingly, Catherine of Valois had become part of the family who would rule England for three centuries. Her Tudor husband and children went on to defend the crown on behalf of her first son, King Henry VI, and when Henry was murdered in the Tower of London, they took control for themselves.

For Catherine, her ultimate loyalty was for her children, both Henry VI and her Tudor sons, Edmund and Jasper. Though Henry VI was weak, mentally ill, and not suited for the kingship he inherited from his royal father and grandfather, Catherine worked hard to create a strong family unit around the young king and herself. Owen and the

Tudor children rallied around their mother, their father, and the Lancaster king, who offered them favors and beneficial marriages when he was able.

It was because of this secondary family unit, centered around Catherine of Valois, that the Tudor dynasty had the bloodlines and the familial strength to take over from the Plantagenet line of kings. Due to the need of the displaced French princess to forge her way ahead and make a stable life for herself, Queen Catherine was a formidable Tudor woman without whom the bulk of English history would be very different. If not for the character, hard work, and motherly support of Catherine of Valois, the Tudor men would not have possessed the ability to accomplish what they did.

Chapter 4 – Margaret Beaufort, Second Tudor Matriarch

The men who established the post-Plantagenet line of English kings would have done very little had it not been for the powerful, motivated women behind the scenes. Margaret Beaufort was one of the primary forces behind the formation of the powerful Tudor family within England, and the first female member of the Tudors whose ambition was channeled into their eventual rise to power.

Born around the year 1443 in Bletsoe Castle, Margaret was descended from John of Gaunt through her father, who was Gaunt's illegitimate grandson. The connection was too tenuous for Margaret or her father to claim the throne, but it was remembered nonetheless and the family was very close to King Henry VI. Margaret was the only surviving child of her father, John Beaufort, and her mother, Margaret Beauchamp, which meant that she inherited a great deal of money and land when John died. Unfortunately, since Margaret was only a baby at the time of her inheritance, her property and fortune was placed in the wardship of William de la Pole, the first Duke of Suffolk.

Margaret was used as a pawn in two marriage plots to get control of her lands and money, both of which occurred during her early childhood. To keep Beaufort's wealth in his control, William de la Pole had his son John marry Margaret sometime between the years 1444 and 1450. She was no more than three years old at the time of the wedding, but John de la Pole was probably only one year old himself. The marriage was annulled three years later when William de la Pole was killed, and King Henry VI transferred the wardship of Margaret's property to his half-brothers, Jasper and Edmund Tudor. Once more, the girl was married off to one of her patrons: Edmund Tudor. She was 12 and he was 24, and the country had just been thrown into the chaos of the civil war. Edmund fought for his half-brother's Lancastrian forces during the war, and soon after his marriage he was taken prisoner by the Yorkist army. There, he contracted the plague and died.

Margaret was a 13-year-old widow with a newborn son, the first Henry Tudor. She gave birth at her brother-in-law Jasper's residence at Pembroke, Wales, and very nearly lost her own life, as well as that of her baby. Perhaps because she was such a very young mother, and Henry an only child in his mother's care, the two were very loyal and attached to one another. Theirs was a lifelong bond which motivated Margaret to do everything in her power to ensure the best future for her son. She recognized the fact that Henry's safety lay in the hands of his Tudor family, who were so close to the Lancastrian king, and she forever sang the praises of her lost husband, Edmund.

Due to her trust in the Tudor's best intentions for their young relation, Margaret peacefully allowed her young son to remain with family in Wales. There, he was among his ancestral countrymen and far away from the violence and uncertainty of the ongoing Wars of the Roses.

Despite her foresworn loyalty to Edmund and his relations, Margaret married a third time, one year after the birth of Henry. This time, her husband was Henry Stafford, a member of the nobility some 20 years Margaret's senior. She was still a teenager at the time of her third wedding. Possibly due to the difficult labor she'd experienced with Henry, Margaret had no children with Henry Stafford. She did, however, enjoy a reasonably stable marriage to her third husband. She took over the administration of her inherited lands and received Woking Palace from King Henry VI.

Pragmatism alone was an excellent reason to keep young Henry Tudor in Wales, but there was another motive behind the decision. Stafford, oddly, did not support the Lancastrian cause and instead fought for the Yorkists. Margaret perhaps played the role of dutiful Yorkist wife in an effort to keep her enemies – and the enemies of her son – close. When Stafford died fighting for Edward York at the Battle of Barnet, Margaret quickly married for a fourth time to Thomas Stanley. In marrying another York favorite, the Tudor mother gained the ability to serve at the court of England's first York king, Edward IV, and after his death, the court of Richard III.

At court, Margaret kept her eyes and ears open. She was taking care of Henry from afar by staying abreast of the gossip and news from the changing English royals. She found the co-conspirator she needed in Elizabeth Woodville, the widow of Edward IV and mother of the princes presumed murdered by usurper Richard III. The two women both had significant reasons to desire the overthrow of the new king and soon became embroiled in an elaborate and dynamic plot.

The two women are historically implicated in Buckingham's Rebellion of October 1483, as well as the idea to marry Henry Tudor to a York princess. The rebellions were unsuccessful but the marriage plan was not. Margaret and Elizabeth both wanted to play up Henry Tudor's Lancastrian bloodline to boost him to the throne, but they were smart enough to realize one bloodline alone wouldn't be enough to put an end to the constant succession of kings or rebellions. Henry needed to marry into the York family to create the perfect mixture of Lancaster and York.

Margaret Beaufort was not the only one who believed in such a plan. In fact, Richard III was rumored to have seriously considered marrying Elizabeth of York after the death of his wife Anne. It would have served him well in terms of consolidating his power with that of his dead brother, but his plan lacked the vital element that Margaret, Elizabeth Woodville, and the Tudor family's featured: the connection of the two Plantagenet bloodlines. Furthermore, Elizabeth and her daughter would have been disgusted at the idea of marriage to Richard III – he was the younger Elizabeth's uncle, and believed to be the murderer of her young brothers.

The Tudors and the widowed Queen Elizabeth Woodville, with full support of Margaret despite her marriage to a Yorkist, put together fresh armies prior to the Battle of Bosworth. Jasper and Henry Tudor had significant support from France and Wales that bolstered their numbers, and Margaret's husband failed to declare loyalty to either side. Since he was traditionally a York supporter, this was a great success for Margaret and Henry's coup. The plan succeeded, and it was Margaret Beaufort's husband, Lord Stanley, who placed Richard III's lost crown upon the head of his stepson. Both Margaret and Elizabeth had succeeded in placing their children on the throne of England.

With Henry Tudor proclaimed King of England, Margaret's life improved greatly. She was granted titles and authority by her son and called "My Lady the King's Mother" at court. Henry's Parliament allowed her to own lands in her own right, separate from her husband, and even act as a judge in the northern part of the realm. She enjoyed every freedom and luxury during the latter half of her life and remained exceptionally close to the son she'd helped to achieve such greatness. As an older woman, Margaret tired of married life and took a vow of chastity with the Catholic Church. Her husband, Lord Stanley, was peaceful concerning the decision, and often visited his wife though she lived apart from him.

At the end of Margaret Beaufort's life, she was the most powerful woman in England. Her body was interred next to that of Edmund Tudor, the father King Henry VII never knew.

Chapter 5 – King Henry VII

Henry Tudor was born, like his ancestors, in Wales. His claim to the English throne was legitimate but tenuous: His royal English bloodline came from his mother instead of his father, and he was possibly illegitimate. Nevertheless, the descendant of Ednyfed Fychan of Gwynedd became King Henry VII of England and France and Lord of Ireland on the 22nd of August, 1485.

To prevent uprisings by the vanquished Yorks, the new king was fair with the remaining members of the family and their supporters. Henry spared both the life and the lands of Richard III's heir, the Earl of Lincoln. Furthermore, the king made it clear that any man who had fought alongside the Yorks would be pardoned so long as he swore an oath of loyalty.

The self-proclaimed king also recognized the wisdom of forestalling a meeting with the English parliament until he had strengthened his claim to the throne. In October of 1485, Henry celebrated his kingship with a coronation ceremony at Westminster Abby. The following January, he was married to Elizabeth of York in the same venue. These important royal tasks accomplished, King Henry VII met with his parliament and began the daily work of running the Kingdom of England and Ireland, as well as England's lands in France.

Henry immediately began to implement changes that would discourage any continuation of the Wars of the Roses. One of the first practices he outlawed was the nobility's keeping of immense livery and maintenance staff. Such staff were required to wear the emblem of their noble employer and often displayed fierce loyalty to their lord's house. Henry had witnessed many uprisings over the previous thirty years, many due to the fact that a potential candidate for the throne could quickly gather an army of his friend's staff. His claim to the throne insecure, Henry cut off these potential armies at their source.

In addition to stripping the aristocracy of their excessive staff, Henry VII brought in much stricter taxation laws and means of collection. There was very little the nobility could do to avoid this increased taxation: Henry's laws stated that if a noble house spent excessively, it must be able to afford higher taxes. On the other hand, law also stated that if a noble house spent little, it could also afford higher taxes because its income must be saved. In this way, Henry VII refilled the royal coffers and eventually calmed the incessant rebellions of nobles who believed they had a legitimate claim to the throne.

This restriction of the nobility was one of the most important strategies the king employed during his reign. There were, nevertheless, continued uprisings in the first years of Henry's reign. Various claimants to the English and Irish thrones gathered supporters and attacked Henry's armies over the course of the next decade. In 1486, 1487, 1491, 1495 and 1497 the king was forced to protect himself from would-be usurpers, many of whom had blood ties to previous kings just as he did. Henry VII crushed every attempt to steal his throne and continually passed legislation that made it more difficult for any faction of the nobility to hold enough power and staff to challenge him. To further stabilize the kingdom and his position, Henry created the King's Council. These council members were all appointed by the king himself, and therefore a separate entity than the existing English Parliament. Though Henry realized the necessity of meeting with the Parliament, which was essentially a gathering of noble heads of household, he did so as infrequently as possible. Unlike today, the monarchs of the 15th and 16th centuries could wait years before summoning a Parliamentary meeting. Henry VII preferred to confer with his own council, half clergy and half nobility, while making decisions. The Parliament was generally only necessary when the king wanted to change taxation laws.

Henry's council, unlike Parliament, met frequently. There were as many as 150 councilors at any given time, though slow transportation typically restricted meeting size to about 40 members. As Henry's reign progressed, he sought out the most educated and knowledgeable of his kingdom to join the council. The king required the best minds to assist him with questions of law, feudal land disputes, taxation, finance and myriad other categories of monarchal administration. The nobility was understandably disgruntled by the shifting balance of power in the kingdom, but it was the King's Council that kept Henry better-informed than any recent king.

To maintain his authority outside of London and major cities, Henry appointed a Justice of the Peace in each county to act as local law enforcement. The job was unpaid, but the stature and power involved appealed to members of the nobility. This kingdom-wide network of law and order was unprecedented.

As Henry brought the most serious in-fighting amongst English nobility to an end, he began to turn his attention to important matters beyond England's shores. Like his predecessor, Henry VI, Henry Tudor wanted peace and prosperity for his kingdom. In the late 15th century, this meant directing his foreign policy towards Spain and France.

The latter half of the 15th century was a tumultuous period on the Iberian peninsula. The marriage of Isabella I of Castille and Ferdinand II of Aragon in 1469 united Iberia's two most powerful Christian kingdoms and provided the framework for expansion. Isabella and Ferdinand were a power couple. In 1478, they conquered the Canary Islands. In January 1492 they oversaw the conclusion of the Reconquista with the victory over the Emirate of Granada, the last Muslim kingdom in Iberia. Later that month, they funded Christopher Columbus' voyages to the west, the first steps towards the creation of a massive Spanish empire in the Americas.

Henry VII wanted to cement a positive relationship with the new Kingdom of Spain as soon as possible. In 1489, he entered into an agreement with Isabella and Ferdinand that saw his eldest son, Arthur, married to their eldest daughter, Catherine. In addition, the Treaty of Medina del Campo promised that England would come to Spain's aid against France, if ever the need arose.

Henry's dealings with France, just three years later, were somewhat problematic given his prior agreements with Spain. Though the ruler of England believed himself to inherit the French throne, most England's holdings in France had been lost by the time Henry VII became king. Since England and Ireland were struggling financially, the king proposed a solution to the problems of war and money with one document: The Peace of Etaples. The treaty was signed by Henry Tudor and French King Charles VIII on November 3, 1492. The Peace of Etaples signified the end of England's invasions of French lands. The English conceded French ownership of Brittany and, in exchange, France agreed to pay Henry 742,000 crowns at the rate of 50,000 crowns per year. It was a huge financial win for Henry, who in signing the document increased the annual income of the crown by 50 percent. Henry's diplomatic skill led to a comfortable co-existence with France for the remainder of his reign.

The last decade of Henry VII's life and rule were the most emotionally difficult. His eldest son and heir to the throne, Arthur, had married Catherine of Aragon, but died mere months after the wedding took place. Distraught, the usually placid King Henry VII wept over his son's death. One year later, the death of his wife Elizabeth led him to shut himself in his rooms for days without speaking to anyone.

Following the death of his eldest son and wife, Henry Tudor decided to leave the Tower of London, which had been their family home. His son Henry lived sporadically in the Tower, but it had generally fallen out of favor and was eventually used for everything but long-term housing for kings and queens. After Henry VII's son moved on, the Tower was used as a military base, storage center, armory, prison and tourist attraction, but never again as the home of an English monarch.

Henry remained close to his young mother for his entire life, allowing her a gentle hand at court and in royal proceedings. Addressed as My Lady the King's Mother, Margaret remarried several times after the death of Edmund Tudor, but her will declared her desire to be buried alongside her second husband.

The king died of tuberculosis on April 21, 1509, having remained unmarried after the death of Elizabeth. His mother, the young widow of Edmund Tudor who bore her son at the tender age of thirteen, died two months later. Her death came one day after the eighteenth birthday of her only living grandson, heir to the English throne: Henry VIII.

Chapter 6 – Arthur Tudor

Henry VII was a clever man who was very aware of the role symbolism played in the hearts of the English people. He was, after all, the king who created the melded Tudor rose to unite the Houses of York and Lancaster, and who married a York to compliment his Lancastrian bloodline. He wanted to create a powerful, almost mythical story around his family and his reign so that he would be respected, feared, and beloved in equal measure. With the birth of his son, Henry continued to weave together his tale, pulling a name from one of the most treasured stories in English history: King Arthur and the Knights of the Round Table.

Though Henry VIII would ultimately inherit the throne from his namesake, the eldest boy born to King Henry VII and Elizabeth of York was actually Arthur Tudor. Born in September 1486, Arthur was the first child born of the union between the York and Lancastrian lines. He enjoyed all the best that his kingly father could give him and was the first in a long succession of Tudor princes and princesses who were provided for lavishly during their childhoods.

Arthur's entire childhood was focused on two things: His education and the future marital alliance of England and Spain. The boy received the best tutors and probably the most comprehensive education any royal child had ever had in England. John Reed, Thomas Linacre, and Bernard Andre were responsible for most of the prince's studies. These and other teachers taught him Greek, Latin, writing and reading, ethics, rhetoric, and history, as well as the sports and military knowledge that were becoming of an heir to the throne of one of Europe's great monarchies. He was also very well-versed in the laws and philosophies of Roman Catholicism. Arthur was a good student whose particular aptitudes lay in Greek philosophy, dancing, and archery.

King Henry VII and his queen put a great deal of thought into the future of their eldest son, especially in terms of who might become his wife – and they did so from the moment of his birth. Catherine of Aragon was ultimately chosen as the best mate for Arthur as early as 1488 when the king signed the Treaty of Medina del Campo with Spain. The two countries agreed that Catherine of Aragon would travel to England in 1500 to marry Prince Arthur.

From the time of the betrothal until Catherine embarked upon her long trip to England, both Arthur and his future bride exchanged letters. As the boy aged, he wrote letters to his Spanish fiancée in Latin, a language that both could understand. Catherine wrote back, and at first these letters were stilted and childish. As both the future bride and groom got older, however, the letters became sweet and endearing, with both professing great love for one another. By the time the two were nearing the age of majority, they felt they knew each other quite well despite never having even set eyes upon one another.

Unlike his younger brother Henry, Arthur was a tall and lean boy with a gentle nature. He was not as athletically-inclined as Henry but was still considered fit and handsome by his contemporaries. He had reddish hair like his brother, a trait that is still considered a common family attribute within the English royal family. A contemporary portrait painted when Arthur was probably a teenager shows him with shoulder-length reddish-brown hair, pale skin and brown or hazel eyes.

Prince Arthur was not only a potential political tool in terms of marriage, but in terms of the variety of royal titles and duties he could hold within his own kingdom. His foremost role was as the Prince of Wales. King Henry VII and his family had their roots in Wales, which made him want to cement his ties there first and foremost. The Tudor Royal Coat of Arms was designed with a red dragon on the left side of the field of Tudor roses, a clear nod to Henry's proud Welsh lineage since that part of the realm had used a dragon as its emblem since at least the 9th century. Henry VII made Arthur the Prince of Wales so that his Welsh neighbors felt connected and respected by their former countryman. As a child, the title pinned to Arthur Tudor was mostly for show, but after he became married his father planned for him to occupy Wales personally. Jasper Tudor, Arthur's uncle, oversaw the administration of the cooperative realms of Wales until that time. It was an important and strategic move on the part of Henry VII. During his reign, entire ancient kingdoms within Wales kneeled to the authority of England.

Prince Arthur had a vast household of servants from all parts of the realm, Wales and Ireland included. Sons of the nobility were sent to his palace to serve their prince in a great variety of ways, including dressing and undressing him, serving his meals, keeping the fires of the palace lit, and keeping inventory of his jewelry. Many of these roles had not existed prior to the rule of Henry VII, who continually developed the proprietary rules of the king's privy chamber throughout his reign.

At one point, Arthur was served by the former Lord Deputy of Ireland following that man's treasonous promotion of Lambert Simnel, pretender to the throne. Simnel had gained a following in Ireland in the latter part of the 1480s for allegedly being the lost Prince Edward Plantagenet, son of King Edward IV. The ruse was enough to incite an uprising led by John de la Pole, Earl of Lincoln, but once Henry's forces overpowered the rebels, the boy was put to work in the kitchens of King Henry VII's castle. Similarly, the false heir's main surviving supporter in Ireland was sent to serve Arthur.

Arthur finally met his bride-to-be in 1501 at the age of 15. The couple was married at St. Paul's Cathedral in London and immediately sent to Ludlow Castle to begin their administration of Wales from the Welsh Marches. Both the young prince and his wife contracted an unidentified illness in March 1502. Catherine of Aragon survived, but in April of 1502, Arthur passed away. His father and mother were heartbroken, both breaking down in tears at the news. They gave their eldest son a magnificent funeral and had his body embalmed and entombed at Worcester Castle in England.

Chapter 7 – King Henry VIII

Henry VII's son received what may be considered the first example of a classic royal education. He learned from many top-rate tutors and could speak French, Latin and some Italian. He received many royal appointments from his father, who wanted to keep the majority of leadership roles in the family. Though young Henry wanted for nothing and enjoyed an easy childhood in comparison to his older brother Arthur, all responsibility for the future of the family and country fell to him when Arthur died unexpectedly.

When the elder Tudor son died of what was then called "sweating sickness," his marriage to Catherine of Aragon was only a few months old. Still insistent on forging a marital bond between the English and Spanish thrones, Henry VII arranged for Arthur's wedding to be annulled and for Catherine to be newly married to his son Henry. Several complications put off the marriage, but soon after his eighteenth birthday, the new King Henry VIII announced he would go ahead with the wedding.

Henry and Catherine married in June of 1509 at a small ceremony in Greenwich. Two weeks later, the couple celebrated their coronation at Westminster Abby.

Henry VIII was not cautious about beginning his rule. He was clearly of age, married and ready to fill his many palaces with a large collection of royal heirs and spares. Almost immediately after his coronation, Henry set his sights on two of his father's advisors: Richard Empson and Edmund Dudley.

Empson and Dudley had been two of the most prominent members of Henry VII's King's Council. Prominence, however, was not the same as popularity. The public despised Empson and Dudley, as they represented the high tax laws of the former King's Council. The nobility in particular blamed the men for Henry VII's tax increases. The two were charged with treason, found guilty and executed by beheading on Tower Hill.

It was exactly how Henry VIII wanted to introduce his reign. Henry believed in swift, decisive action. He wanted it made clear that he was prepared to have even those closest to him killed if necessary. Not only did the deaths of Empson and Dudley overjoy the masses, they revealed the kind of king that Henry VIII intended to be: a strong, single-minded and ruthless one.

No amount of determination could accomplish for Henry VIII one of his dearest goals: the birth of a son. Queen Catherine became pregnant almost immediately after her marriage to Henry. Sadly, their first child was a stillborn daughter. Only four months after the stillbirth, the queen was pregnant again, and this time she gave birth to a boy. In obvious Tudor fashion, he was called Henry. The much-celebrated royal child, however, only lived for a few weeks. Years passed, and Henry and Catherine experienced two more stillbirths before Princess Mary was born in 1516. She was healthy, vivacious and devoted to her parents.

King Henry had grown up with parents who loved and respected one another, and though Henry VII and Elizabeth of York experienced their share of infant loss, they produced four healthy children. Most importantly, given how lines of succession operated in the late medieval period, they produced two boys. The new King Henry had likely expected to find himself in the same situation as had his parents, but after seven years of marriage he only had one daughter. Furthermore, Queen Catherine was six years older than the king, making her 31 years old after the birth of Mary. Given the environment and time frame in which she lived, Catherine was not expected to remain fertile for much longer, and this worried the king.

With domestic issues weighing on his mind, Henry VIII tried to focus on the administration of the country's foreign affairs. His first problem was with France. Though Henry wanted peaceful relations with his neighbors, as his father had, he was also consumed with the desire to regain all of England's lost lands in France. By the time Henry VIII ascended to the throne, only Calais remained in English hands.

In the early years of Henry's reign, France was allied with the Holy Roman Empire, and therefore much too powerful to even consider provoking. Instead of making demands, Henry met with King Louis XII of France on friendly terms. Immediately afterward, he met with King Ferdinand II to establish himself as an ally of Spain. It was the same political move his father had made, except that Henry VIII intended only to bide his time, keeping peace until it better served his wishes not to do so.

Pope Julius II, meanwhile, had no such concerns about keeping the peace. He drew monarchs across Europe into his wars against his neighbors: first Venice, the once-prosperous but declining republic to the northeast of the Papal States, and later the French, who were encroaching on Lombardy to the north. As the pope's wars drew on, the European monarchs grew weary of the conflict, and anxious to regain lands they had lost along the way. A series of treaty discussions began, into which Henry VIII threw himself wholeheartedly. If European borders were to be redrawn, he wanted some of France for himself – particularly Aquitaine, which had been in English hands for three centuries until it was lost by Henry VI.

To facilitate sympathy for his cause, King Henry pledged military aid to the Pope and his allies in the event of a French attack. True to his word, he sent English troops into Italy when the French launched their counterattacks in 1513. Henry's army was strong, capturing first Therouanne, then Tournai from the French. The king was fiercely dedicated to his task, having been promised the title of "Most Christian King" by the pope himself. Henry's ultimate dream was to be crowned by the pope, in Paris, as king of France.

Meanwhile, at home, Scotland took full advantage of the fact that England's king was overseas. James IV was on the Scottish throne, with Henry's sister Margaret by his side as queen. According to the Auld Alliance of 1295, Scotland and France were pledged in friendship and service to one another. While the English king fought the French directly on the continent, James IV upheld his ancestor's part of the agreement by attacking his southern neighbor.

England was not without a leader, however, nor was she without an army. Henry had left his wife in charge during his absence, and Queen Catherine proved a very capable commander. The Scottish army was ultimately defeated and the king killed in combat before Henry VIII even returned to England.

Chapter 8 – Margaret Tudor, Sister of Henry VIII

Margaret Tudor, eldest sister of Henry VIII, was the second of Henry VII's children to be strategically matched with a foreign power. She was born in October of 1489, three years after her brother Arthur and two years before Henry. By the time she was 13 years old, Margaret was promised in marriage to King James IV of Scotland. It was an earnest attempt on the part of the English king to join England and Scotland in a peaceful union.

The girl accepted her duty as a princess of the realm and probably quite enjoyed the festivities put on by her father at the time of the proxy wedding in January of 1502. There was feasting, jousting, games, and many gifts to the young queen. She received a brand-new trousseau and Italian bed curtains to bring with her to Edinburgh in summer of 1503 for the official journey. Her friend and Maid of Honor, Lady Catherine Gordon, was also bestowed with fine new clothes befitting her station. Gordon was something of a ward of the English crown at that point, as she'd come from Scotland as the wife of pretender to the throne, Perkin Warbeck. She was one of the only servants to stay with Margaret Tudor after the long journey to Scotland, as was tradition.

Margaret's travel plans were put off until both her father and James IV had exchanged several properties named in the marriage agreement. When the time finally came to leave England, the princess' mother, Elizabeth of York, and her brother Arthur had died. The Tudor household was morose and forlorn, with King Henry struggling to pull himself out of his grief. There was precious little left of the family Margaret had grown up with and loved, a fact that must have made the northward journey particularly bittersweet. She reached the border on August 1 and traveled onward to Dalkeith Castle to rest and prepare for her formal meeting with King James IV the next day.

James, 16 years his bride's senior, was too impatient to wait to meet Margaret now that she was within riding distance. Without bothering to change into formal attire, the king set off for Dalkeith and surprised the young bride in her appointed rooms within the castle. She was dressed for the occasion in a golden dress, though James appeared to have just been hunting. They had an amicable meeting followed by supper and dancing. That night, two of Margaret's horses were killed in a fire on the grounds which sullied her mood a great deal. The king was very quick to replace her horses and gift Margaret with richly-adorned velvet saddles as well.

The royal couple rode into Edinburgh together and were married in person on the 8th of August. While Margaret settled into her new home, her official affairs (and those of England on her behalf) were conducted by the Earl of Surrey, Thomas Howard. Though Margaret was still a young girl, she had become Queen of Scotland and as such did not appreciate her business being conducted by Surrey and his wife. Shortly after the wedding, she wrote to her father to assure him all was well, and could not help alluding to her distaste at being treated like a child.

Letter from Margaret Tudor, Queen of Scots, to her father, Henry VII

"My most dear lord and father, in the most humble wise that I can think, I recommend me unto your Grace, beseeching you of your daily blessing, and that it will please you to give hardy thanks to all your servants the which by your commandment have given right good attendance on me at this time. And especially to all these ladies and gentlewomen which hath accompanied me hither, and to give credence to this good lady the bearer hereof, for I have showed her more of my mind than I will write at this time.

Sir, I beseech your Grace to be good and gracious lord to Thomas, which was footman to the Queen my mother, whose soul God have pardon; for he hath been one of my footmen hither with as great diligence and labor to his great charge of his own good and true mind. I am not able to recompense him, except the favor of your Grace.

Sir, as for news I have none to send, but that my lord of Surrey is in great favor with the King here that he cannot forbear the company of him no time of the day. He and the Bishop of Murray ordereth everything as nigh as they can to the King's pleasure. I pray God it may be for my poor heart's ease in time to come. They call not my Chamberlain to them, which I am sure will speak better for my part than any of them that be of that counsel. And if he speak anything for my cause, my lord of Surrey hath such words unto him that he dare speak no further.

God send me comfort to his pleasure, and that I and mine that be left here with me be well entreated such ways as they have taken. For God's sake, Sir, hold me excused that I write not myself to your Grace, for I have no leisure this time, but with

a wish I would I were with your Grace now, and many times more, when I would answer.

As for this that I have written to your Grace, it is very true, but I pray God I may find it well for my welfare hereafter. No more to your Grace at this time, but our Lord have you in his keeping.

Written with the hand of your humble daughter

Margaret [sic]"

Henry VII's treaty of peace lasted for the remainder of his reign, giving his daughter and King James enough time to start their family. As Margaret was only 13 years old at the time of the marriage and not necessarily physically ready to have children, the couple's first child was not born until 1507. Queen Margaret gave birth at least six times but only one of her children reached adulthood: James V, born April 10 1512.

After the death of King Henry VII in 1509, Margaret's younger brother Henry inherited the throne and was not much interested in upholding the diplomatic work accomplished by his father. Almost at once, Henry VIII embarked upon a military campaign in France which clearly overstepped the careful rules of the Treaty of Perpetual Peace that his father had signed with James IV. France and Scotland were long-time allies, so once the new English king stepped foot in France intent upon conquering the nation piecemeal, King James IV was obligated to wage war on England. He did so first by sending ships to France and then by personally leading an attack south of the border to try to capitalize on the English king's absence from his own realm. The plan went terribly wrong and James was killed at the Battle of Flodden, leaving Margaret widowed with a young son at the age of 23. The king's body was collected and embalmed but eventually lost somewhere in England.

James' will designated his wife as regent over their baby son James Stuart but stipulated that she remain a widow. She did so during the following year as she faced detractors who wanted to place John

Stuart, her husband's closest relative apart from his son, in her place as regent. Margaret kept her head and negotiated with her adopted countrymen until most of the would-be revolutionaries had lost their sense of urgency. She was at the forefront of a peace pact between Scotland, her brother's kingdom to the south, and France, which was under the rule of Louis XII.

Despite her intelligence and legitimate claim to the Scottish regency, Dowager Queen Margaret found herself alone in a position of power and struggled not to become overwhelmed. She'd been used to ruling at the side of her capable husband, not relying solely on her own counsel in all matters. She sought out a powerful companion, though perhaps not consciously.

The queen's eye fell to Archibald Douglas, a Scottish nobleman born in the same year as she was. Douglas' father had just died alongside King James IV at the Battle of Flodden, and with the death of his grandfather soon afterward, Archibald began the 6th Earl of Angus. His family was an important force within Scottish politics, which is why he came to the attention of the widowed queen. Margaret fell in love rapidly and married Douglas in a secret ceremony on August 6, 1514. When the Scottish nobility and the other members of the royal family found out about the marriage, they were extremely upset.

The first order of business for John Stuart and his supporters was to strip Margaret of her role as regent. She knew this would be a consequence of becoming someone's wife, but what she didn't expect was for the new regency's Privy Council to take away her right to be involved in her children's lives at all. Furious, she took her sons James and Alexander to Stirling Castle with some of their supporters to keep the boys out of the hands of the new regent, Duke of Albany. Douglas ran home to Forfarshire.

It was a move that caused a tug-of-war over the boy king and nearly sparked civil war throughout Scotland. John Stuart knew that his role as regent was useless if he were not in possession of little James V, but he couldn't simply send an army to Stirling and knock down the door, since such a move would endanger the life and wellbeing of the young king. In the summer of 1515, however, the Duke of Albany received both the Stuart children into his custody after Margaret discovered she was pregnant and vulnerable. Her brother, King Henry VIII of England, wrote to her with great concern and begged her to return to his kingdom so he could ensure her safety. Once the boys were out of her custody, she met with her husband and did just that.

It was August of 1515 when Margaret and Archibald arrived in the north of England. In October of the same year, the Dowager Queen gave birth to a daughter, Margaret Douglas, at Harbottle Castle, Northumberland. A few months after delivering her healthy baby girl, Margaret learned that her youngest son, Alexander, had died under the protection of John Stuart. He was not quite two years of age. Margaret was further entrenched in misery when Archibald left her to return to Scotland and beg the Earl of Albany for forgiveness. He was forgiven and took up with a new woman, the Lady Jane of Traquair. Margaret was down, but not beaten. She remained in England for several years and bided her time, only being allowed to visit with her son once. When her son turned 12, she seized a chance to regain her authority and power.

The Scottish Regent traveled to France in 1524 to oversee his troops' performance in the ongoing Italian Wars. While he was gone, young King James V turned 12 and was considered by many to be of a sufficient age to rule the kingdom without the guidance of a regent. The time was right for Margaret, who re-entered Scotland, met up with her allied families, and took her son from Stirling Palace to Edinburgh. Parliament met in the summer and officially declared James V the undisputed, independent leader of Scotland. A winter Parliament recognized Margaret Tudor Stuart's right to act as an advisor to her royal son. After his deposition by Parliament, the Earl of Albany remained mostly in France.

While the ousted regent backed down peacefully, the Earl of Angus, Margaret's estranged husband, did not. He'd had another daughter with his mistress and forsaken his wife politically. He'd been charged with treason and exiled to France but escaped to England where Margaret's brother eventually allowed him to return to Scotland. Margaret did not respond positively. When Angus attempted to join the Parliament upon his return to his own country, she actually fired cannons in his direction.

Margaret was unable, ultimately, to keep her husband out of parliamentary proceedings, nor was she immediately able to obtain a divorce. Douglas took full advantage of his leeway and kidnapped his step-son James V. Angus kept control of the king for three years, acting as the major power behind the crown until 1528, when the fifteen-year-old king forcibly removed himself from the custody of his self-appointed protector. The same year, Margaret was granted a divorce from the Pope. She married Henry Stuart, another relation to her first husband, and was welcomed back to court by her son.

Once he'd obtained the throne for himself and could act as he saw fit, King James V embraced the advice and nearness of his oft-estranged mother. Probably as a kindness to Margaret, James named her new husband Lord Methven. Together, the family arranged peace once more between Scotland and England by the year 1534. Four years later, King James V married Mary of Guise, a girl who was very friendly with her husband's mother.

There were no more political upheavals during Margaret Tudor's lifetime, though her third husband took up with a mistress and fell very much out of her favor. She was not granted a second divorce, and so continued to reside often at Methven Castle. In 1541 at the age of 41, the Dowager Queen of Scotland died at home at Methven. She was interred at the Perth Charterhouse. Her son had been summoned shortly before her death but arrived too late to make his farewells. He had his mother's belongings packed up from her husband's house and delivered to his own residence.

Margaret's only other surviving child was Margaret Douglas, who lived a long life and enjoyed a close relationship with her uncle

Henry VIII. She married Matthew Stuart, 4th Earl of Lennox and was grandmother to King James VI of Scotland, eventual inheritor of the English realm from Queen Elizabeth I.

Chapter 9 – Mary Tudor, Queen of France

Mary Tudor was the youngest surviving child of King Henry VII and Elizabeth of York. Born on March 18, 1596, she was brought up in her own household, which was traditional for all royal children of the era. From the age of six, Princess Mary had her own household of servants, educators and advisors. She was taught embroidery, Latin, French, music, and dancing like her sister Margaret.

From a young age, Mary was considered a beautiful and talented girl – which for a princess meant that she could be easily used in political strategies between kingdoms. An early engagement to Charles of Castile was canceled in lieu of a peace treaty crafted by her brother's advisor, Cardinal Wolsey. She didn't have long to wait before Henry and his council found their ideal use for her as the third wife to the elderly French King Louis XII. France and England were in a constant state of rivalry, particularly over Calais and many other regions on the continent that had changed hands between them more than a few times. A marital match between the French and English crowns stood to accomplish much for both parties.

King Henry VIII's little sister was 18 years old when she set out to France to marry King Louis, a match 34 years her senior. She was accompanied across the English Channel by Lady Joan Guildford and four younger ladies-in-waiting, one of whom was Mary Boleyn. Once the party reached Paris, Mary's retinue was joined by Anne Boleyn. On the 9th of October 1514, Mary Tudor married King Louis XII at Abbeville before moving with her new husband to the court at Paris. She'd already had a proxy wedding at her brother's palace in England, as was tradition. There had been a lavish party in August of 1514, two months before the couple met face to face. The royals and their guests had a wonderful time, Mary dressed in her finest new clothes, and the French Duc de Longueville acted as proxy for his king. The two even climbed into a bed together so Longueville could touch Mary with his unclothed leg – simulating marital consummation.

At 52 years of age, King Louis had no living sons and still harbored hopes that he may yet beget a son with his young English wife. When Louis died three months after the wedding, the French court laughed that he must have overdone himself in the marital bed, though given his age and ongoing battle with gout, it was more likely the latter that ended his life. Whatever the reason for Louis' death, it signaled freedom and relief for Mary, now Dowager Queen of France.

Before the young girl could go home to England, however, she had to wait and see if she'd become pregnant with an heir to France. At the bidding of the Francis I, cousin to the deceased king, Mary stayed in isolation for six weeks to determine whether or not Louis had impregnated her. When it was clear she was not growing a French heir in her womb, Francis I officially took over the throne of France and Mary was cleared to leave.

In England, Henry VIII sent one of his closest friends, the newly-created Duke of Suffolk (Charles Brandon), to collect his sister and bring her home. It was a risky move since Henry knew full well that Mary was in love with Brandon, but the king trusted the latter not to make anything of it. The King made Brandon promise not to be charmed by Mary and urged him simply to ensure her safety on the voyage back to England. Suffolk promised and set off to do as he was bid.

Henry and Charles had a particularly special friendship because they had spent part of their childhoods in the same household. At the Battle of Bosworth, at which Henry VII had defeated Richard III and taken the English throne, it was Brandon's father who had borne the Tudor standard. William Brandon was killed during the battle, so the first Tudor king had Brandon's son Charles educated with his own children. As adults, Henry and Charles had a very familial and trusting relationship. It was for exactly this reason Brandon was entrusted with the most delicate and personal of tasks on the part of Henry VIII.

When Mary's traveling companion arrived in France, Francis I had questions about the future of the Dowager Queen of his country. The French king wondered what the future would hold for this girl who was still very young and politically valuable. He wanted to know if she required another marriage within France, and if so how he could help. There were discussions of perhaps arranging a wedding between Mary and Antoine, Duke of Lorraine, or Charles III, Duke of Savoy.

Mary did indeed have marriage in mind, but it was to no one in France or on the continent. She told Francis that she wanted to marry Charles Brandon and said she would be very grateful for his blessing in doing so. Since the French king saw no reason such a marriage shouldn't go forward, he made all the arrangements. Charles, for his part, was surprised at how far his secret betrothal had gone without him knowing a thing about it. Mary was adamant, however, and she knew very well that he'd married his first two wives solely for ambitious purposes. Her instincts were good, since Charles could surely do no better than an English princess and a French queen. More than that, the two had a history together thanks to Henry VII and were probably very comfortable with one another. Worse marriages had been arranged without the knowledge of one of the parties.

Though Mary wrote to her brother asking for his blessing, Henry didn't have time to respond in the negative before she and Charles went through with the wedding. It took place on March 3, 1515, in the presence of King Francis I and only nine other witnesses.

King Henry was not amused. At a time when the nobility required the permission of the king to marry, it was incredibly disobedient and insulting of his sister and friend to do such a thing. Whether he approved of the match or not, Henry was an egotistical king who certainly resented not having been consulted properly.

He wrote angry letters to both his sister and the Duke of Suffolk, remonstrating them for moving so quickly in a foreign land and without so much as his knowledge, let alone his consent. His sister wrote back, reminding Henry that he had promised her she could marry whomever she pleased after the old French king died. She appealed to his brotherly love and asked forgiveness.

Letter from Mary Queen-Dowager of France to Henry VIII:

"My most dear and entirely beloved brother,

In most humble manner, I recommend me to your grace.

Dearest brother, I doubt not but that you have in your good remembrance that whereas for the good of peace and for the furtherance of your affairs you moved me to marry with my lord and late husband, King Louis of France, whose soul God pardon. Though I understood that he was very aged and sickly, yet for advancement of the said peace and for the furtherance of your causes, I was contented to conform myself to your said motion, so that if I should fortune to survive the said late king I might have affixed and clearly determined myself to marry with him; and the same [I] assure you hath proceeded only of mine own mind, without any request or labour of my said lord Suffolk, or of any other person. And to be plain with your grace, I have so bound myself unto him that for no cause earthly I will or may vary or change from the same. Wherefore my good and most kind brother, I now beseech your grace to take this matter in good part, and to give unto me and to my said lord of Suffolk your good will herein. Ascertaining you, that upon the trust and comfort which I have, for that you have always honourably regarded your promise, I am now come out of the realm of France, and have put myself within your jurisdiction in this your town of Calais, where I intend to remain till such time as I shall have answer from you of your good and loving mind herein; which I would not have done but upon the faithful trust that I have in your said promise. Humbly beseeching your grace, for the great and tender love which ever hath been and shall be between you and me, to bear your gracious mind and show yourself to be agreeable thereunto, and to certify me by your most loving letters of the same till which time I will make mine abode here, and no farther enter your realm. And to the intent it may please you the rather to condescend to this my most hearty desire, I am contended and expressly promise and bind me to you, by these presents, to give you all the whole dote which delivered with me, and also all such plate of gold and jewels as I shall have of my said late husband's. Over and besides this I shall, rather than fail, give you as much yearly part of my dower, to as great a sum as shall stand with your will and pleasure; and of all the premises I promise, upon knowledge of your good mind, to make unto you sufficient bonds. Trusting, verily, that in fulfilling of your said promise to me made, you will show your brotherly love, affection, and good mind to me in this behalf, which to hear of I abide with most desire; and not to be miscontented with

my said lord of Suffolk, whom of mine inward good mind and
affection to him I have in manner enforced to be agreeable to
the same, without any request by him made; as knoweth our
Lord, whom I beseech to have your grace in his merciful
governance. [sic]"

Charles Brandon also wrote to his friend, the king, apologetically. He had no particular excuses and simply stated that he knew he'd upset Henry but that he didn't truly expect much to come of it. His overconfidence in his friend probably didn't help the situation, because the newly-married couple decided to stay in Calais until Henry's mood lightened.

Technically, Charles Brandon had committed treason by marrying a royal princess without the king's consent. There were those among the king's council who wanted him to be put to death, or at least imprisoned. Henry decided to fine the couple. He charged them an astonishing 24,000 pounds for their recklessness, confiscated the 200,000-pound dowry Mary had received from King Louis XII and took all the traditional marriage gifts Mary had received from the French king. In Mary's letter, she handed the money and plates – a customary marriage gift, for fine dining sets were expensive – over to her brother happily.

The costs of the fine itself were insurmountable. Henry agreed to let Mary and Charles pay 1000 pounds per year for their rights to return to his court and continue on in their privileged lives as before. Of course, Mary and Charles agreed, however even wealthy nobles could not afford such annual payments. After the first part of the debts were paid, a second wedding was arranged at Greenwich Palace in the presence of King Henry VIII and his courtiers. The English ceremony took place on May 13, 1515, after which both the bride and the groom were soon back in the good graces of King Henry.

Mary Tudor was Brandon's third wife, so upon their marriage she became stepmother to two girls named Anne and Mary. She spent most of her time with the girls and her own children at Westhorpe Hall in Suffolk, though Brandon was often in London at court with Henry. The couple had two daughters, Francis and Eleanor, and a son named for his father.

Though she was referred to as the French Queen for the rest of her life, Mary Tudor Brandon lived the life of a Duchess of Suffolk. She raised her children, cared for the household and attended important events at her brother's court from time to time. Having already been acquainted with Mary and Anne Boleyn when the sisters had attended her in France, Henry's sister had developed a strong disliking of Anne that resurfaced in the 1530s. As King Henry distanced himself permanently from Queen Catherine of Aragon and attempted to make Anne Boleyn his wife, Mary spoke out against her brother's mistress. There was only so much displeasure and anger she could allow herself, however, since Henry had graciously lowered her debts and was responsible for her financial wellbeing.

In 1528, Mary contracted the sweating sickness, a little-understood disease of the time. The symptoms of the illness came on rapidly in its victims, beginning with the feeling of cold, shivering, and light-headedness. After an hour or so of cold, those infected began to sweat heavily and suddenly. An oppressive feeling of heat then followed, as well as thirst, headache and delirium. Often, victims of the sweating sickness died within hours of the first symptoms. If they survived, they had not gained immunity, since people could contract the same illness again and again.

Mary survived her ordeal but was never fully healthy afterward. It has been theorized that perhaps the Duchess of Suffolk suffered from a form of cancer or heart disease that was exacerbated by her bout with the sweating sickness. Six months after her brother married Anne Boleyn, Mary died at her home in Suffolk.

The French Queen was beloved by many and her death resonated throughout England and France. At her funeral, a French delegation attended to offer their condolences. Both her biological and stepchildren jostled for position behind her casket as it made its way to the abbey. Mary's was interred at Bury St. Edmonds Abbey in Surrey, then later moved to St. Mary's Church when Henry had the monasteries dissolved. Since custom forbade a monarch or a grieving spouse to attend a funeral, neither Charles nor Henry were present at her final ceremony.

Her children were integral to the future of the royal court – particularly Frances Brandon. She was born on July 16, 1517, in Hertfordshire but she spent the bulk of her childhood at the Brandon home in Suffolk. Unlike many children of noble parents, Francis and her siblings were raised together in the same household as their mother. All the Brandon children received a good education just as their father and mother had at the pleasure of King Henry VII. Francis visited her uncle Henry's court in London regularly and became very fond of Queen Catherine of Aragon. She met her cousin Mary there and developed a friendship that would be lifelong. Francis married into the Grey family and was mother to de facto Queen of England, Jane Grey.

Chapter 10 – The Birth of the Church of England

Despite her military victory, Catherine continued to fail in her most essential task as queen: producing a male heir. Henry VIII respected his wife and trusted her completely, but he was not satisfied with only a daughter as an heir. Henry was adamant that he needed a son to inherit the throne of England. The Wars of the Roses ultimately stemmed from the question of whether the line of succession could pass through female descendants; Henry VIII wanted no such ambiguity to cripple the Tudors. The king grew desperate for sons.

When the king's daughter, Princess Mary Tudor, was nine years old and her mother was 40, King Henry fell in love with his wife's lady-in-waiting. Her name was Anne Boleyn, and she was of the noble birth required to serve at court. The king wrote numerous letters to Anne and sent her extravagant gifts of jewelry. Anne, however, was well aware that Henry had multiple mistresses at court – included her own sister, Mary. Anne refused the king's gifts and advances, asserting her belief that no happiness would come to her in the role of mistress:

> "*If you ... give yourself up, heart, body and soul to me ...*" wrote Henry, "*I will take you for my only mistress, rejecting from thought and affection all others save yourself, to serve only you.*"

> To which Anne replied: "*Your wife I cannot be, both in respect of mine own unworthiness, and also because you have a queen already. Your mistress I will not be.*"

Henry was not a man used to being told *no*, and soon became determined to secure Anne Boleyn for himself. The devoutly Catholic king found permission to discard Catherine of Aragon and marry the woman he loved passionately in an unlikely source: the Book of Leviticus.

> "*And if a man shall take his brother's wife, it is an unclean thing: he hath uncovered his brother's nakedness; they shall be childless.*"

Whether Henry genuinely believed that his lack of sons was God's punishment for his marriage to Arthur's widow, or whether his thorough study of the Bible had rewarded him with the perfect excuse to exercise his lust, the king began to consult his councilors and spiritual advisors on the matter.

Divorce was initially out of the question for a Catholic king, not to mention completely unprecedented for a royal couple in the 16th century. When Henry convinced his lawyers and the Archbishop Thomas Cranmer that he intended to remarry, whatever the consequences, they decided the best course of action was to seek an annulment on the basis that Queen Catherine had consummated her previous marriage to Arthur Tudor.

Popes were not in the habit of granting annulments to adult couples who had a child together. The courts struggled with the king's mandate for six years, waiting for approval from the Catholic

Church that never arrived. Henry had promised Anne Boleyn they would marry as soon as it was legally possible, but with no permission from the Church forthcoming, Henry and Anne wed in a secret ceremony in November of 1532. The marriage was legalized in a second wedding the following January. In May of 1533, Archbishop Cranmer presided over a special court that rendered null and void the king's marriage to Catherine and certified his new marriage to Anne as valid—without the approval or consent of Pope Clement VII.

Catherine of Aragon was beyond insulted and humiliated at the public display her husband made of dissolving their marriage. Catherine had fought fiercely against the annulment proceedings, insisting that she and Arthur had never consummated their marriage. She had the Catholic Church on her side, as well as the support of her family in Spain. In the end, neither was sufficient to change Henry's mind.

In 1535, Henry had Catherine taken to Kimbolton Castle in Cambridgeshire. She was deeply depressed and never conceded to Henry's wish that she no longer call herself the Queen of England. His jilted first wife locked herself in her own rooms at the castle, only leaving to attend Catholic mass and meet with visitors.

One precious visitor who was not permitted to see Catherine was her daughter Mary. Henry repeatedly asked mother and daughter to recognize Anne Boleyn as their queen in exchange for visitation rights, but they both refused. Mary was incredibly loyal to her mother, and both women were staunch Catholics. They could not conscientiously bow to Anne, nor could they disobey the orders of the pope, now Paul III, who had excommunicated Henry. Friends of the former queen and her daughter smuggled letters between the two, but at court they had both fallen out of favor.

Catherine of Aragon died on January 7, 1536, after a long period of constant fasting and self-deprivation. On the day she was buried as a Dowager Princess of Wales at Peterborough Cathedral, Henry did not attend the service, and forbade his daughter Mary to pay this last respect to her mother.

Henry VIII's decision to go forward with the marriage to Anne Boleyn, despite the explicit instructions from the Pope not to do so, caused a split between him and the Catholic Church. In 1532, after waiting years for word from the Church on his proposed marriage to Anne, Henry had reached a breaking point. On the king's behalf, Henry's chief minister Thomas Cromwell drafted the Statue in Restraint of Appeals. The Act, passed in April of 1533, made the king the final authority in England on all matters, including religious questions—and made it illegal to accept the authority of the pope. In November 1534, Parliament passed the First Act of Supremacy, which proclaimed Henry the Head of the Church of England. Henry's kingdom had become a Protestant nation.

The signs of this religious reformation became quickly visible throughout England. Ornate churches were robbed of their gargoyles, angels, and other Catholic symbols, and monasteries were knocked down. Statues of the saints were removed from their pedestals, many of which remain empty half a millennium later. New printing presses shared the stories of the Bible for everyone to read – whereas Catholics were expected to hear the Bible only as interpreted by their priest.

Henry VIII, in his insistence to marry his wife's lady-in-waiting, ended up changing his entire kingdom for centuries to come. He was fiercely proud of this fact, and took seriously his responsibility to educate his people on matters of religion.

To the confused ranks of religious leaders during the Reformation, Henry said:

> *"Alas, how can the poor souls live in concord when you preachers sow amongst them in your sermons debate and discord? They look to you for light and you bring them darkness. Amend these crimes, I exhort you, and set forth God's word truly, both by true preaching and giving a good*

example, or else, I, whom God has appointed his vicar and high minister here, will see these divisions extinct, and these enormities corrected."

Henry VIII may have gotten his way in his battle with the Church, but he had not yet gotten his son. On September 7, 1533, Anne Boleyn gave birth to Elizabeth Tudor, much to Henry's disappointment. After Elizabeth's birth, Anne, like Catherine before her, endured several miscarriages. On the same day Catherine of Aragon was buried, the now-unquestioned Queen Anne delivered her last baby—a stillborn boy. Her misfortune would only increase.

Chapter 11 – King Henry VIII: Wives Two and Three

Henry VIII was considered a very handsome and athletic king when he began his reign. He was quite tall for the time period—probably above six feet in height—and he was an avid sportsman. Henry enjoyed hunting on horseback and jousting with his courtiers and knights. The Henry VIII who married Anne Boleyn was a man who truly seemed to have it all. His physique in later years was a stark contrast to this original image. In fact, when he died, the king could only be described as obese and ill; he was suffering from several chronic medical problems. One of these ongoing ailments was ulcerated legs, an injury generally attributed to a jousting accident at the age of 44, mere months before Henry ultimately lost his temper with the new queen.

A contemporary witness to the scene wrote about what he saw on the mock battlefield:

> *"On the eve of the Conversion of St. Paul, the King being mounted on a great horse to run at the lists, both fell so heavily that everyone thought it a miracle he was not killed, but he sustained no injury. Thinks he might ask of fortune for what greater misfortune he is reserved, like the other tyrant who escaped from the fall of the house, in which all the rest were smothered, and soon after died."*

Both jousters crashed at the pinnacle of the match and fell heavily to the ground. Despite the commenter's assertion that he was uninjured, Henry suffered a serious head injury. He was reported "unable to speak for two hours."

It was by no means the first time Henry had suffered an injury from his favorite sport, and in all other cases Henry had healed and recovered his health in full. His accident in 1536 was different. In time, Henry was well enough again to speak and work, but he never joined in a jousting competition again. His accident is thought by many historians and medical researchers to have marked an important transition between the first and second parts of Henry's life. Whereas before the accident the king was athletic, confident and boastful, afterward he was considered sullen and considerably less sporting in nature. In particular, some believe that the king's temper would never quite recover.

Anne's final miscarriage occurred in the days following Henry's accident. Despite the fact that his wife was still quite young and healthy, Henry was not content to keep waiting. Fewer than three years after the most controversial marriage in English history, the king once more sought to remarry.

Henry's second annulment was politically simpler than the first, but just as emotionally draining. Anne was constantly furious with her husband for his affairs with various ladies at court,. He excused himself by blaming her for their continued lack of a male heir. When their relationship was too volatile to continue, Henry called in his advisors and lawyers.

The king's prime advisor, Thomas Cromwell, was all too happy to find a new wife for his monarch. Cromwell did not have a good relationship with the Boleyn family and he was eager chance to do away with an enemy while simultaneously pleasing the king. To speed along the annulment, Anne was imprisoned and put on trial for several charges. These included adultery, high treason and incest – the latter based on the claim that she'd had an improper relationship with her own brother. Historians believe that the king's allies falsified most, if not all, of the charges brought against Anne.

Found guilty, Anne's marriage was annulled and she was sentenced to die. Her brother, George Boleyn, shared the same sentence and was executed two days before Anne. The final victim of the charges against the queen was William Brereton, a servant to the king. Brereton was found guilty of committing adultery with Anne. He died on the same day as George.

At the executioner's block, Anne was serene and calm. Prepared for death, she spoke to the people gathered before her.

> "Good Christian people, I am come hither to die, for according to the law, and by the law I am judged to die, and therefore I will speak nothing against it. I am come hither to accuse no man, nor to speak anything of that, whereof I am accused and condemned to die, but I pray God save the king and send him long to reign over you, for a gentler nor a more merciful prince was there never: and to me he was ever a good, a gentle and sovereign lord. And if any person will meddle of my cause, I require them to judge the best. And thus I take my leave of the world and of you all, and I heartily desire you all to pray for me. O Lord have mercy on me, to God I commend my soul."

It is impossible to say whether the king's head injury truly did change his character, but we do know that mere months after his fall, Henry had Anne Boleyn - the wife for whom he changed all of England - imprisoned, denounced as queen and executed. He would continue to acquire and discard wives in quick succession, never truly content with any of them—with the exception of his third wife, Jane.Anne Boleyn was executed on Tower Hill on May 19, 1536. Less than a fortnight later, Henry VIII married Jane Seymour, former lady-in-waiting to both Queen Catherine and Queen Anne. Jane was seven years younger than Boleyn and remarkably different than the king's first two wives.

Jane Seymour also came from a good family but had not received the extensive education that her predecessors had. She was not an avid reader or writer, like Catherine and Anne, and is said only to have been able to read and write her own name. She enjoyed more traditional homemaking skills such as embroidery and gardening. Known generally as a sweet and mild-mannered young woman, Jane nevertheless had strong conservative views concerning the way her household should be run. She banned her serving ladies from wearing the vibrant French dresses that had been so popular with Anne Boleyn and other young women at the time.

Jane was the opposite of Catherine and Anne, which is quite possibly what enticed Henry VIII to her in the first place. He was a boisterous and confident king who, at that point in his rule, desired very little input from his spouse. He wanted a woman who was happy in herself, and content to know her place within his life and palaces. For her part, Jane was perfectly aware of the fate that met Henry's first and second queens, and would have thought very carefully before speaking out against her powerful husband.

There were, however, two matters for which she sought Henry's ear. A few months into his third marriage, Henry faced the first major internal challenge to his break with the Catholic Church. Unhappy with the king's suppression of the Catholic church, a group of nobles organized what became known as the Pilgrimage of Grace. Led by Robert Aske of London, the Pilgrimage gathered the support of some 40,000 people in the north of England. The pilgrims marched to Lincolnshire Church and occupied it in the name of their Catholic rights. They continued onward to Doncaster, where they were met by lords from nearby counties who represented the king. Seeing the great number of people, Henry's representatives decided to talk with Robert Aske and see if the two parties could come up with a peaceful solution to the Catholics' grievances. When the Duke of Norfolk, Thomas Howard, told Aske that the king would grant the people a parliament, Aske accepted this proposal and told his followers that they should be grateful.

Henry VIII, of course, had not been consulted, and was not at all willing to hold any such parliament with the Catholic faction. Jane Seymour appealed to her husband for leniency, but Henry ignored her defenses of Aske and his pilgrims. After several more forays between Aske and the king's men, the leader of the pilgrimage was executed, as were thousands upon thousands of his followers. It was an unprecedentedly ruthless move on the part of the king, but as he saw it, protecting the Church of England was vital. He would no longer deal with any talk against his reformation of England.

Jane Seymour had more success with a second matter: the status of Henry's two daughters, Mary and Elizabeth. Queen Jane, as she was known despite her lack of official coronation, held family in the highest regard. For this reason, she wanted her husband to accept his young daughters back into his life, as much for his own emotional and spiritual welfare as for theirs. Because Mary and Elizabeth had been made illegitimate upon the annulments of their respective mothers, they were no longer part of the royal household, nor were they considered potential heirs to the throne of England. Jane hoped to restore the girls to their rightful titles. In particular, she bonded with Mary and felt deep sympathy for the plight of Queen Catherine. Her sympathy for Catherine, and for Robert Aske's pilgrims, suggests that Jane may have been a Catholic sympathizer, though this potential private leaning was never revealed to the public.

On October 12, 1537, Queen Jane gave birth to Edward Tudor. The baby boy was healthy and strong – the first of Henry's sons to thrive. It was the biggest achievement of Queen Jane's short life. While Edward endured his elaborate christening ceremony, Jane became very sick. Over the next twelve days, she experienced a high fever and bouts of delirium. She craved sweets and wine, both of which were provided for her, but there was nothing to save her life. Jane Seymour died on October 24.

King Henry VIII was genuinely pained by the death of his third wife. He wore mourning clothes of deep black for over three months following Jane's burial, and even took up her quiet hobby of embroidery to keep her pensive, calm ways in memory. Most surprisingly, Henry waited two full years before marrying again.

Chapter 12 – King Henry VIII: The Last Three Wives

When the mourning period was emotionally past and Henry found time once more to desire a woman at his side, the king's advisors and friends made haste to procure one to his liking.

Anne of Cleves was selected for her noble status and her nationality. Born in Dusseldorf, then part of the Holy Roman Empire, Anne of Cleves came from a family that had also rejected the rule of the pope. Thanks to Henry's Reformation, England had a strained relationship with most countries in Europe, and the king wanted to forge new bonds outside of his own realm. With both Anne and her younger sister, Amalia, under consideration to become his next wife, Henry sent his court portraitist to visit the Cleves household and create true likenesses of the women on canvas.

The artist, Hans Holbein the Younger, had the difficult task of creating a very quick portrait that would be sent back to Henry and his advisors. Art historians have suggested that Holbein had already marked up much of the canvas before the actual portrait sitting, meaning that the women's features were quite generic. Whatever the exact process, Holbein sent back his completed portraits on time. King Henry VIII was happy with the picture of Anne and decided to move forward with the marriage contract.

Shortly before the wedding, Anne traveled to England to take up residence in London. Excited to meet her, Henry arrived in costume so that he might playfully tease the lady before unmasking himself and revealing his true identity. Upon seeing her for the first time, the king rushed back to his advisor, Thomas Cromwell, and shouted "I like her not!" Unfortunately, though Anne of Cleves had many genuine admirers of her beauty, Henry was not one of them. Anne was quite tall and broad-boned, with a large nose. Though these features were well-blended given her frame, the king had simply envisioned a smaller woman from the portrait he'd studied.

Henry met with Anne before the wedding ceremony took place, when there was still time to back out of the marriage. For unknown reasons, he chose to move forward with the wedding despite his misgivings at Anne's physical features. Perhaps he placed a great deal of importance on his reputation in the rest of Europe; perhaps he decided to see if, in time, he would grow to appreciate the young woman.

Anne was only 25 years old when she married the 48-year-old Henry VIII. There was very little to attract a man like Henry to young Anne, since she was not as well-educated or as dainty and small as his former wives and lovers. Nevertheless, the two were married on January 6, 1540.

Whatever made Henry go forward with the wedding was not enough motivation to actually consummate the marriage. After his first night with Anne, Henry confessed to his manservants they he had put his hands all over the new queen in an attempt to become aroused, but it was to no avail. Confused about just what constituted marital consummation, Anne wrote happily to her mother, claiming that she was happy in the marriage and everything was going as it should.

King Henry would never spend the night with Anne of Cleves. Instead, true to form, he decided to have the marriage annulled so that he could marry one of her ladies-in-waiting. By July of 1540, just six months after their wedding, Henry VIII and Anne of Cleves had their marriage declared illegal and illegitimate. The jilted bride was neither executed nor cast out of the royal houses, however. In a rare show of empathy and respect, King Henry declared that henceforth, Anne of Cleves was his "sister" and the owner of several beautiful, rich estates throughout the kingdom. She was given a luxurious annual salary from the crown and lived the rest of her life a rich woman in England. She died in 1557 at the age of 41.

On the July 28, 1540 – the very same year in which Henry had married and divorced Anne of Cleves – the king married his fifth wife: Catherine Howard. She was merely a teenaged girl at the time of the wedding, estimated at 16 or 17 years of age. Henry was nearly 50.

The king was delighted at the youth and vivacity of little Catherine Howard. Catherine enjoyed dance lessons and could read and write, but was otherwise quite uneducated. The fifth Queen of England by Henry VIII's side had been raised at the large estate house of her father's step-mother, the Dowager Duchess of Norfolk, but her upbringing there was somewhat controversial.

At the estate of the Dowager Duchess, many young girls from noble families were in the care of the lady of house. This was a common practice at the time, intended to help the girls learn aristocratic manners while saving their families money on their upbringing. The Dowager Duchess was not particularly strict with respect to how the girls spent their spare time. Given free reign, Catherine and her roommates had a habit of letting neighborhood boys into their sleeping area at night. Much worse, however, was Catherine's experiences with her music teacher, Henry Maddox. Catherine would later admit that, from the age of 13, Maddox had molested her at the Duchess' estate.

At the age of 15, Catherine had begun a long-term romance with an employee of her patroness: Francis Dereham. According to sources close to the Catherine, she and Francis had a sexual relationship and referred to one another and "wife" and "husband." When the Dowager Duchess discovered the young couple's relationship, she sent Dereham away to Ireland.

The very young queen was, therefore, both experienced in the sensual parts of life and accustomed to the control of powerful—and brutal—men. Upon the teenager's marriage, King Henry VIII must have seemed just as much an imposition to her small self as had Henry Maddox. The king was no longer the attractive royal catch he had once been. He was around 300 pounds and quite sick most of the time. At nearly 50, the once-slim and attractive young king had grown unrecognizably fat, soft and rather intolerant. In the wake of his jousting accident, perhaps the king had taken solace in two pleasures that were left to him; food and drink. His body had expanded rapidly over the course of his rule, adding up to 20 inches of girth around his chest. As the same time, he grew less patient with his wives, less empathetic with his advisors and less merciful towards the people of England and Ireland. At this point in his life, women most likely feared telling him "no."

The relationship between Catherine Howard and King Henry VIII was brief. While living at the palace, she soon fell in love with one of the king's servants, Thomas Culpeper, and the two of them began an affair. Queen Catherine was not a practiced writer and must have taken a great deal of time to form each word in the following letter to Thomas Culpeper:

> *"I never longed so much for a thing as I do to see you and to speak with you, the which I trust shall be shortly now. That which doth comfortly me very much when I think of it, and when I think again that you shall depart from me again it*

makes my heart die to think what fortune I have that I cannot be always in your company."

The king's staff uncovered letters between Catherine and Culpeper, and Henry had Catherine imprisoned in the winter of 1541. Thomas Culpeper and Francis Dereham, Catherine's former lover, were found guilty of high treason and executed that December. Catherine's sentencing came late in January, after Parliament created a brand-new law by which she would retroactively be found guilty of treason. On February 13, 1542, Catherine Howard was helped up the steps to the executioner's scaffold and decapitated. Her body was disposed of in the same mass grave as her cousins, Anne and George Boleyn. King Henry VIII did not attend the execution.

Henry VIII's final choice for queen was Katherine Parr. She was 31, twice-widowed and childless—a complete turnaround from Howard. With Parr, there was no chance to accidentally assume her virginity and find her lacking; there was no reason to expect children that would never come. At 51, Henry's legs were covered in very painful boils that had to be regularly lanced by his doctor. Because of his size and pain, he could barely move around the Palace of Whitehall. The reason for his marriage to Katherine Parr at such a difficult point in his life was actually quite pure and simple: Henry VIII wanted female companionship from an experienced woman he could trust. The two married on July 12, 1543, at Hampton Court Palace.

Mary, Elizabeth and Edward were all in attendance and would receive much positive attention from their new stepmother. When she became the Queen of England, Katherine Parr had already seen two husbands grow sick and die; she must have known that this particular bout of nursing and caring for a sick man would come to an end soon enough.

Katherine had been raised in the rural north of England and knew little about the exciting life of courtiers and kings, but she was an educated woman who never stopped learning. When she moved to Henry's palace as his sixth queen, Katherine was pleased to join in the frequent philosophical and spiritual discussions of the day. She was a devout Reformer, and as she learned more on the subject of religion, she made sure that Henry's children learned alongside her. In particular, she took on the education of Elizabeth and Edward, creating perhaps the most well-educated noblewoman England had ever seen. The two future monarchs became stoic Protestants, due in no small part to Katherine's guidance.

Unfortunately, some of the Catholic advisors at court believed that the queen went too far in her constant Protestant campaign. They convinced Henry that she was perceived as an evangelical and a heretic. The king arranged for a contingent of guards to arrest his wife the next day, but also had a courtier slip the arrest warrant under Katherine's door to warn her. The queen rushed immediately to her husband's rooms and spoke with him, assuring him that she deferred to him in all matters, including theological ones. He smiled and seemed pleased with her.

The next day, however, the arresting officials returned. They approached the royal couple while Katherine, ever a gentle and caring wife, sat beside the king and massaged his swollen legs. Lord Wriothesley announced that he had come to arrest Queen Katherine and take her away.

Katherine must have struggled to hold on to her senses – after all, two wives before her had been mercilessly killed for displeasing the king. But Henry VIII knew very well that many of his advisors and courtiers sought to use his characteristic anger and swift judgment for their own purposes. He had orchestrated the entire incident to demonstrate to his court that he was the master of his own mind. When the guards came to arrest his queen, he physically struck them and sent them all away humiliated. Katherine was safe under Henry's protection.

Parr remained a dutiful wife to Henry VIII until his death in 1547 at the age of 55. Henry spent his last days suffering greatly in bed. His infected boils stank and none of his courtiers or attendants dared tell him the end was near, since Henry himself had enacted a law that forbade anyone to speak of the death of a monarch.

Modern medical professionals have speculated that the king suffered a variety of illnesses, including diabetes and syphilis. These could explain his ulcers, night sweats, extreme thirst and mental degradation in the last few years of life. Another potential culprit, a neurological disorder known as McLeod's syndrome, could account for the rapid change in Henry's health and demeanor starting in 1536, as well as the repeated miscarriages and stillborn births suffered by his many wives.

King Henry VIII died on January 28, 1547. He was not yet 56 years old. He was interred beside Jane Seymour, the woman he claimed was his one true wife.

Katherine Parr's relationship with her royal stepchildren continued long after the king was gone, as she remained their most eager tutor. A few short months after becoming a royal widow, Katherine married for a fourth time to Thomas Seymour, the brother of Henry's beloved Queen Jane. She loved him deeply but died in childbirth the following year.

Anne of Cleves outlived both Henry VIII and his other five wives. She stayed at Hever Castle on her ex-husband's generous allowance for nearly two decades, a frequent and beloved guest at the English court. She died in 1557 at the age of 41.

Chapter 13 – King Edward VI

Henry VIII called little Prince Edward the kingdom's "most precious jewel." He gave his prized son all the toys and comforts he could ever want, and provided him with a thorough education in European languages, philosophy and religion. Despite the romantic entanglements of his father, Edward enjoyed the sort of family life that his own father had. He spent holidays with Katherine Parr, Henry VIII and his sisters, Mary and Elizabeth. In 1546, the family spent their first Christmas together thanks to the persuasion of Queen Katherine. At that time, Henry officially claimed both daughters as legitimate and welcomed them as part of the Tudor family. Each of Henry's children was henceforth an heir to the throne of England.

The siblings were all close, but Edward preferred the company of Mary the most. He had a bit of a rivalry with Elizabeth, who was a spectacular student in the siblings' combined lessons. Edward was also credited with great intelligence; his main interests were finance and military history and strategy.

Young Edward had a relatively healthy childhood. Hoping to protect his sole male heir from disease, the king ensured that his son's rooms were scrupulously cleaned. Like most children, Edward contracted several illnesses during his childhood, including a form of malaria. Overall, however, he was considered a vivacious and fast-growing boy.

As was tradition, Edward Tudor was the subject of various marital schemes by his father and other royal families throughout Europe. Since Henry VIII wanted to unite Scotland and England, he decided that the best course of action was to marry young Edward to Mary, the infant queen of Scotland. Mary was only six days old when her father, King James V, died. He had no other legitimate heirs. With Scotland under the power of various regents, Henry VIII saw an opportunity. The Treaty of Greenwich, signed in 1543, promised that the six-month-old Mary would marry Edward, then age five, upon reaching her tenth birthday. Part of the treaty included the stipulation that Mary be sent to the English court to be raised as Henry VIII saw fit.

Ultimately, Scotland reneged on its agreement and instead made a new contract with its old ally, France. Mary was to be sent to the French court for her education and eventual marriage to the Dauphin Francis, heir to the French throne. Edward's father was outraged. In retaliation, and in the hope that the Scots might respond to more heavy-handed persuasion, he ordered Edward Seymour—brother to Jane Seymour and uncle to Edward—to lead an invasion of Scotland. The fighting lasted from 1543 to 1551, and later became known as the "Rough Wooing." Though Scotland sustained horrible losses at the hands of Seymour's forces, it refused to marry off its little queen to the English.

Before Henry VIII died, he stipulated in his will that, should Edward inherit the throne before the age of eighteen, a party of sixteen personally-selected executors would share the power of the crown. In the final weeks and days of Henry's life, the will was amended so that the old king's wishes were less clear. Upon Henry's death in

1547, his son was crowned King Edward VI in a short ceremony befitting a child. Afterward, though Henry's intended executors did take power, state affairs were almost wholly handled by Edward Seymour. Seymour named himself Lord Protector of the Realm and Governor of the King's Person. It was not the Regency Council that the old king wished for, but Edward was too young to understand such matters or make corrections. Until the age of fifteen, King Edward VI watched a never-ending power struggle between relatives and council members.

At first, Seymour's war against Scotland gave him great respect at court and established him as the king's main regent. Soon, however, popular opinion collapsed into revolts across England. The people were angry that further Protestant measures—fully supported by the Edward, the first English king to be raised a Protestant—were being imposed in their churches. Particularly egregious was the translation of the Bible into English. The kingdom-wide distribution of the first England-language liturgical text, called Book of Common Prayer, enraged Catholics as well as conservative Protestants. Both groups believed that Latin was the ideal translation for their holy texts, and were angry at the fact that now the Bible could be read and interpreted—or, worse, misinterpreted—by any literate English person.

Only two years into Edward's reign, his uncle Edward Seymour was overthrown from his position in the Regency Council charged with various crimes against the crown, including ambition, reckless war and stealing from the royal treasury. The ambitious John Dudley replaced Seymour as head of the council. With his uncle in prison, Edward VI happily deferred to Dudley in matters of state. In fact, entries in his personal journal portray Edward VI as quite emotionally detached from his authoritative uncle and most other members of the Regency Council. When Seymour, sensing that his time as Lord Protector of the Realm was nearing an end, fled to Windsor with the young king, Edward wrote in his journal: "Me thinks I am a prisoner." A later entry proclaimed, with little sympathy, "The Duke of Somerset had his head cut off upon Tower Hill between eight and nine o'clock in the morning."

In his teenage years, Edward VI grew into a potent and opinionated king, though he could not yet rule independently: "I will say with certain intention, that I will see my laws strictly obeyed, and those who break them shall be watched and denounced." Edward was dedicated to the new regime his father had established and enacted several measures to increase the influence of the Church of England. These included government-appointed church ministers, rights of the clergy to marry, and communion for common people. Clergy who outright disapproved of the reformations of the church – such as the Bishops of Winchester and London - were imprisoned in the Tower of London.

Most of the work of officiating church reform fell to Edward's chief advisor, the Archbishop of Canterbury Thomas Cranmer, who had also served Henry VIII. The Archbishop wrote extensively in order to clarify the reformation laws. One of the most important of these documents was the Forty-two Articles, in which Cranmer outlined the Church of England's stance on various religious questions. For example, Cranmer explained that, while traditional Catholics believed that the bread and wine taken at communion were literal pieces of Jesus Christ's body, members of the reformed religion should treat the reference to Christ's body as merely symbolic. These and other highly-contested issues of the time needed clarification from King Edward so that clergy, commoners and law-keepers understood how to perform their roles and avoid punishment.

In 1553, when Edward VI was fifteen years old, he fell ill with tuberculosis and did not recover. Fearing the worst, he decided to choose his potential successor rather than leave the kingdom to his half-sister Mary. Though Mary had already been declared heir after Edward by Henry VIII, the 37-year old Catholic was not the ideal candidate for a newly-Protestant kingdom. The obvious choice for

Edward seemed to be his Protestant sister Elizabeth, but the teenage king surprised everyone by picking his first cousin, Jane Grey.

Jane Grey was the great-niece of Henry VIII by way of his younger sister, Mary Tudor. She had been raised in the household of Katherine Parr, often joining her cousins Edward and Elizabeth for their studies. But it was not merely Jane's devoutness and her relationship with Edward that inspired the young king chose his cousin to succeed him. Jane's father-in-law was none other than John Dudley, Edward's chief advisor. The wording of the dying king's succession document was jumbled, but tell-tale signs of corrections were present. The line "Lady Jane heirs male" had been changed to "Lady Jane *and her* heirs male," which meant that Jane herself, not only any male offspring, was part of the line of succession.

The last words of King Edward VI were recorded for posterity:

> *"I am faint; Lord have mercy upon me and take my spirit."*

Four days after Edward's death on July 6, 1553, Lady Jane Grey was proclaimed Queen. She never made it to her coronation.

Chapter 14 – The Nine Days' Queen, Jane Grey

Born the same year as Edward, Lady Jane was a teenage newlywed when she ascended to the throne. Though she did indeed possess royal Tudor blood, she was never groomed for the crown, nor did she at any point in her life – including during Edward's illness – expect to become Queen. However, her father-in-law, John Dudley, was all too eager to pave the way for her, and he was perfectly positioned to do so as Edward VI's self-proclaimed regent.

Upon Edward VI's death, any successor to Edward VI needed to trace his or her lineage back to Henry VII, the first Tudor king—and there was a strong preference for candidates who were male. There were, however, no male Tudors available. A quick look backwards through the royal family tree proved that there were only two other candidates for the throne beside Henry VIII's own two daughters.

Henry VII had produced four children: Arthur, Henry VIII, Mary and Margaret. Arthur died before he could become a father; Edward Tudor was Henry VIII's only son. Mary Tudor's eldest child was daughter Frances Grey, whose eldest child was daughter Jane Grey. Margaret Tudor had married King James IV of Scotland. Of their six children, only James V survived into adulthood. James V's only living child was Mary Stuart.

Mary Stuart was an unlikely choice. This was the same Mary whom Scotland had promised, and then denied, to five-year-old Edward as a future bride. Now ten years old, Mary was living in the court of the French king, where she would one day be married to his son. Furthermore, her uncle Henry VIII's will had excluded Mary, and the entire Stuart line, from succession. If, as many argued, both Mary and Elizabeth were illegitimate by virtue of Henry VIII's annulments, and if Mary Stuart had been eliminated by Henry VIII's last will and testament, then Jane Grey was the only possible heir to the throne. John Dudley, Jane's powerful father-in-law, arranged to have her Jane Grey taken to the palace and sworn in as Queen.

While Edward lay on his deathbed, Mary was at home in Hunsdon, Hertfordshire. When the king died, she was making preparations to visit her half-brother at his request. Before she could make the journey, she received an important warning from a friend. Mary was told that Edward VI wanted to entrap her and have her imprisoned, so that once he was dead she could not raise an army against Jane. It was the ultimate insult to Mary, who had been very close to her brother in his early youth.

Mary took this warning to heart and fled instead to East Anglia, where she did indeed put together an army. There were many Catholics in East Anglia, and they supported her with horses and armed men. She wrote immediately to Edward's Privy Council and made it clear that she intended to take what she believed was rightfully hers. Henry VIII's eldest daughter had such strong numbers behind her that riots broke out in London. In the name of Queen Mary, Queen Jane was captured and deposed only nine days after she had been brought to the palace. Mary had not even arrived in the capital before her enemy was charged with treason and imprisoned in the Tower of London.

Crowds cheered as Mary Tudor rode into London on August 3, 1553, alongside her half-sister Elizabeth. More than 800 members of the nobility marched with her. There was no more question of the validity of Mary's rule. Mary was a strong woman who knew her mind; Jane, twenty years her junior, was girl afraid of causing trouble. Nevertheless, the Nine Days' Queen, as she came to be known, had proven herself a threat to be contained. Jane, her husband Guildford Dudley, her father-in-law John Dudley, and her own father were all arrested and imprisoned at the Tower.

During her imprisonment, Jane wrote to her cousin Mary in an attempt to explain herself.

> *"Although my fault be such that but for the goodness and clemency of the Queen, I can have no hope of finding pardon.... having given ear to those who at the time appeared not only to myself, but also to the great part of this realm to be wise and now have manifested themselves to the contrary, not only to my and their great detriment, but with common disgrace and blame of all, they having with shameful boldness made to blamable and dishonourable an attempt to give to others that which was not theirs...[and my own] lack of prudence...for which I deserve heavy punishment...it being known that the error imputed to me has not been altogether caused by myself. [The Privy Council] ....who with unwontd caresses and pleasantness, did me such reverence as was not at all suitable to my state. He [Dudley] then said that his Majesty had well weighed an Act of Parliament...that whoever should acknowledge the most serene Mary...or the lady Elizabeth and receive them as the true heirs of the crown of England should be had all for traitors...wherefore, in no manner did he wish that they should be heirs of him and of that crown, he being able in every way to disinherit them. And therefore, before his death, he gave order to the Council, that for the honour they owed to him...they should obey his last will...As to the rest, for my part, I know not what the*

Council had determined to do, but I know for certain that twice during this time, poison was given to me, first in the house of the Duchess of Northumberland and afterwards here in the Tower…. All these I have wished for the witness of my innocence and the disburdening of my conscience. [sic]"

With Jane Grey and John Dudley locked up, Mary turned her attention to the Catholic Bishops who had been locked in the Tower for nearly the entirety of her brother's rule. Thomas Howard and Stephen Gardiner were immediately released and given new titles. Gardiner was restored to Bishop of Winchester and created Lord Chancellor. He crowned his redeemer Queen Mary I on October 1, 1553 at Westminster Abby. The next month, Jane and her fellow prisoners were put on trial. They were found guilty and sentenced to death.

On February 12, 1554, Jane was beheaded at the Tower of London. Before her death, she addressed the crowd assembled below the scaffold:

"Good people, I am come hether to die, and by a lawe I am condemnded to the same. The facte, in dede, against the quenes highnesse was unlawfull, and the consenting thereunto by me: but touching the procurement and desire therof bt me or on my halfe, I doo wash my hands thereof in innocencie, before God, and in the face of you, good Christian people, this day."

Jane tied a handkerchief around her eyes, laid her head on the block, and echoed the last words of Jesus on the cross:

"Lorde, into thy hands I commende my spirite! [sic]"

Chapter 15 – Queen Mary Tudor I

Mary was a powerful mixture of her parents; She was ruthless like Henry VIII and faithfully Catholic like Catherine of Aragon. Though she had publicly forgiven her father for keeping her away from her mother in final years of Catherine's life, Mary had never accepted that England was a Protestant kingdom. To Mary, there was only one thing she must do during her reign: reunite with the Catholic church. This plan had been growing in her mind since she and her mother were forced out of Henry VIII's court. A letter from Catherine of Aragon at that time urged Mary to do as her father said and avoid causing problems, for her own sake and safety:

> *"Daughter,*
>
> *I heard such tidings today that I do perceive (if it be true) the time is very near when Almighty God will prove you; and I am very glad of it for I trust he doth handle you with a good love. I beseech you, agree of His pleasure with a merry heart; and be sure that, without fail, He will not suffer you to perish if you beware to offend Him. I pray you, good daughter, to offer yourself to Him...And if this lady [Shelton] do come to you as is spoken, if she do bring you a letter from the King, I*

am sure in the self same letter you shall be commanded what you shall do. Answer with few words, obeying the King, your father, in everything, save only that you will not offend God and lose your own soul; and go no further with learning and disputation in the matter. And wheresoever, and in whatsoever, company you shall come, observe the King's commandments.

But one thing I especially desire you, for the love that you do owe unto God and unto me, to keep your heart with a chaste mind, and your body from all ill and wanton company, [not] thinking or desiring any husband for Christ's passion; neither determine yourself to any manner of living till this troublesome time be past. For I dare make sure that you shall see a very good end, and better than you can desire...And now you shall begin, and by likelihood I shall follow. I set not a rush by it; for when they have done the uttermost they can, then I am sure of the amendment...we never come to the kingdom of Heaven but by troubles. Daughter wheresoever you come, take no pain to send unto me, for if I may, I will send to you,

Your loving mother,
Katherine the Queen [sic]"

After years of letting herself be pushed around by King Henry and his advisors of the reformed church, Mary had no remaining patience left for her tenure as queen. Though she superficially accepted England's dual nature with reference to religion, she truly believed that Catholicism was the one true faith. Alone, Mary could do little to reinstate Catholicism in her country, so she sought an ally abroad. Philip II fit the role perfectly, and he came recommended by his father, King of Spain.

Born in 1527, Spain's heir to the throne of Catholicism's most faithful nation was eleven years younger than Mary. Still, the match made sense to England's new queen, who undoubtedly wanted to reconnect with her mother's Spanish side of the family. The marriage was arranged quickly, much to the pleasure of Mary, who was both enamored with Philip and very eager to become pregnant. She was 37 years old but hopeful that she could produce an heir of her own. If she did not, upon her death the kingdom would fall into the hands of her Reformist half-sister, Elizabeth. Her anxiety over that potentiality drove her to imprison Elizabeth in the Tower of London.

When she discovered her fate, Princess Elizabeth wrote promptly to her half-sister:

> "March 16, 1554.
>
> *If any ever did try this old saying, 'that a king's word was more than another man's oath,' I most humbly beseech your Majesty to verify it to me, and to remember your last promise and my last demand, that I be not condemned without answer and due proof, which it seems that I now am; for without cause proved, I am by your council from you commanded to go to the Tower, a place more wanted for a false traitor than a true subject, which though I know I desire it not, yet in the face of all this realm it appears proved...*
>
> *And as for the copy of the letter sent to the French King, I pray God confound me eternally if ever I sent him word, message, token, or letter, by any means, and to this truth I will stand in till my death.*
>
> *Your Highness's most faithful subject, that hath been from the beginning, and will be to my end,*
>
> *ELIZABETH,*
>
> *I humbly crave but only one word of answer from yourself."*

To ensure that his son Philip would be named King of England, Charles V of Spain gave his son the kingship of Naples and Jerusalem before the proposed wedding. Mary ensured that her husband would be called King of England, with his name beside her own on all royal documents. The couple was married on July 25, 1554 at Winchester Castle.

Mary's court was afraid that under the kingship of a Spaniard, England would lose its independence. This fear was exacerbated when the queen showed classic signs of pregnancy. At her advanced age, many expected her to die in childbirth, and a document was drawn up by Parliament declaring King Philip the Regent of England upon Mary's death. Impervious to the dangers and gossip, Queen Mary was excited and full of joy with her Catholic husband from Spain and a baby on the way. She was happy and comfortable enough to have Elizabeth released from prison. Unfortunately, her projected due date for the baby's delivery came and went. Several months after the false rumor that she had given birth to a boy, Queen Mary's pregnancy symptoms disappeared. There was no baby.

Soon afterwards, King Philip II departed his wife's side to attend to matters in the Netherlands, then a part of the Spanish Empire. Mary was devastated. Lonely and depressed, she blamed her failure to conceive and give birth on her having been too accepting of the rampant Protestantism of her country. She became more fixated than ever on eliminating from England those she deemed heretics. It was this moment in Mary Tudor's life that changed her into the infamous Bloody Mary of legend.

Desperate to make up for her self-perceived sins against the Catholic Church, Mary orchestrated her own version of her grandparents' Spanish Inquisition. Queen Mary and Pope Julius spent several months negotiating England's return to the Catholic realm. Under the restoration agreement, anti-heresy laws were passed and Protestants were rounded up and burned at the stake en masse. It was both reminiscent of the rule of Ferdinand and Isabella of Spain, who ruthlessly prosecuted Jews and Muslims in their kingdom, and of

Henry VIII's punishment of the anti-Protestant protestors in the north of England. Mary was ruthless and became feared throughout the country.

Thomas Cranmer, the Archbishop of Canterbury and Edward VI's most trusted religious advisor, was an immediate and obvious target for Queen Mary. As England's most powerful member of the Church of England, aside from the monarch, Cranmer had created new rules, doctrine and biblical interpretations that infuriated Mary and the Catholic Church. Mary made the Archbishop watch his colleagues being burned alive. Cranmer agreed to become a Catholic after being tortured, but his words were not enough for the queen. She ordered him to be burned at the stake on March 21, 1556. Before the fire consumed his body, Cranmer confirmed his belief in the Protestant Reformation.

King Philip II returned to England in 1557 to ask for his wife's help protecting the Holy Roman Empire, of which his father had been emperor, from the conquest of France. She agreed, despite contrary advice from her council. Severe flooding in England had caused meager harvests and very few resources; the costs associated with sending troops to the continent further depleted the country's treasury. Although English and Spanish troops successfully guarded Spain's authority in Italy, England lost its last piece of land in France: Calais.

Queen Mary suffered one more false pregnancy before becoming very sick – possibly from a uterine disease – and dying on November 17, 1558. During her five-year reign, she had an estimated 300 people burned alive.

Chapter 16 – Elizabeth Tudor

Mary's crown fell directly to the last remaining child of King Henry VIII: Elizabeth Tudor. No longer imprisoned by her sister, Elizabeth was living in Hatfield, Hertfordshire, when Mary's condition degenerated drastically. Upon Mary's death, she came directly to London and was immediately pronounced Queen of England.

England was in sorry shape when Elizabeth was crowned on January 15, 1559. Queen Mary's death ended a chaotic and violent reign that earned her the nickname "Bloody Mary." The quick succession of four monarchs in the relatively short time since King Henry VIII's death was reminiscent of the flurry preceding Henry VII's rule. Once again, the people craved the kind of stability in the monarchy that would enable peace and prosperity. Elizabeth needed to address the financial crisis and a food shortage in addition to the intense distrust between Catholics and Protestants in the kingdom.

Elizabeth's first obstacle was her gender. That her predecessor was also a queen may have been a disadvantage to Elizabeth, as Mary was considered an over-emotional ruler. Though only 25 at her coronation, Queen Elizabeth was an intelligent woman and she fully intended to prove herself:

> *"As for my own part I care not for death, for all men are mortal; and though I be a woman yet I have as good a courage answerable to my place as ever my father had. I am your anointed Queen. I will never be by violence constrained to do anything. I thank God I am indeed endowed with such qualities that if I were turned out of the realm in my petticoat I were able to live in any place in Christendom."*

The Protestants who had endured five years of persecution under Mary were less concerned about the queen's gender; they were desperate to feel safe and free to worship in their own way. When Elizabeth quickly declared that England was to be a Protestant kingdom again, they rejoiced. The country and the international community remembered that Elizabeth was the child of Anne Boleyn, the very woman for whom Henry VIII had broken with the pope and established the Church of England. For Protestants, this fact bolstered their appreciation for the new ruler and gave them hope for the future of their country. After years of unprecedented persecution, the reign of terror had come to an end for the die-hard members of Henry VIII's religion.

Elizabeth's decision to reinstate the Reformation was celebrated by half her people, but the other half feared for their lives in this world and their souls in the next. She had a lot of work to do to allay the fears of everyday Catholics, and to subdue the most radical Catholics who would challenge her reign. Most Catholics agreed that the burning of supposed heretics needed to stop, and were willing to make some concessions to the Protestants in order to live peacefully. When Elizabeth canceled her sister's re-association with the pope, the decision was expected and not fiercely contended. The queen tried to blend some elements of traditional Catholicism into the Church of England's rulebook, including vestments for the clergy and the use of crucifixes. This more moderate approach to religion offended many, but it was not so strict so as to cause immediate revolt or backlash. Elizabeth required her parliament and advisors to swear an oath of allegiance to herself as the Supreme Governor of the Church of England, but she also did away with heresy laws so that anyone who refused would not face torture and death.

Elizabeth's panel of advisors—many of whom had served her brother Edward as well as her sister Mary—were primarily concerned with two things: whether Catholic Europe would invade the island, and who the young queen would choose as a husband. At first, Elizabeth graciously played hostess to an onslaught of potential suitors from home and abroad. Mary's widower, King Philip II, was happy to continue on as England's king beside Elizabeth instead of Mary, but Queen Elizabeth refused his proposal. Furthermore, since Spain remained devoutly Catholic, the arrangement between the two countries no longer made sense. Proposals followed from kings and princes of Austria, France and Sweden. Elizabeth, considered flirtatious and very much entertained by the endless line of suitors, kept most of her suitors guessing, often for years. It became clear very soon into her reign that Queen Elizabeth was already in love with an Englishman and therefore unlikely to marry anyone else. Unfortunately, the object of her affection was already married.

Robert Dudley, the queen's childhood friend and apparent love interest, was the son of John Dudley, the man who had orchestrated Jane Grey's ascension to the throne. Robert Dudley had rallied troops for Jane before she was stripped of her crown, and as a consequence was sent to the Tower of London alongside his father and brother. Coincidentally, Elizabeth was imprisoned at the same time by her sister. Both were released and eventually restored their family's titles and lands.

Robert had served King Edward VI, most auspiciously by helping the king's army crush the Catholic rebellion of 1549. By the time Elizabeth Tudor became the Queen of England, she and Robert had known each other for many years. According to courtiers, the two often flirted publicly and were suspected of being in love with one another. Of course, though the Council and Parliament were eager for their queen to find a husband, Dudley's wife, Amy Robsart, stood in the way of such a match.

Rumors were rampant at Elizabeth's court that she was waiting for Dudley's wife—apparently very ill—to die so that she could marry Robert. As the years wore on and the queen still refused all marriage proposals, her suitors generally believed this rumor to be true. In 1560, when Amy Robsart died after a fall down the stairs, many believed that Robert or even the queen herself had arranged for the woman's murder. Aware of such gossip and concerned about how a wedding would reflect on them, the couple never did marry.

In 1562, the queen contracted smallpox. Without a husband, a child or even a chosen heir, Elizabeth's government worried that the country would succumb to civil war upon her death. It was very telling that on her sickbed, Queen Elizabeth hastily chose someone as Protectorate of the Realm: Robert Dudley. This decision was never acted upon, however, since the 29-year-old queen was nursed back to health.

Much of the work of caring for Elizabeth during her long days of sickness fell to her friend and lady-in-waiting, Mary Sidney. Unfortunately, Mary herself fell victim to the same disease while she played nursemaid. She also survived but was terribly disfigured. Her husband wrote of the ravages of smallpox on his wife:

> *"When I went to Newhaven [Le Havre] I lefte her a full faire Ladye in myne eye at least the fayerest, and when I retorned I found her as fowle a ladie as the smale pox could make her, which she did take by contynuall attendance of her majesties most precious person (sicke of the same disease) the skarres of which (to her resolute discomforte) ever syns hath don and doth remayne in her face, so as she lyveth solitairilie sicut Nicticorax in domicilio suo [like a night-raven in the house] more to my charge then if we had boorded together as we did before that evill accident happened.[sic]"*

Though Elizabeth was not terribly scarred by her ordeal, the illness had left her with marks. She took to wearing heavy white lead makeup after her recovery, as well as a wig that may have covered small patches of baldness from scarring.

During the beginning of Elizabeth's rule, her cousin Mary Stuart was in France while regents and councils ruled Scotland. Following the death of Mary's husband, the French king, the Queen of Scots finally returned to the country of her birth.

During her reign, Queen Elizabeth saw the formation of a country that had truly moved out of the Middle Ages. England's first theatre was built by Richard Burbage; William Shakespeare wrote plays and performed at the queen's palaces. Francis Drake navigated the world's oceans and explored North America in the name of England. England's armies defeated the Spanish Armada in 1588 and 1597. She chose never to marry, but instead to carry the burden of the monarchy alone. She was proud and defensive of her position:

> *"[F]rom my years of understanding ... I happily chose this kind of life in which I yet live which I assure you for my own part hath hitherto best contented myself and I trust hath been most acceptable to God. From the which if either ambition of high estate offered to me in marriage by the pleasure and appointment of my prince ... or if the eschewing of the danger of my enemies or the avoiding of the peril of death ... could have drawn or dissuaded me from this kind of life, I had not now remained in this estate wherein you see me. But so constant have I always continued in this determination ... yet is it most true that at this day I stand free from any other meaning that either I have had in times past or have at this present."*

Queen Elizabeth of the House of Tudor reigned England and Ireland for over 44 years, a time which is looked upon as the Golden Age. Her era was not just defined by political strategy, strife with Scotland, France and Spain, and an onslaught of royal suitors.

Though the mid-16th century was largely defined by poor harvests, war with Ireland, a population boom of around one million people, and an increase in poverty, the last part of the century brought better tidings. For the first time, the whole of Ireland came under English control. Harvests and economies improved, lessening the suffering of the common people so that they might enjoy some leisure time at the theater or pub.

The first theaters were built throughout the kingdom when Elizabeth was on the throne, and due to her love of plays she kept them open despite an outcry from clergy who believed actors, costumes, drama, and stories all posed a threat to the immortal soul. It was even suggested that the black plague, which swept through English cities every summer, was sent by God as punishment for acting in or watching plays. The queen found this preposterous and continued to attend the theater. Many of her courtiers became patrons of the arts, commissioning plays, books, and poetry by the likes of William Shakespeare and Christopher Marlowe.

William Shakespeare arrived in England during the early part of the 17th century and wrote many plays that were performed for the queen herself. Theater was just the start of the entertainment and arts renaissance, however. While the poor and rich gathered together in playhouses, writers and university students resided side-by-side in London's inns and boarding houses. It was an explosive environment in which the artistic minds of so many influential people flourished and developed. Nicolas Hilliard created fine portraits in miniature form, silver jewelry became vogue among England's growing upper middle class, and architects designed manor houses for the nobility based on classical Greek styles and modern Dutch patterns.

The arts thrived thanks to a stable and strengthening economy within England and Ireland. Elizabeth enacted several laws that had a positive impact on the local economy, including several referred to as the "poor laws." The poor laws affected homeless and disabled people, as well as those who were out of work. In a general sense, Elizabeth made vagrancy illegal, but she also wrote legislation that told her local Justices of the Peace what to do with a vagrant. The disabled, aged, or underaged homeless, for example, were cared for in the newly-established almshouses. The Justices of the Peace were allowed to collect taxes in their towns to fund the almshouses and provide the most basic care for anyone housed within them. Anyone deemed fit to work was employed in whatever labor force was available, though treatment of such workers was by no means what modern laws would consider humane.

With more people at work, England's primary fabric-weaving industry held strong, but there were more products incoming from the New World. Elizabeth had commissioned Francis Drake and Walter Raleigh to sail to the American continents throughout the latter 1500s, and there they claimed lands in her name, bringing back gold, tobacco, potatoes, tomatoes, and other valuable goods. Merchants during this time frame had much to celebrate and the industry boomed as English people discovered a love of tobacco. Though vegetables from the New World were less popular and often considered poisonous, they eventually caught on and revolutionized British agriculture and cuisine.

Queen Elizabeth also attempted to boost the economy by requiring individuals to work in the same area in which they were born – this was intended to stop poor farmers and tradespeople from flocking to the city in search of work, and thereby keeping food production up. She also fixed wages, but this was less than effective since food prices kept rising. Despite ongoing difficulties in helping the people earn enough money to care for themselves, Elizabeth did manage to pay down the considerable debts amassed by her father and other royal predecessors.

Elizabeth never did marry, for which reason she was sometimes referred to as the Virgin Queen. She proclaimed herself "married to England," and when pressured about the problem of the succession after her death, she avoided answering or changed the subject. As the last child of Henry VIII, without an heir of her own, Elizabeth's crown would have to go to another branch of the royal family. Her two Tudor aunts had passed away, leaving only Margaret Douglas or James VI of Scotland the most probably contenders.

At the beginning of the 17th century, an aging Queen Elizabeth retired to Richmond Palace on the River Thames and mourned the loss of many of her close friends and servants. Her health deteriorated quickly, beginning with depression. The coronation ring she had not removed since it was placed upon her finger in 1558 was forcibly removed after having grown into her finger – some believe this caused an infection that led to sepsis. Ladies-in-waiting on the queen reported that she either could not or would not sit down, standing for as many as fifteen hours a day before collapsing onto piles of cushions on the floor. One serving lady even reported that Elizabeth suffered visions of ghosts who gave her guilt – including Mary, Queen of Scots and Katherine Grey, sister of Nine Days' Queen Jane Grey. At the end, she lost the ability to speak or stand from the floor. Her ladies arranged her on the bed and councilors visited, paying their respects as well as looking for her answer to the succession.

When James VI's name was mentioned, Elizabeth apparently signified her desire for him to act as her heir by circling her head with a finger to indicate a crown. She died aged 69 years on March 24, 1603 and the honor of filling her place on the throne of England fell the King of Scotland. It was the first time one monarch ruled over both kingdoms.

Queen Elizabeth's body was sealed in a lead coffin with her likeness carved on the cover, then driven by barge on the Thames to Westminster Abbey. The coffin was pulled through the streets of London on a horse-drawn hearse before its permanent interment at Westminster. She shares her tomb with her half-sister, Queen Mary I.

Chapter 17– Mary Stuart, Queen of Scots

Queen Elizabeth's main rival during her reign was her cousin Mary Stuart, the child of the English queen's cousin Margaret Douglas and King James V of Scotland. Mary was born in December 8, 1542, just six days before her father died from a sudden illness. She inherited the Scottish throne upon James' death and the Duke of Arran, James Hamilton, became her main regent. Almost immediately, the royal infant received two serious marriage proposals from England and France.

The first proposal came from King Henry VIII, who wanted to match Mary to his son, Prince Edward. Arran informally agreed to this proposal on behalf of his ward, but broke his promise soon afterward. The second proposal came from King Henry II of France, who wanted Mary to wed his own son, Francis. As France and Scotland were long-standing allies, Arran ultimately decided to accept the French offer and forsake Henry VIII. To cement the deal, Mary herself was sent to France in 1550 to be raised at the side of her future husband. In Mary's absence, her mother Mary of Guise ruled Scotland as regent, having put aside Arran in 1544.

Mary Stuart stayed in France with her future in-laws for 13 years and completed her education there as part of the inner circle of the French court. Her father-in-law was kind and fatherly to her, but apparently Mary's mother-in-law, Catherine de Medici, had a disliking for the girl. The royal children married in 1558 and became King and Queen of France in 1559 after Henry II died in a jousting accident. Mary was 16 years old and Francis II was 15. Only 17 months later, Francis died from complications from an ear infection and left Mary Dowager Queen and a widow. The same year, Mary's mother died in Scotland. Nine months after the death of Francis, Mary Stuart returned to Scotland.

She was 18 years old, Dowager Queen of France, ostensibly next in line to the throne of England, and active Queen of Scotland. Mary was the most powerful woman in Europe, but she lacked political prowess. She also lacked familial support, since the Tudor queen was suspicious of her, and the unfriendly Catherine de Medici ruled France as regent for Francis' younger brother Charles IX. At home, there was violence and derision between Catholics and Protestants that was inflamed by Mary's staunch Catholicism. Hers was not an easy transition from one kingdom to the other.

She had not been in Scotland since she was a very small child and was unsure of the local customs and culture. Further, she was a devout Catholic arriving to a small kingdom of Catholics and Protestants who were constantly at arms with one another. She was the rightful Queen of Scotland, but she felt powerless and out of place. In 1565, Mary married her cousin, Henry Stuart, the Lord Darnley, hoping to solidify her position. Mary's southern neighbor, Queen Elizabeth Tudor, was immediately apprehensive.

Not only had English King Henry VIII purposefully overlooked the Stuarts for the line of succession, but Mary had been raised and educated in an enemy nation as far as he was concerned. In marrying

Henry Stuart, the Scottish queen was essentially pairing her Tudor blood with that of another distant Tudor; Elizabeth was not impressed. She knew well enough how easy it could be for relations of the crown to find supporters and build an army; if the Catholics among her own people were unhappy enough they might well join the ranks in support of Mary.

Upon her return to Scotland, Mary's life became rather chaotic. She'd likely hoped that the marriage to another Stuart would solidify her authority and give her the emotional and political support of her wider family, but that wasn't what happened. Instead, Mary's half-brother James Stuart, Earl of Moray, saw his chance to make a play for the crown. James Stuart was also a child of the late King James V, but his mother was a mistress of the king. Nevertheless, he had designs on the throne and once Mary wed Henry, he knew how to proceed: By joining the Protestant rebels and giving them a figurehead to rally behind.

Moray raised troops, as did Mary; the armies both set out in the summer of 1565 but neither accomplished much of anything as they did not meet head-on. Finally, in October, Moray set down his arms and fled to England. Queen Mary immediately sought to strengthen her Privy Council by bringing in popular members of the Protestant nobility. Eventually, Moray was allowed to join them.

Mary's husband was a jealous and ambitious man who only added to the queen's problems. First, he insisted that he be crowned equal to her and be given the right to succeed her as Scotland's only monarch if she predeceased him. Second, he believed she was having an affair with her private secretary, the Italian David Rizzio. In the first case, Mary refused. In the second, Henry conspired with friends and murdered Rizzio in plain sight of the queen.

Mary gave birth to another James Stuart in June of 1566, and near the end of that year she had a secret meeting with her most trusted advisors to discuss how to remove her husband from court. In February of the next year, he was found murdered. James Hepburn was accused of the murder by the slain Lord Darnley's father, and under pressure to punish the killer, Mary held a trial for Hepburn. He was acquitted. What happened next has never been properly explained.

Hepburn gathered officials and documented support from many members of the nobility to pursue marriage with the queen. In April of 1567, Hepburn either kidnapped Mary or convinced her to accompany him to Dunbar Castle, where they remained for several days. When they married each other mere weeks later in a Protestant ceremony, the queen's advisors and subjects alike were baffled. The marriage put everyone at odds and led to Mary's forced abdication of the Scottish throne. Her son, James VI, merely an infant, was named king and placed under the care of a regent.

Mary Stuart escaped prison and fled Scotland, seeking the help of her cousin Queen Elizabeth of England and Ireland. Hepburn was exiled from Scotland and eventually died in a Danish prison. Under the guise of compliance, Elizabeth had Mary sequestered at Bolton Castle in Wensleydale and ordered an investigation into the Scottish queen's conduct north of the border. A court hearing was set up to determine whether Mary was guilty or complicit in the death of Henry Stuart. Elizabeth would not allow Mary to attend, but the latter refused outright anyhow. The deposed queen believed that as a foreign monarch she was not subject to the courts of any nation other than her own.

During the hearing, a set of letters were shown as evidence against the Scottish queen. These were not signed, but they seemed to be in Mary's handwriting and they were interpreted as love letters between the queen and James Hepburn. The letters were considered very uncertain proof of Mary's involvement in the death of Scotland's king, and yet they were a very real threat to her. At a Conference between Scotland's Regent, James Stuart, and Elizabeth, the English court declared as their queen wished: Nothing had been proven for or against Mary Stuart. The Regent returned to rule Scotland and Mary remained in English custody.

Queen Elizabeth was simply unsure how to deal with Mary, and therefore left her to languish in Tutbury Castle. The location of Mary's house arrest was very strategically planned to keep her far from the Scottish border and away from the sea. Contained in the middle of England, Queen Mary could not be easily freed by her supporters back home. Mary was well provided for, with a staff of at least 16 ladies-in-waiting and a personal chef. She merely was not allowed to leave the estate.

In 1587, Elizabeth ordered her royal cousin to be executed following her spy's discovery of a plot to replace herself with Mary on the throne of England. By the time of her death, the Scottish queen had been kept in England for 20 years.

Chapter 18 – King James I and the Tudor Legacy

James Stuart was born on June 19, 1566, and he inherited the Scottish crown as the infant son of Mary, Queen of Scots. Though court portraits show James posed next to his royal mother, the boy was less than a year old when he last saw Mary Stuart. He was twenty years old when she was executed for treason against Queen Elizabeth – rather ironic given that he would eventually inherit Elizabeth's kingdom upon her death in 1603.

The succession of James of Scotland to the English throne was a momentous occasion and it would be the basis for the eventual formation of the United Kingdom of Great Britain and Northern Ireland.

Though technically under the rule of James I, England's Tudor Dynasty came to an end, the monarchy after James were still closely related to the Stuarts, Tudors and even the Plantagenets. In fact, Great Britain's current monarch, from the House of Windsor, is directly descended from King Henry VII and can trace familial roots all the way back to that servant of the Welsh Kingdom of Gwynedd, Ednyfed Fychan. Still, the Tudors are considered a stand-alone epoch of English history.

Under the leadership of Henry VII and his descendants, England changed its religious identity, developed its colonial identity and became Europe's financial center. Henry VIII invested in the Royal Navy and the predecessor to the Royal Mail, while his daughter Elizabeth granted the creation of the Royal Exchange. Ships sailed around the world and brought colonists – as well as the religiously persecuted – to the Americas. Explorers brought back tomatoes, squash and potatoes, the latter of which would eventually become a new superfood in the Old World. Merchants and stockbrokers gathered in London to borrow, lend and invest money. The English fashion industry blossomed, influencing everyone from the future Queen of France to emigrant Puritans. Slowly, over more than a century of Tudor rule, England became more unified, more stable and more self-aware of its place in the world.

Of the dynasty's founder, King Henry VII, the historian Henry Bertram Chrimes said:

> *"If it be true that England showed a greatness and a marked flowering of her spirit and genius in the course of the sixteenth century, such a development would have been inconceivable without the intermediation of Henry of Richmond's regime. Not for him were the vast egoisms of his son Henry nor the gloriations of his granddaughter Elizabeth. But without his unspectacular statecraft their creative achievements would have had no roots."*

It is true that England was forever changed because of the actions of the first Henry Tudor, but historians often overlook the roles played by the women of the family, particularly those who married into the House of Tudor. Without the dedication, commitment, support and personal risks of women like Catherine of Valois and Margaret

Beaufort, the magnificent story of Henry Tudor versus Richard III at Bosworth Field may never have existed. If the Tudors hadn't seized the throne, England may have fallen into permanent civil war and the dissolution of the monarchy altogether.

It is easy to see the many ways this powerful and authoritative family changed the world, because of so many things they left behind. The Church of England is not only the largest religion in Great Britain, but Anglicism has spread throughout the Americas as well. Law and order, public support for the poor and even medicine have developed into finely-tuned programs thanks to Queen Elizabeth and King Henry VIII, the latter of whom legalized human dissection and funded public education.

Even the arts blossomed during the Tudor era thanks to the country's stability and growth. No longer constantly focused on internal war, the middle and upper classes of English people discovered talents and appreciation of architecture, paintings, theater and literature. Still today, the plays, poetry, artworks, sculpture and buildings are considered things of great intelligence and beauty.

Truly, the Tudors gave England the strong foundation upon which many great things were – and are still being – achieved.

If you enjoyed this individual book on the Tudors, can you please leave a review for it?

Thanks for your support!

Part 2: The Wars of the Roses

A Captivating Guide to the English Civil Wars That Brought down the Plantagenet Dynasty and Put the Tudors on the Throne

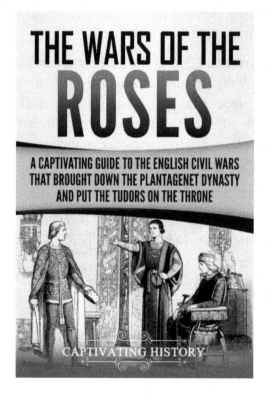

Introduction

The Wars of the Roses were a complex set of battles, skirmishes, and kidnappings during the 15th century in England. They had their roots in the nearby Civil War of France, which greatly influenced English politics for years to come. Though there is no one universally-accepted start or end date for these wars, the major events throughout the wars occurred between 1455 and 1485.

The central reason for the Wars of the Roses, otherwise referred to as the 15th century English Civil War, was a tug-of-war between two families for the throne of England. Though both families were in fact closely related, they had split half a century earlier. Instead of one unified Plantagenet family, the cousins became Lancasters and Yorks. While the Lancasters remained on the throne, the Yorks were overlooked in the succession of kings. The Yorks became jealous, given their equal relation to England's ancient monarchy, and when the Plantagenet-Lancaster dynasty appeared tragically weakened by the succession of Henry VI, the royal cousins took the opportunity to demand a new ruler.

Henry VI took over the rule of England upon the death of his father when he was not yet one year old. A scramble over leadership in the boy's appointed Regency Council led to the prominence first of Henry's Lancaster uncles, then Richard of York. Upon Henry's coming of age, Richard of York was unwilling to give up his power and under many pretenses he raised an army.

Over the course of several decades, the royalist army and rebel armies fought throughout the country. Led first by Richard of York, then by his son Edward of York, the rebels gained and lost the power of the crown multiple times, as of course did the royal Plantagenet-Lancaster side. Fighting continued until both sides eventually lost their grip on the crown into the hands of the founder of a brand-new royal dynasty.

Chapter 1 – A Short History of the House of Plantagenet

Every history buff knows who the Tudors were. But what about the dynastic family who ruled England for nearly 300 years before the Tudors had even left Wales, seeking greatness beyond the borders of their homeland? The Plantagenets were the English monarchs who took control of a confused and fractious nation after the Norman Conquest and smoothed down the roughest of its edges. They were violent, heavy-handed, and lacked even a hint of the highly-touted civility and gentleness of later eras. Yet, without their brute force, England and Great Britain would be very different today.

European history is rife with long-lived family names, each one heavy with the weight of centuries of nobility, war, and royal entanglement. The name "Tudor," "York," or "Plantagenet" calls up images of swords, throne rooms, and the heavy golden livery collars of people who helped shape history. It may be surprising to learn that the historical surname, or House, of Plantagenet began its infamous life as a simple nickname for conqueror Geoffrey V d'Anjou. In the 12th century, d'Anjou was the powerful Duke of Normandy and count of several domains within modern France.

Historians hypothesize that the name "Plantagenet" was given to Geoffrey because of the yellow straw-like flowers he wore in his hat, which were named "plantagenets." Whatever the reason for the moniker, Geoffrey V d'Anjou is considered the founder of House Plantagenet, which was also referred to as the Order of Anjou before the Tudor era. The Plantagenet title was not actually used in reference to Geoffrey and his descendants until the reign of Henry VII. It was a purely retroactive House denomination created simply to refer to the ruling dynasty that came before Henry Tudor and his descendants. By the 17th century, the term was commonplace and fully accepted by historians and royal genealogists who had become used to this type of familial departmentalization.

The original Plantagenet, Geoffrey, was a continental Norman who married into the English royal family in 1128 to King Henry I's daughter, Matilda. It was a political marriage arranged primarily by Henry I, who wanted to cement the aging ties between Normandy and the English descendants of Normandy's William the Conqueror. Both England and Normandy were politically tied, but their administration was not centralized until Henry I pushed leaders in both regions to pledge their loyalties to his daughter.

Despite Henry I's best efforts to protect his crown for Matilda, it was taken by his nephew, Stephen of Blois, after his death in 1135. King Stephen had many supporters, but so did Matilda and the Duke of Anjou. The usurpation of the throne caused civil war in 1139 when Geoffrey Plantagenet and Matilda marched into London with an army and took the crown by force. Only a few years later, Stephen stole his position back and the deposed rulers fled to Normandy.

By that time, Plantagenet was the ruler of Normandy, so the family remained there. The couple had three sons together, one of whom would inherit England: Henry II. When Henry II became king, it marked the beginning of a three-century dynasty of Plantagenets that didn't end until Richard III's death in 1485.

The Duke of Anjou gifted the kingdom to his son Henry in 1150. Henry married Eleanor of Aquitaine, thereby gaining control of most of France, and then invaded England twice before securing the right to succeed to the throne following the death of King Stephen. Henry II became the King of England in 1154.

King Henry II began his rule by attempting to erase the legacy of his predecessor. He required the noble houses of England to destroy all castles they had built for Stephen. The new king established the federal finance ministry and brought back the royal justices, whose job it was to travel throughout the kingdom and judge criminal cases.

Descendants of Geoffrey Plantagenet and Henry II were often at war and at odds with the nobility or the Papacy, but they held tight to the fundamental principles that kept the country's economy running – taxation and the implementation of localized law and order.

The Plantagenet dynasty was a formative era for England and the future United Kingdom. Geoffrey Plantagenet's successors oversaw the formation of an English Parliament, the official institutionalization of feudalism, the domination of Wales, and several political alliances with Scotland following the rebellions of William Wallace. It was during the Plantagenet era that England and France embarked upon the Hundred Years' War, an era of constant land disputes that usually involved the continental regions of Aquitaine, Normandy, Brittany, Anjou, and Maine – most of the regions Henry II and his wife Eleanor held in their possession. Both England and France had reason to believe these places fell under their own jurisdiction, and neither was willing to permanently concede defeat.

Though the Plantagenet family did indeed rule England from the 12th century, the dynasty was split into two factions of cousins in 1399. That year, following the death of John of Gaunt, the Plantagenet line broke into two separate sub-houses: Lancaster and York. Both retained an equal relationship with John of Gaunt, heir to King Edward III, meaning both had a solid claim to the throne. The controversy between the cousins came about due to which heir on which side was closest to the previous monarch. In a family feud over the crown that lasted 86 years, it was these Lancasters and Yorks who were responsible for bringing England to civil war in the 15th century.

The Lancasters retained the throne after the death of King Edward III, while the Yorks were installed in important positions at court and throughout the kingdom. Balance held, though delicately, and both sides of the family developed their own identity. The Lancasters adopted the red rose as their sigil, while the Yorks adopted the white rose. In the 15th century, the Yorks usurped the English throne from the Lancaster king, and the two sets of roses declared war upon each other.

Chapter 2 – Civil War in France

Though the English Civil War did not break out until King Henry VI reached adulthood, the most prominent factor behind the future Wars of the Roses was the succession of this child. Upon the death of Lancastrian King Henry V while campaigning in France, the nine-month-old heir became king of England in his stead in August of 1422. Just months later, the infant king's grandfather, French King Charles VI, died, having made England's rulers the rightful heirs to France. Not yet a year in age, Henry VI was the ruler of all England and France.

The young king's mother, Catherine of Valois, was the daughter of the deceased French king, which could have made her a very powerful regent. However, Parliament stepped in to create a Regency Council that excluded Catherine and appointed only men. The council was comprised of 18 people, including John of Lancaster and Humphrey of Lancaster, who were the most prominent councilors of the group since they were brothers of the old king and uncles of the new. John went to France to govern the

English lands abroad while Humphrey stayed in England as Lord Protector of the Realm.

The most controversial issue facing Henry VI's Regency Council was the ongoing Hundred Years' War with France. Though England's own monarch was, in name, the King of France, it was impossible for the English to govern an entire country in which there were immense forces aimed against foreign rule. The disinherited son of the old French king, Charles Valois, garnered great support for his cause and waged civil war against the English and their French allies. Infamous patriotic warrior, Jean d'Arc, joined the fight on the side of Charles VII, changing the momentum of the war.

Charles VII was crowned king of France at Reims Cathedral in 1429. Charles built on this victory by adding more soldiers to his forces and more districts of France to his own group of allies. They fought hard against the English but had much ground to recover, which was particularly difficult given that Charles was still not accepted by all French provinces as their king. Jean d'Arc herself wrote to the English king and his council, asking them to give up France to the French or suffer the consequences.

The Regency Council thought little of France's beloved female knight and continued its fight on the continent for another 15 years before an armistice was agreed upon in 1444.

King Henry VI turned 16 in 1437, finally coming of age to rule his kingdoms. He took over England and England-allied France from his Regency Council, at which point it became known as his Privy Council. The English privy councilors were split between a desire for peace and a desire to press onward in France. Richard Plantagenet, a York cousin of the king, had taken one of the coveted Regency positions just one year prior to the king's birthday; he strongly favored continued military efforts abroad.

The acting king, however, was not in favor of continued fighting. He wanted to put an end to the Hundred Years' War and come to some kind of final agreement between England and France, whatever that may mean for England's holdings abroad. Haste would have been ideal, since the Royal Treasury was in deep debt from war expenses. The king was no match for his political rival, Richard of York, however. Richard was a powerful force within the council, and so war continued, less and less to England's advantage.

King Henry VI was not without his own strategy, however. He worked together with his favorite advisor, William de la Pole, to put a stop to the war and restore peace in France. De la Pole organized the Treaty of Tours, intended as the armistice of 1444. It was signed by Henry VI and Charles VII and laid out the stipulations of marriage between the English king and a member of the French aristocracy. France asked Henry VI to give up his claim to the French throne, offering him several regions in the south of France as motivation to do so. He also demanded the return of Anjou and Maine to French control. Charles VII was unwilling to give England any territories without maintaining ultimate ownership, so these negotiations wore on without ever reaching a firm conclusion.

Arrangement of the meeting between envoys of the kings was lengthy and perpetually delayed. De la Pole would be blamed for negotiations that failed England in favor of France, though he acted on his king's orders and stated he had promised nothing concrete to Charles VII. While the ownership of several French regions, including Anjou, Maine, and Brittany were still under negotiations, the marriage contract between countries held strong.

In 1445, the king married Margaret of Anjou, the Princess of Naples, in-law of Charles VII, member of the French House of Anjou, and daughter to the Duchess of Lorraine. The Duchy of Lorraine was officially part of the Holy Roman Empire, but at the time of Margaret's wedding, it was effectively ruled by members of the House Valois. The marriage was the keystone to Henry VI's plan for peace between the Valois and Plantagenet families, and by extension, France and England. At the time of the wedding, Henry was 23 years old and Margaret was 15.

Originally, the Treaty of Tours promised 21 months of peace between the two countries, but the treaty was extended at the insistence of Henry VI. The king believed that his marriage and a long-term peace treaty would cement affable relations between the two countries, but his plan didn't succeed. In 1448, Charles VII threatened England with warfare if Maine and Anjou were not handed back to the French; King Henry VI did so, but it did not halt the onslaught of war. Fighting resumed in 1450, and Valois' forces defeated the English in several crucial battles, pushing them out of France and ultimately out of their own continental French strongholds, except for Calais. By mid-century, the Hundred Years' War had all but ended, with England on the losing side.

England's loss signaled the end of the French Civil War, and the beginning of the wars at home.

Chapter 3 – England's Loss and a King's Illness

Several important events occurred during the final years of the Hundred Years' War. One of Henry's uncles, the Duke of Bedford, died. The wife of his remaining uncle, Humphrey Plantagenet, was found guilty of performing witchcraft intended to bring on the death of the king. She was forced to divorce Humphrey, the Duke of Gloucester, and live in prison for the remainder of her life.

Soon after King Henry's marriage to Margaret of Anjou, the new queen became suspicious of her husband's uncle, the Duke of Gloucester. Humphrey Plantagenet stood to inherit the throne of England upon the death of Henry VI, a fact that the queen felt certain he would take advantage of. The king was convinced that his uncle plotted against him, which may or may not have been a reality, and Humphrey was arrested. He died only a few days later in prison in 1447.

In 1450, King Henry VI's most influential councilor, the Duke of Suffolk (William de la Pole) was scapegoated by the rest of the council as the reason England lost its lands in France. The king was forced to banish him from England. Upon making his exit to the mainland, Suffolk was intercepted and decapitated by an angry mob.

That same year, Jack Cade, a northern Yorkist from Kent, published his Proclamation of Grievances. He believed, as did Richard of York, that the king had surrounded him with poor counsel and was not personally heeding the laws of the land.

Without Suffolk, Henry VI came to depend heavily upon his wife, Margaret of Anjou. Margaret was young, but she was clever, ambitious, and trusted by her husband. As it became clear that King Henry was not only a weak ruler but that he suffered from bouts of psychological instability, Margaret's role as queen of England grew less supportive and more vital. She knew, given Henry's mental illness, that the crown was in constant danger from close rivals. After the death of the Duke of Gloucester, that threat came in the form of Richard Plantagenet, also called Richard of York.

Richard Plantagenet was given a position on the Great Council, an emergency authoritative council created in 1453 at the onset of Henry VI's first major illness. After having heard that the last of his English forces had been pushed out of France, the king became mute and ceased to govern. The Great Council tried to make do, hoping the illness would be short-lived, but it proved a lengthy battle. The next year, the Great Council elected Richard of York as Lord Protector of the Realm.

Margaret of Anjou was not pleased with this promotion, since Richard Plantagenet arguably had a firmer claim to the throne of England than did her own husband. Both Henry and Richard were direct descendants of King Edward III; however, Richard's birth was a generation closer to his great-grandfather than Henry was to the same great-great-grandfather.

Richard of York did indeed want to claim the English crown, but his life and ambitions depended on pretending that he was a firm supporter of Henry VI.

The first order of business for the newly-appointed Lord Protector of the Realm was to imprison his biggest competition and friend to the king and queen, the Duke of Somerset. Unfortunately for Richard, Margaret gave birth that same year, 1453, to Prince Edward. By 1455, King Henry VI was ready to rule once more, so Richard of York was set aside, and Somerset freed from prison.

No longer directly in line to the throne nor in charge of the kingdom, Richard Plantagenet took matters into his own hands and called together an army. He met King Henry VI with Queen Margaret, Somerset, and other allies traveling north near St. Albans and attacked them. Somerset and 300 others were killed. Henry VI was wounded and taken hostage by the York faction.

A strange and drawn-out civil war had officially begun.

Chapter 4 – Treason by the Duke of York

The Battle of St. Albans was a clear victory for the Yorkists, but it was not their goal to kill the king. They wanted only to subdue him and keep him in their possession. Since there was already an heir apparent in Henry's son Edward, the king's death would have likely led to another regency council headed by the boy's powerful and influential mother. Probably only for this reason, Henry VI was captured but largely unharmed.

When Richard of York took Henry VI back to London the next day, he did so under the pretense that he was once again acting as the king's regent. York had his royal hostage kept comfortably in a variety of castles and apparently Henry did very little complaining about his circumstances. Months later, when the king's Parliament held a rare meeting, it was informed by York that Henry was once more unfit for the throne. The Parliament declared Richard of York the Protector of England, a title he held until early 1456 when Henry once more rallied and joined his council. Instead of punishing his captor, Henry reinstated York as a leader of his army and commissioned him to respond against regular threats at the Scottish border. York was also made Lieutenant of Ireland and spent most of his time in that part of the realm.

Henry's desire for peaceful relations with all factions was strong, a fact clearly exemplified by his forgiving treatment of Richard of York. Henry organized a meeting between his kidnapper, York's in-laws the Nevilles, and the crown's own representatives. This was a classic medieval-style cease-fire, known as a Loveday. The meeting took place on March 24, 1458. Negotiations were made between all parties, and ultimately the Lancasters, Yorks, and all their major allies agreed to maintain peace and forgive one another for real or imagined trespasses. Though King Henry was proud of the affair, to most involved, the event was considered largely ceremonial.

Margaret of Anjou, for her part, had begun to believe that her husband was incapable of protecting his position and dealing with threats to himself and his family. Fortunately for Henry and their children, the Queen of England was a strong and intelligent woman. She took a firm hand with her husband for both their sakes. Margaret knew that despite the illusion of friendship and forgiveness between the two Plantagenet lines on Loveday, there were armed forces at the ready on both sides. The next summer, Margaret called for a Great Council meeting to which Richard of York and his main allies in the Neville family were not invited. York and his supporters knew what this meant—they were about to be accused of treason.

Before the council met, Richard recruited as many fighting men to his cause as he could with the help of the Nevilles. On the royal Lancaster side, Margaret of Anjou personally recruited soldiers to fill her army ranks, gathering twice as many as the rebels. The first clash between the two armies came at the Battle of Blore Heath in Staffordshire on September 23, 1459. Part of the Yorkist army marched south to join the rest of Richard's forces, and the royal army met them before they could complete the journey.

The Lancaster army had around 10,000 men assembled, whereas the incomplete York army had only 5,000. A creek passed between the two armies with deep banks that made forging the water a tricky endeavor, and to avoid needless fighting, the leaders of the armies, Lord Aubrey for the Lancasters and the Duke of Salisbury for the Yorks, attempted to find a diplomatic solution. Ultimately, they failed to do so. Both sides advanced.

Despite having all possible advantages, the royal army was besieged into retreat under vicious attacks from the rebels. Lord Aubrey was killed, as well as 2,000 of his soldiers. Hundreds of royalists switched sides mid-battle, which probably had more to do with saving their own lives than it did with their political beliefs. Under the secondary leadership of Lord Dudley, the Lancaster army fled, leaving Salisbury to continue southward and join Richard of York.

Less than a month later, still awaiting reinforcements from Salisbury in the north and Lord Warwick in Calais, the Duke of York and his partial army occupied Ludlow along the Welsh border. They'd been pushed back from London by the king's forces and knew they'd need full numbers before it would be possible to enter the capital city.

Richard, his father and Richard Neville (the Earl of Warwick) arrived with their troops in mid-October to face the royal army as it approached with the king himself at its head in full armor. It was a surprising moment for many of York's assembled soldiers since Richard had insisted that his fight was not against the king, but the king's advisors.

When Henry VI offered pardons to anyone in the Yorkist army willing to switch sides, all 600 men from Calais joined the Lancaster troops. York, Warwick and Salisbury fled, pretending to return to Ludlow for a night of discussion but actually deserting their own soldiers. They ran to Wales, leaving the army facing the king without any leadership. There was no alternative for the rebel troops except to kneel to Henry, which they did. York's family was taken into custody.

Despite the lack of any large-scale fighting, this stand-off came to be known as the Battle of Ludford Bridge. It momentarily cemented King Henry VI's place on the throne, both in the minds of the rebels and the royal supporters. The Lancastrians returned home to enjoy their victory as Henry and Margaret's enemies fled. Once safe at a distance in Wales, York returned to Ireland and Warwick to Calais. Parliament, at long last, denounced the Duke of York as a traitor.

Amazingly, Richard Plantagenet had not yet run out of supporters. Warwick and Salisbury would return to England to battle the king's forces again the very next year.

Chapter 5 – The Battle of Northampton

In the spring of 1460, Warwick sailed from Calais once more to meet Salisbury in Ireland and make plans for their upcoming attack. Both had garnered more support for York's claim to the throne, particularly in Ireland where the younger Richard had served as Lieutenant for several years. Though King Henry had named a new Lieutenant of Ireland in place of Richard and a new Captain of Calais in place of Neville, citizens of Ireland and Calais did not recognize any authority but that of the old leaders.

York decided to stay in Ireland, safe, while the Nevilles led the attack on Henry VI's troops. Warwick and Salisbury did as York commanded, gathering their armies and marching into London at the beginning of July. The city was unsure how to prepare for the onslaught, eventually remaining true to Henry VI and stationing soldiers along the London Bridge to prevent the Yorkists' entrance. Thomas Scales and Robert Hungerford were stationed at the Tower of London with armaments, ready to face a siege. Locked up within the compound were members of the public who could not fight or were unwilling to do so.

The Earl of Salisbury's army broke through the ranks of Lancastrians at the London Bridge but could not penetrate the walls of the Tower. The two sides fought fruitlessly, Scales opting to use the weapons at his disposal to fire into the city. His imprecise bombardment killed many Londoners as well as Yorkists, but the opposing army did not back down. Salisbury continued to press on the walls of the Tower while his son, Earl of Warwick, marched towards Henry and his army at Northampton on July 10.

At Northampton, the royal forces were outnumbered by the rebels, though they did have a few cannons on their side. Warwick sent messengers repeatedly asking to speak with the king but was denied every time, finally being told that an attempted meeting would end in Warwick's death. Neville's final message stated that at two o'clock he would either speak with King Henry VI or die. Promptly at two o'clock, the Yorkist army advanced.

Luck was not with the Lancaster forces, as a steady rain robbed them of their only advantage by soaking the cannons. Worse than the loss of the artillery was the fact that an entire flank of their army had arranged to commit treason on behalf of the rebel faction. Lord Grey of Ruthin was the army leader responsible for letting Warwick's troops through his ranks and into the royal camp, where they seized King Henry. In exchange for giving the king's enemies easy access to the camp, Grey received York's support in a land dispute and was later named Treasurer of England.

Four of Henry's top advisors sacrificed themselves on his behalf, but the king was taken captive for a second time despite their efforts. Three hundred troops were killed at the Battle of Northampton. Afterward, Warwick took Henry VI back to London and his army joined with Salisbury's to insist London's protectors open the gates of the Tower. Scales and Hungerford fought viciously against the attackers but saw the numbers against them were too great to overcome. They were forced to admit a few men with whom to discuss terms of a ceasefire, and the Tower was surrendered to the rebels. Hungerford escaped the city but Scales was captured by his own citizens, furious at his haphazard shooting, and killed.

Following the battle at Northampton, Richard of York believed he'd won the war. He triumphantly re-entered England, heading straight for London. He brought his own council to court, confirmed that Henry VI was caged in the Tower and rode into the city that September under a banner which displayed the Royal Arms of England. When York reached Henry's palace, however, he did not receive the welcome or celebration he had expected. No one hailed him as king, and they refused to do so no matter how plainly he made his case.

The fact was that both Henry VI and his son were alive, and therefore it was only in the hands of Parliament to grant the Duke of York the ultimate position of power. The parliamentarians met and discussed the situation, deciding that it was not for them to put a living king aside. After all, monarchs were considered appointees of God and therefore subordinate only to the administration of the Catholic Church; certainly not to a congregation of politicians.

Parliament did not grant Richard of York the kingship, but it did recognize its potential chance to stop the endless infighting between the two Plantagenet factions. It was obvious that the Duke of York wanted nothing less than ultimate control over England, and without that, he would wage war ceaselessly until he was satisfied. In an attempt to satisfy him, Parliament granted him the ongoing role of Lord Protector of England. At least this way, York would harness the control he desired and England would benefit from having a sane person in possession of Henry VI's power. In addition, York and his progeny were granted the right of succession over Prince Edward of Lancaster. So, when Henry VI died, his son would be overlooked in favor of Richard or Edward of York.

King Henry did not begrudge the slow usurpation of his crown, but instead lamented all the violence and death that went into each attempt to take it. He was a generally complacent prisoner, happy to occupy himself in his own rooms and hope that his obedience saved lives. If he was angry at the Act of Accord, which cut his son out of the succession of kings, he did not make a fuss. Margaret, who had escaped the fighting with young Edward, would make it for him.

Though he was without the title "King of England," Richard Plantagenet held the most prominent position in the kingdom and Henry VI remained locked away in the Tower of London. For several months, the Lord Protector remained in London to organize his affairs. It was not long before his army was needed again.

Chapter 6 – Margaret's Army

After the Battle of Northampton, King Henry was placed under the custody of York's allies and kept away from court. The king's quarters were comfortable and he was well-cared for, though every visitor, letter and move he made were monitored closely by York's enforcers. As before, the king made no attempt to free himself and may not even have considered himself to be in a predicament. In some reports, the king considered his captor a friend and protector and was happy to follow Richard's instructions.

His wife and son escaped the fray unharmed and ran to Wales to avoid being captured by Richard's forces. By this point, Margaret very clearly understood her role within the royal family: matriarch. She was young and not particularly experienced, but she was motivated by the need to take care of her little son and keep herself safe from political enemies. The queen had a loyal contingent that made sure she and young Edward were whisked away even as Henry VI was being captured and placed into the custody of Richard Plantagenet. She was not content to cower behind her guards, however, and started to formulate a plan to win back her family's position.

When she felt it was safe, Margaret traveled with Edward to Scotland to plead for help from Queen Mary of Guelders. Guelders was Scotland's acting regent for her underage son, King James III, and though her country had a constant record of violence and land disputes with England, she recognized the good sense in helping her neighbor queen. The Scottish queen knew that if England's monarchy could be overthrown by its cousins, the same thing could happen in Scotland. Mary of Guelders made the best of the situation and agreed to equip Margaret with troops in exchange for the disputed city of Berwick-upon-Tweed. While the Queen of England negotiated, adding Scots and Welsh troops to her existing English armies, the loyal lords in northern England put together their own armies and took over Richard Plantagenet's key city of York.

The Duke of York had no choice but to ride north from London and face the insurgents. He sent his son Edward to quell the Lancastrian influence in Wales and left the Earl of Warwick in charge of troops in London. On December 21, 1460, York's army arrived at Sandal Castle, his own estate just outside of Wakefield, Yorkshire. He took back and occupied Sandal Castle with troops numbering 5000 to 6000. Meanwhile, Margaret's army traveled south to Yorkshire and set up camp nearby for the week of Christmas. Messengers traveled back and forth between the castle and the Lancastrian camp and a pact of non-violence was agreed over the holiday.

Though Margaret of Anjou was in control of the combined forces of Lancastrians after the Battle of Northampton, she most likely stayed in York or even Scotland while the army did her bidding. Once out of her immediate range, Margaret's army fell under the combined leadership of Henry Beaufort, Henry Percy, Henry Holland and many other family heads close to the Lancasters. Many of these men had lost brothers, fathers and sons in the previous battles and had personal agendas against the Duke of York.

Over the Christmas break, York's forces faced a shortage of supplies and were forced to leave the fortified estate to forage and hunt for food. They were running out of the basic foodstuffs necessary to stay and fight, which may explain York's decisions when the violence commenced.

York's military maneuvers during the ensuing Battle of Wakefield were ultimately a very rapid failure. Richard stayed with his army nine days at Sandal Castle before engaging the enemy, and during that time sent a messenger to ask his son Edward for reinforcements. Neither Edward nor any of his soldiers arrived in time, though there were no major skirmishes between Margaret and Richard until the second-last day of 1460.

On December 30, Margaret commanded her military leaders to approach Sandal Castle and arrange themselves for battle a mile from York's residence. The Lancastrians are said to have outnumbered their enemy perhaps two to one, a fact that helped them spread out through the land with at least three battalions facing the castle. They remained steady, perhaps finalizing the details of their attack, but York beat them to it.

Freshly-supplied with more troops gathered by Lord John Neville, York was ready to face the Lancastrians. Plantagenet kept command of the troops he'd brought to the castle, while Neville maintained command of the troops he'd gathered. While strategizing, Neville convinced the Duke of York to make his stand in the field rather than from within his fortified compound. It was a very poorly-planned move that made little sense to those fighting on either side. As long as Richard held his castle, his soldiers could benefit from the fortification, doors and thick walls of Sandal Castle while forcing his enemies waste their strength trying to break through. Nevertheless, Richard was buoyed by the arrival of Neville's battalion, possibly influenced by the fact that food was scarce at Sandal Castle, and confident enough to meet the Lancastrians in the field east of Wakefield.

The Yorkists followed their leader out of the compound and towards the line of the enemy. as almost immediately the Yorkists were surrounded on all sides by the royal army. Fighting was fierce and violent, and a section of York's army had clearly agreed beforehand to betray him. Under the leadership of Sir Andrew Trollope, hundreds of Richard Plantagenet's allied soldiers changed allegiance mid-battle, confusing the Yorkists and causing localized chaos that spread through the ranks.

The Battle of Wakefield was the biggest and bloodiest battle of the civil war, though it probably lasted only about an hour. Trollope's turncoat actions made things difficult for York, but the real turning point of the engagement was John Neville's entrance into the fray – on the side of his apparent enemy. It turned out that Neville had distanced himself from York's troops only to give himself room to turn on them and help the Lancastrians surround him. Soon, Richard Plantagenet was killed and the battle finished. Thousands lay dead, including York's son Edmund and John Neville, the man who'd made such a difference the outcome of the battle.

The Lancastrians put the Duke of York's head on a spike next to his son's. They were displayed on the Roman Micklegate Bar in York, Richard's head wearing a paper crown. His body was buried at Pontefract and later reburied at a church in Fotheringhay, the location of Richard's favorite residence. At the end of the 19th century, a monument was erected to mark the fall of Richard Plantagenet at Wakefield.

Because Richard of York had been granted the right of succession by English Parliament, his death meant his remaining son, Edward, was next in line to the throne following the death of King Henry VI. Henry, of course, was still very much alive, though he remained unofficially imprisoned under York's orders in London.

Chapter 7 – Mortimer's Cross and the Battle of Towton

The death of Richard Plantagenet did not bring the civil war to an end. Immediately upon the defeat of his father and brother at the Battle of Wakefield, 18-year-old Edward Plantagenet—also called the Earl of March—took up the Yorkist cause for himself. Neither army could desist and go home, as the battles were by no means finished. Less than a month after the clash at Wakefield, troops began strategic movements on both sides. At this point, the Tudor family joined the war.

Jasper and Owen Tudor, half-brother and step-father to King Henry VI, gathered pro-Lancaster troops in their native Wales before marching into England to confront Edward, the Earl of March. At the beginning of February 1461, the Tudor's army met with the remaining York army, now under the leadership of young Edward VI. The fighting occurred at Mortimer's Cross near Hereford, which had been Edward's stronghold while his father led the Yorkist armies.

The Lancaster forces were ultimately bested by the Yorkists, with the former forced to flee southward. It has been documented that thousands of troops were killed, though historians believe the numbers were not so high. Among the dead was Owen Tudor, husband to dowager queen Catherine of Valois. His son escaped with his life.

Just weeks later, a separate faction of the York army, led by the Earl of Warwick, fought Margaret's army at the Second Battle of St. Albans. Margaret's forces were triumphant, sending Warwick away from London and rescuing King Henry VI from the Tower of London. Warwick's troops retreated and joined with Edward's own army marching north to Yorkshire.

Edward marched into London after the victory at Mortimer's Cross and proclaimed himself king of England on March 4, 1461. At that point, most Londoners had grown to dislike Margaret of Anjou, an ambitious foreigner whom they had never warmed to. The court did not make it difficult for Edward to seize the empty throne. Queen Margaret was not willing to let go of power so easily, however, so she rallied and sent her troops to chase down Edward's when they went to reclaim York in mid-March. The two sides clashed many times before meeting a final time just north of Towton, Yorkshire.

Both armies camped nearby the town of Towton on March 28, preparing for battle in the morning. It was unusual for a battle to take place on a religious holiday, but that particular Palm Sunday, the Duke of Somerset and Edward of York lined up a combined 50,000 to 200,000 soldiers. Various contemporary sources and historians do not agree on the number of troops; however, they do agree that this was by far the largest battle of the Wars of the Roses.

The morning of March 29 was cold and snowy, but the battle was not to be avoided. The Lancaster army had significantly more support from the English nobility, as well as a larger number of individual horsemen, spear-throwers, archers, and swordsmen. The Lancaster side was led by a cousin of King Henry's, Henry Beaufort.

The king himself, with Queen Margaret and Prince Edward, was safely settled at York. The York army was led by teenaged Edward of York himself.

The armies met between Towton and Saxton, with the Lancasters given an early advantage in placement. They were protected on two sides by marshlands and a steep riverbank. Safe, the king's men waited for Edward to make the first charge. York's archers let loose in the direction of the wind, but they were eventually beaten back by an immense force of Lancastrians pushing south.

The Plantagenet king's army kept its overall advantage for several hours in the snow, but mid-way through the fight, York's troops were joined by their final contingent, led by the Duke of Norfolk. Positioned such as they were, the king's men could not see the incoming ranks of fresh soldiers until they were nearly upon them. Strong-armed from the rear, the Lancastrian troops lost their grip on the battle.

After up to ten hours of fighting, small contingents of the king's army began to flee, tossing their heavy helmets, shields, and armor aside to escape more quickly. Seeing they'd won, the Yorkists had no mercy for the Lancaster troops. Runaways, surrendered nobles, and captives were slaughtered as they saw the cause was lost and tried to save their own lives. By the thousands they ran across the river, crushing the bridge, with many drowning, and soon afterward, they began climbing over the piling bodies of their own troop. Records from that day reported 28,000 casualties.

Their forces overcome, the deposed King Henry VI and Queen Margaret of Anjou, with their son Edward, ran for shelter in Scotland. Edward had won the throne and was crowned Edward IV, King of England on June 28 that same year.

In a letter from royal supporters to Queen Margaret following the Towton clash, the queen was advised not to attempt to leave her safe place in Scotland before they arrived.

Some of the casualties of that long-ago battle were discovered in a mass grave in Towton in 1996. After careful archeological excavation and record-keeping, the Towton Skeletal Collection of 43 almost-complete bodies was taken to the University of Bradford for preservation. The bodies show tell-tale signs of extreme violence indicative of the use of war hammers, polearms, knives and swords. Further archeological exploration in the area revealed multiple mass graves as well as the single grave of a presumed noble knight. Further scientific studies are ongoing.

The emotion, drama, fear, violence, and death that marked the decades of war in 16th-century England has left an unforgettable archeological and political legacy. It is even said that the spiritual world bears permanent scars from the terror of those gruesome battles. Many visitors to Towton, for example, have reported sightings that mirror those of the long-ago fight between Edward of York, Richard Neville, and the royalist House of Lancaster. At least one visitor to the historical battlefield has captured paranormal images on film.

The decisive battle in which Edward of York took the crown from Henry VI has provided physical researchers with a treasure-trove of knights, soldiers, buckles, and arrowheads – but its supposed metaphysical properties are more difficult to study. The battle took place in a blizzard at the end of March in 1461, 14 years before Henry Tudor took the throne of England, and believers in the paranormal claim that every year, a similar snowfall hits Towton. They say that if visitors peer far into the snow, they see a massive army fighting the same battle in the name of England's long-dead king. The battle lasts several hours as knights on horseback and foot soldiers meet their deaths again and again.

A pub near the ancient battlegrounds of the Yorks and Lancasters claims to be the regular haunt of a poltergeist. The spirit moves heavy objects, throws kitchen pots and tools on the floor, and pushes over large pots of vegetables that have been left safely level on the stove. Pub owners say the ghost is not malevolent, but very active and generally troublesome. Unable to communicate with the spirit, they simply call it "Nancy."

Nancy isn't the only supernatural being reputedly left behind by the Wars of the Roses. The Cock Beck – the stream in which thousands of soldiers drowned, froze, and were crushed to death under the feet and corpses of their own comrades-at-arms – has its own stories to tell. The innocent-looking stream of water was a major feature of the Battle of Towton, cutting huge lines of men off from freedom in the last hours of the siege. It ran red with blood and was dammed with bodies by the time Edward had won his victory.

People who live near the Cock Beck say some days they can hear the moaning and screaming of dying and injured soldiers who passed away centuries ago. Such tales may be difficult to prove, but they hold great significance for those who believe in them and want to honor the memory of the tens of thousands that died fighting for both sides during the Wars of the Roses. All the ghosts of the battlefield, in their own way, contribute to an ongoing memorial and respect for that bloody and dangerous era in English history.

Chapter 8 – York Takes the Throne

The country's first York king was crowned on June 28, 1461, at Westminster Abbey. It was two days after Edward's triumphant return to London. Immediately upon entering the capital city, King Edward IV called together Parliament and knighted 32 of his most loyal supporters.

While Henry and Margaret remained in Scotland along with some of their exiled English allies, the king had all slain Lancastrian nobility posthumously stripped of their rank and holdings. This act thereby took all privilege, property and income from the families of York's murdered enemies. The Lancastrians and allied families who remained alive were given the chance to change sides or face the same fate. In this way, Edward removed his remaining opposition at court, bullied his cousins into showing respect, and elevated the Yorks and his greatest non-familial supporters to positions of high rank.

There were still hold-out factions of Lancasters in the north, but this was expected and the rebellions were kept relatively under control by the new king. With peace in place throughout the bulk of the kingdom, Edward IV chose to focus on the consolidation of his fractured land. It meant a great deal to the nobility and the commoners alike that Edward had been officially crowned and the bloodiest part of the war was at an end. By the time the Lancaster king was deposed, the country had suffered for six years to provide constant arms, food, supplies, and soldiers to both the Yorks and the Lancasters. Great cities like York and London had come under fire so often that their gatekeepers were loath to open up for anyone, no matter their rank. Finally, most of the country could focus on healing, settling down, and prospering. Moreover, Edward was a young, strong, tall and seemingly intelligent man whose figure commanded a room. He was well-liked.

While Edward IV and Richard Neville, Earl of Warwick, effectively ruled England, the exiled monarchs in Scotland coordinated with northern allies in England and Wales. Margaret never rested, causing clash after clash in the northern region that sapped much of Edward's resources. He and Warwick discussed entering Scotland and facing their enemy once more, as proven by this letter from Warwick to the king in October of 1463. The letter, written by Warwick to the king, expresses the former's satisfaction at the monarch's decision to invade Scotland, and promises to do whatever is necessary to make that campaign successful.

Indeed, after three years being safely hidden by allies in Scotland, Henry VI was removed to northern England because of fears that Edward's negotiations with the Scots would go badly for him. Several small battles ensued between the diplomatic party and the Lancaster king's protectors. In 1464, Henry VI was captured by Edward and brought back to London. He was locked in the tower once again, with Margaret and his son back in Scotland. He stayed there for five years while the deposed queen continued to rally small groups of armed Lancaster allies at every opportunity.

Chapter 9 – The King in the Tower

Henry Lancaster languished in his luxurious prison. Like his imprisonment under Richard of York, the true king of England seemed pleased enough to do the bidding of Edward IV and did indeed consider the usurper a close friend. Whether this was only his attitude during moments of dementia and delusion, or whether Henry truly felt comradery with his kidnappers, neither history nor contemporary sources can say. It does seem telling that Henry VI made no large effort to free himself or to negotiate with his jailor. It was his meek and mild manner that had cost him many loyal supporters throughout the years of the war, but without Queen Margaret to rally him, Henry was unwilling or unable to change his temperament.

Called the "Mad King" due to his random bouts of dementia, the deposed king would have been considered unsuited for his royal position even if he'd enjoyed constant sanity. Extremely devoted to Catholicism, Henry disliked blood and violence, had no desire to torture or kill enemies, and considered nudity in men or women lewd. His empathy made him quick to forgive debts to the crown. He also used much of his treasury's money to help alleviate the poverty of his people, a fact that would be remembered by them much later. During his time as king, unfortunately, Henry's methods for ruling the realm were overwhelmingly unappreciated.

Henry VI had been extremely popular due to his name and the legacy of his family, but on a personal level he was not well-liked. Henry was awkward, soft-spoken and many found him quite feminine. He did not conform to the men's fashions of the times, notably dressing in plain clothes and avoiding the upturned shoes preferred by other gentlemen of the court. The boastful and self-aggrandized behavior of most European monarchs was polar opposite to Henry's kind and unimposing manner. Essentially having been a political prisoner from his first year of life, it is possible that Henry VI was predisposed to following the orders of stronger, more authoritative members of the royal house.

King Edward provided his docile rival with food, clothing, and a personal chaplain with whom to say the Catholic Mass. He could receive some visitors, but many of those only wanted to spy on the Mad King for their own curiosity.

While locked away, the gentle king wrote poetry. His words expressed his belief that the hunger for riches and power was a dead end in life. After being little but a political pawn his whole life, it is not particularly surprising that Henry VI merely sat back in his comfortable prison and allowed those around him to make decisions. It was the same power dynamic he'd learned in childhood and continued to accept in his marriage.

To his credit, King Edward IV could easily have chosen to kill Henry, but was satisfied at having him locked away. His decision to keep the deposed king in the Tower seems to solidify his father's statement that he was never an enemy of King Henry VI, but an enemy of those who advised him. Edward may have kept Henry alive for the simple fact that Richard of York had no intentions of killing him, or he may have worried that Henry's death would reflect badly on him personally. It may have been as simple as that Edward didn't truly see Henry as a threat—after all, the man was content to read and write and keep to himself.

Few records exist from Henry's time in the Tower of London, but it seems he caused little trouble and did as he was told. Five years after he was taken hostage, his people came for him.

Chapter 10 – The Kingmaker Repents

Richard Neville had been dubbed "The Kingmaker" after the series of battles that led Edward IV to the English throne; unfortunately, Neville did not enjoy the same close relationship with the young Duke of York as he had with Richard Plantagenet. Though they were great allies in the early years of Edward's reign, the friendship turned sour after 1464.

With Henry Lancaster safely within his reach, Edward IV looked to other issues facing the kingdom. Continued war with France was something the new king wanted to put his military might into, but Warwick preferred to call a truce and perhaps arrange a marriage between the nations. Warwick visited France and made an effort to cultivate friendships there, but when he accompanied King Louis XI's ambassadors back to Edward's court, the English king was blatantly disrespectful. This sticking point was the beginning of a rift between King Edward IV and the man who had been his father's staunchest ally.

The Earl of Warwick held out some hope that his king would concede to marry a French noble and cement peace between the two nations. Though Edward showed no inclination to do so, it was still a shock when the king married Elizabeth Woodville, a widowed English aristocrat with two sons. Not only was the marriage unadvisable in Warwick's view, but Edward had married in secret without even consulting him. It was the ultimate insult and signified a final break between the two who had fought the Lancasters side-by-side for so long. Neville realized his great influence over the king was all but gone, and he did not take the news with grace. Instead, he accused the new queen of witchcraft.

Edward never forced Warwick out of court, but the latter spent less and less time there. In 1467, Warwick left court long-term and returned to his lands in the north of the country; he was considerably disappointed in how things were going under the York monarch. King Edward, for his part, focused on forging a powerful relationship with the leader of Burgundy as well as his wife's family. To that end, he arranged a marriage between his own sister Margaret and the new Duke of Burgundy, with plans to invade France with his new allies. When English troops entered France the next year, they captured Jersey for the king, but overall, the campaign was considered an incredible waste of money.

In London and beyond, the Earl of Warwick was becoming more popular than the man he'd placed on the throne. He knew it, too. In 1469, Neville decided he had enough and officially switched sides. Warwick betrayed King Edward IV in favor of the deposed royals he had been fighting for 15 years. He started by orchestrating a royalist rebellion in the north of England, where Henry Lancaster's supporters had yet to be suppressed successfully. It wasn't just another fight because this time Neville had made it personal against King Edward. He'd started negotiating with the king's younger brother, George, and convinced the royal sibling to marry Isabel Neville, Warwick's own daughter.

The rebellions culminated in the battle of Edgecoat Moor on July 26, 1469, and it forced Edward to flee when many of his top supporters were killed. Seizing the moment, the Earl of Warwick offered refuge to Edward that equated to imprisonment. Mere months later, Edward was released and returned to London due to intense pressure from York's supporters. The infighting was still not finished, however. At the Battle of Losecoat Field on March 12 of the next year, Warwick's side lost, and he was forced to retreat to France.

Warwick's presence in France marked an important moment in the history of the wars, since at this point the Earl met with King Louis XI and negotiated a formal alliance with Margaret of Anjou. He returned to England to head the Lancaster army with the help of Jasper Tudor in October 1470. They successfully ousted Edward from the seat of power and forced his retreat from England. Edward fled to Burgundy, while Warwick took Henry from the Tower and placed him back on the throne. Henry VI was crowned again and paraded through London for everyone to see.

To further entrench himself into the royal family, Neville arranged the marriage of his daughter Anne to Edward Lancaster, Henry and Margaret's son. By that time, the heir to King Henry was 16 years old. Anne was thirteen.

The reversion to Lancaster rule was incredibly short-lived, as was Warwick's regained power.

Edward had gone to Burgundy, where he enlisted the support of Charles, heir to King Louis XI of France. With French investments on his side this time, Edward returned to England via the north. When he was recognized, he pleaded that he'd only come back to take back his York estate. The Percy family, greatly influential in that part of the country, owed much of their land to the Yorks and let Edward pass.

Reestablished in his estate, King Edward set out to find his old friend Warwick. Edward convened with his brother George, who had changed sides again once it became obvious his father-in-law never intended to put him on the throne. It was George who attempted to speak with Warwick when the two parties met near Coventry.

George Plantagenet couldn't convince his one-time ally to concede defeat and accept Edward as his king. Diplomacy having failed, the York brothers turned around and raced towards London. Upon their departure, Warwick summoned his own allies and set off in the same direction.

The gates of the capital city swung easily open for their returning king since residents of the city much preferred Edward to the feeble Lancastrian. Henry VI, so briefly removed from his cushioned prison, was promptly returned to the Tower of London. There was no struggle, not even an argument. Henry VI, apparently pleased to see his cousin Edward, offered himself to the usurper and stated pleasantly how he trusted himself to York's custody completely. Having dealt with the old king, Edward set back out to end further rebellion from Warwick.

Chapter 11 – The Battles of Barnet and Tewkesbury

Both sides prepared for an important clash, but they avoided attack until they had been joined by their full forces from all parts of the country. It took several weeks of pacing the countryside before the armies were sufficiently populated.

The battle commenced on April 14, 1471, when over 20,000 soldiers gathered, ready to fight. King Edward IV met the Earl of Warwick near Barnet, Hertfordshire, about twelve miles north of London. The Yorkists, dressed in blue and red livery, were outnumbered two to one. Warwick's forces, which included the king's own brother George, wore red.

The battlefield was covered in thick fog when the front lines woke before sunrise and prepared to fight. Royal and rebel forces were spread across multiple fields separated by hedgerows, so movement was somewhat restricted. Edward attacked first, firing arrows despite the fog that clouded the archers' view. Attacking with archers first was a classic military strategy designed to take out as many members of the opposing side as possible before engaging in hand-to-hand combat. The Yorkists loosened thousands of arrows upon the Lancastrians, reaching over 350 yards per shot.

On Warwick's side, troops were confused by the fog. The lack of visibility was bad enough, but there was a ripple of paranoia through the ranks that crippled the morale of Warwick's army. Many of his soldiers and battalion leaders were worried about further side-changing on the part of their allies-at-arms. It was a poor start for the Lancastrian force, which at one point began to mistakenly attack itself due to the similar banners under which each army marched. Observers of the friendly-fire attack called "Treason!" believing that the Earl of Warwick had crossed over to the York side on which he used to fight.

In the confusion, the Lancastrian army backed away from the clash in search of visual perspective and a chance to communicate with its own factions. Seeing his enemy's forces slow, Edward sent in the reserve soldiers for a fresh wave of slaughter that ultimately caused overwhelming backpedaling from Warwick's army. After fighting for six hours, Richard Neville himself, the Kingmaker and traitor to Edward IV, was caught and killed by the opposing army. Though artwork celebrating the battle showed King Edward murdering his traitorous friend, that is unlikely how it happened.

At the death of their leader, the Lancastrian army broke up and went into full retreat. Both sides lost about 1,500 people, but when the battle was over, the Lancasters still hadn't given up the cause. Queen Margaret of Anjou, her son Edward, and Edward's wife Anne Neville arrived in England the same day the battle took place. Though their defeat had been brutal, the queen's presence rallied the remaining Lancaster army. Those who hadn't deserted marched through the west country and into Wales to recruit once more. When they entered England again, they were met by King Edward and his army for the last time at Tewkesbury, Gloucestershire.

Margaret had done a fine job of recruiting throughout the southwest, but it was to her advantage that Jasper Tudor still had a strong army of Welsh soldiers at her disposal. The loss of Richard Neville had been a crushing blow to the Lancastrians, but they would not give up the fight so long as there was an available Lancastrian heir to the throne. As far as they were concerned, Henry VI and his son Edward were meant to rule England: it mattered not how many battles were fought, or if there were others who might try to claim the throne. The Lancastrian case had become considerably more compelling now that Prince Edward had reached the age of majority.

Now 17 years of age, the son of Margaret of Anjou and Henry VI had a personal vendetta against the Yorks for dethroning his father and taken away his own birthright. He fought with the Lancastrian forces under the leadership of the Duke of Somerset.

Margaret intended for her army to storm the city of Gloucester before facing Edward of York's forces, but the latter sent a message to the city's governor ordering him to keep the gates shut. Denied entry to the city, Margaret decided it would be a waste of resources to fight her way in so the deposed queen rerouted her troops to nearby Tewkesbury. The unplanned extra ten-mile hike exhausted the soldiers, but Edward's troops were also overworked by their rapid chase. On the night of May 3, the Lancastrians camped outside Tewkesbury, and the Yorkists just three miles away.

The River Avon and the Severn were to the Lancastrian's rear; an ancient earthwork fort encompassed Margaret's camp, though the queen herself retreated to a distant church for safety before the battle began the morning of May 4. In front of the Lancastrian army lay a jumble of hedgerows and difficult terrain that the enemy would have to cross.

As was his habit, Edward of York advanced first. He had placed spearmen in the adjacent woods, and these surprised Somerset's section as they tried to surround the Yorkist's left flank. The Lancastrians lost ground and attempted a retreat that proved difficult across the Severn River. Somerset, furious at one of his colleagues, Wenlock, for failing to come to the rescue, killed the man in question before escaping.

Again, Margaret's forces were in full retreat, with many drowning as they tried to reach nearby churches and hide inside. York's men pursued viciously, rounding up the men in churches and killing each one. They saved some of the Lancastrian lords for public execution days later, placing their heads on pikes.

The Prince of Wales, Edward Plantagenet-Lancaster, had been killed during the battle. His mother hid for several days in mourning before sending a message to King Edward that she was at his mercy. She had no hope of restoring her fragile and disinterested husband, Henry VI, onto the throne of England, and without her son and heir, she felt the Lancastrian cause was lost. King Edward took the fallen queen into London and kept her as a prisoner and war trophy.

Chapter 12 – The Death of a King

Edward of York had won an important victory and it seemed there was no one left with the adequate authority to challenge him. Both Henry VI and Queen Margaret were in his custody, the rival Prince of Wales was dead and the traitorous Earl of Warwick was dead. It was a glorious part of the new king's saga and one that was touted fiercely by his family and supporters.

There were still Lancastrians in Wales under Jasper Tudor and rebellions in the north, though without Queen Margaret or Prince Edward to lead them, their dislike of the York king was of relatively little consequence. Centered in Kent, however, was one more haphazard pro-Lancastrian army posed to strike. It was led by Thomas Neville, illegitimate cousin to the Earl of Warwick.

Neville was in possession of several ships and had been patrolling the English Channel during his cousin's military campaign. After the death of Richard Neville at the Battle of Barnet, the remaining Neville pieced together an army with his soldiers at sea and the unhappy people of Kent. He sailed to London via the Thames with artillery and a massive army of 20,000. Orchestrating two attacks, first at the London Bridge and the second at Kingston upon Thames, Neville put everything he had into wresting control from York. The fighting took place between the 12th and 15th of May, 1471.

King Edward's protectors in London fought Neville off fiercely, firing back across London Bridge with their own artillery and ultimately capturing thirteen of his ships. Thomas' last stand was unsuccessful and he was beheaded on the 22nd of September.

The very same night Edward returned triumphantly to his capital city, King Henry VI died in the Tower of London. An anonymous person, identifying themselves only as "a servant to Edward IV," heralded by the king as a hero and wrote a document celebrating Edward's final victory. It was heavily-laden with York propaganda, touting the worthiness of Edward over his enemies and Henry VI. It referred to Thomas Neville as the "Bastard" and claimed that the old king in the tower died of "melancholy."

Historians generally agree that King Edward sentenced the deposed king to death and had one of his trusted supporters carry out the sentence in secret. It is generally believed that King Henry VI was struck heavily on the head while he kneeled to pray in his chapel. His body was exhumed in 1910, and it revealed blood and hair stuck to the skull.

Chapter 13 – The Final Plantagenet Kings

There is much speculation about why King Edward would kill Henry VI after having happily kept his rival in the Tower of London for so many years before. Perhaps he was simply finished with quashing endless rebellions and believed that by cutting down the final Lancastrian with claim to the throne, his rule would gain balance and peace. It could also be true that Henry had been kept alive so long to negate the potential of his more powerful son, Prince Edward. As long as Henry was alive, Edward may have felt capable of overcoming his enemy; perhaps the younger and more fearsome Prince Edward seemed a challenge that was bigger than necessary. Once the threat of Prince Edward had been eliminated, there would have been no reason to keep his father alive.

King Edward IV enjoyed a relatively normal reign once the Lancasters were finally beaten, and he settled into his role with gusto. There were two military campaigns that occupied the remaining years Edward spent on the throne: the alliance with Alexander Stewart of Scotland, and the invasion of France with the support of the Duke of Burgundy.

Desiring a friendly relationship with Scotland, Edward decided the best means accomplish that goal was an alliance with the brother of King James III. Alexander Stewart wanted to replace his brother James on the throne of Scotland, and if Edward would support him with troops, supplies, and money, the two could become firm allies. Edward went ahead and sent his brother Richard, the Duke of Gloucester, north; the mission was a huge success. Gloucester took the capital city of Edinburgh and captured King James III.

Unfortunately for King Edward and Gloucester, Alexander Stewart lost his nerve and reneged on his deal. James was released and England retreated, but not before the Scottish king was forced to hand over Berwick-upon-Tweed. The city had changed hands before, most recently when Queen Margaret had gifted it to Scotland in exchange for the safety and support of her family in 1461.

As for France, Edward found himself allied with another fickle ruler. The Duke of Burgundy failed to provide military support for England's invasion of France, forcing King Edward to negotiate a treaty with King Louis XI.

In his younger days, King Edward had been a pinnacle of health and strength. He was over six feet in height, taut and lean, and ready for battle at a moment's notice. In the later 1470s, however, he spent less time on the battlefield and more on the throne. He seemed to be making up for the extreme violence and exertion of the early years of his rule by sitting back and delegating. He was much less active, gained quite a bit of weight, and suffered from a succession of illnesses.

Despite his failing health, King Edward made some distinctive changes to the kingdom for which he had fought so hard to rule. He reached out to the disgruntled Welsh and made much of naming his son and heir the new Prince of Wales. He rebuilt St. George's Chapel at Windsor, patronized artist and printer William Caxton, and created an impressive collection of books and illuminated texts.

Centuries later, Edward's library went on display at the British Museum.

Edward never quite recovered from the constant threat of treason by those he trusted, which led him to execute his brother George in 1478 following the latter's involvement in yet another conspiracy. Many others were executed for similar reasons.

King Edward became seriously ill in April of 1483, though the reason is lost to history. Some sources claim typhoid, some pneumonia. Whatever the reason for the illness, Edward worsened as the weeks wore on and realized that he needed to take a final look at his will. His son, Prince Edward, was named successor, but the king's brother Richard was named Lord Protector of the young heir. Edward IV died on April 9, making 12-year-old Edward V the new king.

When the elder Edward died, his heir and brother were away from London. The two convened twenty days later at Stony Stratford, and immediately Richard had his nephew's retinue arrested and sent away to await beheading. Richard Grey, one of Queen Elizabeth Woodville's sons from her first husband, was among those who lost his life on Richard's instructions.

When Richard took young Edward V into his personal possession and instructed the boy to follow his orders, dowager Queen Elizabeth Woodville fled with her remaining children to Westminster Abbey.

Edward V traveled with his uncle to London, at which point the young king was placed in the Tower of London—not only a traditional prison for important prisoners, but the traditional place for kings to lodge before their official coronation. Probably unaware that his servants and friends had been sent to their deaths, Edward V would not have thought twice about following and trusting his father's brother. He stayed in the Tower and awaited his coronation, planned for June 25. Two weeks before the coronation was supposed to take place, Edward's younger brother, Richard, was taken from his mother on the premise that he was needed at the ceremony. Richard was placed with the child king in the Tower.

While the children awaited the coronation, an argument raged between the nobles of London that concerned their legitimacy. The proposed illegitimacy of the boys came from the revelation that King Edward IV had been engaged to a woman called Eleanor Butler before he married Elizabeth Woodville. At the time, engagement to be married was binding and no other marriage could take place afterward without the dispensation of the church. Richard Plantagenet pushed this fact on Parliament, who officially claimed both boys illegitimate on the very day Edward V was meant to have been crowned king of England.

In his nephew's stead, Richard Plantagenet became king of England under the title Richard III. He was crowned on July 3, 1483.

Chapter 14 – Richard III and the Princes in the Tower

Technically, Edward V was the reigning king of England from April until July. His kingship was officially stripped from him after Richard convinced Parliament of the invalidity of his parents' marriage at the end of June. Not allowed to attend their uncle's coronation, Edward and Richard seem to have remained in the Tower of London for the rest of their lives. Once they were deemed unnecessary to Richard's rule, the princes simply stopped being seen. They made no visits, attended no royal events and after several weeks no longer received visitors.

John Argentine, a doctor who served the royal family, called on Edward V and his brother several times during the summer of 1483. Though contemporary accounts claim the boys were seen from time to time that summer, eventually they faded from the public altogether. By the end of the year, they were assumed dead. Historians generally agree that Richard III murdered his nephews

Edward V and Richard; however, there is no concrete proof for or against him. Other suspects have been named, including Richard's successor, Henry VII.

Dominic Mancini, an Italian visitor to the English court in the summer of 1483, was captivated by the mysterious events surrounding the princes in the Tower.

No satisfying explanation concerning the whereabouts of either Edward or Richard was ever given. Richard knew perfectly well that his courtiers and the English commoners believed he'd killed the young boys for the crown – but he neither confirmed nor denied the rumors. It would have been simple just to bring the boys out in public to quell suspicion, but again, nothing of the sort was arranged. There were no declarations of death and no funerals, which allowed several young men in the following years to fake their identities as both Edward and Richard.

Thomas More, a philosopher, clergyman, and lawyer who would become an advisor to King Henry VIII, wrote his own account of the incident, claiming to have witnessed several connected events after the deaths. He reported that the boys' bodies were buried under a pile of stones at the foot of a staircase within the Tower complex. According to More's story, years afterward the bodies were moved by a priest and placed into a grave more fitting to a king and his brother. The location of the grave was forgotten, since the man who commissioned the priest to move the bodies, Sir Robert Brakenbury, died soon afterward.

A century later, two small sets of bones were found during a renovation of the White Tower. These were inspected and found to match the ages of the princes who disappeared. The bones were placed into a large urn and interred at Westminster Abbey where they rest to this day. More sets of similar bones have been uncovered in the years since, but no conclusions have been made concerning the identity of the remains or the manner of death. Queen Elizabeth

II has never given her approval for the interred bones at Westminster to undergo DNA and other forensic testing.

Richard III's wife, Anne Neville, died in 1485 before the couple could have any more children to replace their deceased heir, Edward. No one knew better than Richard how important it was to have a son waiting in the wings to take over the throne, and rumors flew around London that he planned to marry his niece, Elizabeth of York. Elizabeth was the daughter of King Edward IV and the sister to the mysteriously lost princes in the tower. Such a marriage would have been a clever political move, since it would connect the deposed Lancaster line with his own York line.

Queen Elizabeth, the younger Elizabeth's mother, had every reason to want to destroy Richard Plantagenet. Not only had Richard III taken the throne from family but he had imprisoned and probably murdered both of her sons. Hearing that Richard III planned to wed her eldest daughter must have been unbearable.

Before any such plans could move ahead, King Richard was forced to defend his crown from the one remaining man who could make the same claim on it: Henry Tudor. Tudor's campaign was heavily influenced by his mother, the dowager Queen Margaret Beaufort. Margaret had always harbored ambitious plans for her son, to whom she was very close. Once every opponent to Richard III had been eradicated from the fabric of the kingdom, she saw the chance for her son to make the great leap from hard-working nobleman to king of the realm.

Margaret was not the only dowager queen to believe in her son's potential. Elizabeth Woodville, fearing further tragedy for her family and desiring revenge, wanted Henry Tudor to succeed as well. The two women met and plotted together to challenge Richard. They did not have to wait long for their plans to come to fruition. Only three years into his rule, King Richard III faced Henry Tudor on the battlefield. Tudor was joined by Queen Elizabeth's eldest son, Thomas Grey, half-brother to Edward V. Grey had joined a failed rebellion in October 1483 and was as loyal as his mother to the new hope of the Lancaster line.

Chapter 15 – The Battle of Bosworth

Richard III's son and heir, Prince Edward, had died at the age of ten in 1484. If he died without further issue, the crown must revert to the closest male heir. With no Yorks or Lancasters left of the Plantagenet dynasty to make a claim, the closest remaining heir came from a Welsh nobleman who had married the dowager queen of England, Margaret Beaufort: Henry Tudor.

Henry Tudor was born in 1457, a nephew to the Mad King Henry VI. His father, Edmund Tudor, was half-brother to Henry VI, making Henry Tudor a Lancastrian relation. Jasper, an important figure in the Wars of the Roses, was Henry's uncle; Owen Tudor, a casualty of the Battle of Mortimer's Cross, was his grandfather.

With the support of two dowager queens, France, and much of the nobility, Henry Tudor made his campaign for the throne. His first attempt, in the same year Richard III claimed the throne, was unsuccessful since a strong storm stopped his ships from crossing the English Channel. Based in Brittany and then in France, Tudor waited until everything was ready to strike again. He set out at the beginning of August 1485 and arrived on Welsh soil on the seventh day of the month. Wales being the ancestral home of his father's family, Tudor found himself very welcome. King Richard's own appointees in south Wales gave up their positions to follow Henry eastward. As he and his troops moved towards the English capital, Henry gathered more support and soldiers along the way.

King Richard was alerted to the impending army and so gathered his own forces promptly. The royal army marched north and met Henry Tudor's troops near Bosworth Market, Leicestershire. They were midpoint between the eastern and western shores of England. The Lancaster side had 5,000 to 8,000 soldiers—half of which were likely French—and the Yorks slightly outnumbered them. Thomas and William Stanley, the latter of whom had married Henry Tudor's mother Margaret Beaufort, gathered thousands of their own loyal troops but refused to declare a side before the battle began. Such moves were customary of the Stanleys who preferred to join the winning side just in time to claim victory and save themselves great sacrifice. They had, however, met secretly with Henry Tudor twice as he swept the countryside looking for more men.

The two armies finally met on August 21. King Richard's troops were positioned to the northeast upon Ambion Hill, while Henry Tudor's were spread along the plains to the southwest. The two sections of the Stanley's army were positioned some distance southeast of Henry's; Richard could see them from his hilltop camp. The problem for the Stanleys, who did seem to hope for a Tudor victory, was that Richard had kidnapped Thomas' son prior to the battle for leverage. In preparation for the battle, King Richard sent a message to the Stanleys advising them to join his army or expect Thomas' son to be killed. Another message came from Henry, asking his mother's husband to formally declare a side.

In answer to Richard, Thomas replied simply that he had more sons. To Henry, he said he would join once the battle plan had been laid out and the fighting started. Both sides had to begin without any certainty where the extra 2,000 to 4,000 soldiers would end up. With no other choice, Henry's side advanced under the leadership of the Earl of Oxford, a man with much more battlefield experience than Henry.

The fight started with cannon fire and arrows loosed by the Yorkists on the hill. They had the immediate advantage given their position, but Oxford was experienced and clever about the art of warfare. The Lancastrians huddled together instead of breaking apart into the traditional three-piece battalion and marched steadily towards higher ground, sending their own deluge of arrows into the opposing side. Once the lines met in hand-to-hand combat, Oxford gained the advantage.

To the northeast of the central battle lay Richard's flank, led by the Earl of Northumberland. Perched on a nearby hill, Northumberland's men were not in a good position to reinforce the king's soldiers; however, Richard signaled to them to do just that. The flank remained where it was, leaving the king to find a different solution. Seeing Henry Tudor within reach, Richard rushed towards him. He knew that if he struck down the leader of the rebellion, the Lancastrians would retreat.

On horseback, Richard charged with a retinue of mounted knights towards his foe, killing Tudor's standard bearer. Henry jumped off his horse and retreated to the relative safety of his bodyguards on the ground, making himself a less conspicuous figure. With Richard separated from his main army and grappling with Henry's bodyguards, the Stanleys decided it was time to show themselves. Their troops raced in and joined the Lancastrians, pressing Richard back until he was unhorsed and thrown into a marsh.

Richard III refused to surrender although he was pressed on all sides by enemy forces. Rhys ap Thomas, one of the Welsh noblemen who defected from his position to join Henry Tudor, is reported to have killed the king while he struggled to find footing in the slippery marsh. At his death, the York army slowly abandoned the battle as they learned their king was gone. Richard's crown was retrieved from the marsh.

In the instant that King Richard III was slain, the kingdom was left without a ruler; Henry Tudor knew it was essential to make his claim immediately or others may deign to take the throne before he returned to London. To cement his triumph and the beginning of his rule, Henry arranged a humble coronation as soon as the king was killed.

When the fighting was finished and the vanquished army had flown, Henry rode into the nearby town of Stoke Golden, surrounded by his commanders and closest supporters. There, they mounted a hill and stopped beneath an oak tree, where Henry kneeled and was crowned with the battered golden circlet taken from Richard III's helmet. He stood, proclaimed King of England by Lord Stanley, and all around him cheered loud and long enough to be heard by the men who remained on the battlefield. That hill was named Crown Hill thereafter, and still exists today – though it has been developed into a residential area.

Henry had the bodies of all those slain during the battle brought to nearby St. James Church to be buried. Richard III's body was not treated so kindly. Tudor did not allow his enemy a Catholic burial, but instead had Richard's body stripped and put on a horse so he could take it to the city of Leicester as proof of his victory. After two days, the body was unceremoniously buried at the church of the Greyfriars, without so much as a marker.

Upon his return to London, Henry Tudor was publicly proclaimed king of England under the title Henry VII. He organized a formal coronation on October 30, 1485 and was hailed as the first non-Plantagenet ruler in three hundred years.

Chapter 16 – The Foundation of the Tudor Dynasty

In claiming the throne of England, Henry Tudor knew that he needed to be different than his predecessors. He wanted all the people of England to accept his rule, including both parts of the Plantagenet line. His first order of business, following the coronation, was to marry Elizabeth of York, daughter of King Edward IV and Queen Elizabeth Woodville. Since Henry's claim to the crown was through his mother, great-great-granddaughter of King Edward III of House Lancaster, he wanted to cement his position by joining the York part of the family with his own. Elizabeth and Henry were married on January 18, 1486, at Westminster Abbey.

Elizabeth and Henry's children would be equally Lancaster and York, the ideal solution to the Plantagenet feud that began over three decades of civil war in England. To celebrate the bringing together of the split family, King Henry VII designed the Tudor Rose: a simple floral emblem whose inner petals were white and whose outer petals were red. It was a symbolic end to the war of the York white rose against the Lancastrian red rose.

Henry's rise to the throne was not without its detractors, though his victory on the battlefield in 1485 is marked by most as the end to the Wars of the Roses which had impoverished the realm and turned cousin against cousin for 30 years. The Tudor king met a few more armies in battle before his reign was through. Each rebellion centered around a supposed Plantagenet claimant to the throne, including a man who said he was the younger of the lost princes in the tower. King Henry's forces squashed the rebellion, and Henry had the boy installed in the palace kitchens. Another potential claimant, the son of George Plantagenet, was lodged permanently in the Tower of London.

With the diminishing rebellions under control, Henry VII focused on peace treaties with his neighboring nations, as well as bringing sorely-needed funds into the royal treasury. The king created a very effective taxation system and raised a great deal of money for infrastructure projects such as Europe's first dry-dock at Portsmouth. He invested in the creation of an English navy and sent ships to the Ottoman Empire to purchase alum—a mineral important to the wool and dyeing industries—and resell it throughout Europe and England.

King Henry VII was very intent on keeping his family safe, healthy, and happy. He remained very close to his mother, who had borne him at the age of 13 and helped him earn his place on the throne. Henry's letters to Margaret were doting and indicative of the love the king had for his wife and children as well.

King Henry VII remained on the throne until his death from tuberculosis on April 21, 1509, 6 years after the death of his beloved wife Elizabeth. His mother died two short months later. The Tudor king's son succeeded him without incident at the age of 18 as King Henry VIII. The first Henry Tudor ruled England for 26 years, giving his kingdom the peace, stability, and time it needed to prosper.

Chapter 17 – Attempts on the Tudor Throne

King Henry managed to stabilize the kingdom, but his rule was not without its own challenges. His detractors claimed he was an illegitimate son of Margaret Beaufort and therefore unqualified to claim the crown. Still others claimed they were Plantagenet survivors whose ties to the kingdom preceded the Tudor kings. The most notorious attempts to gain power while Henry VII wore the crown were made by two young men called Perkin Warbeck and Lambert Simnel. Each claimed to be one of the multiple lost Plantagenet heirs who had vanished after imprisonment in the Tower of London.

Lambert Simnel was the first to make his claim as Edward Plantagenet, though the idea really came from his tutor. The early details of Simnel's life are largely unknown, though he is believed to have come from an average middle-class family who might have been bakers or tradespeople. Born around the same time as Edward Plantagenet, son of George Plantagenet, brother to King Edward IV, Simnel was ten years old in 1487 when he came under the tutelage of a priest called Richard Simon.

Upon becoming acquainted with his young pupil, Simon decided to forego priestly training and instead get Lambert ready to make a noble appearance at court. The priest taught Lambert how to act, think and speak like a member of the royal family, an idea born of the teacher's assertion that his pupil greatly resembled the lost sons of King Edward IV. His initial plan was to have Lambert imitate the younger of those princes, Richard, but by that time it was commonly rumored that both princes had died in their luxurious prison. So, Simon had to make a contingency plan that focused instead on the son of George Plantagenet.

Edward, son of Richard III's brother, had been imprisoned immediately after Henry VII killed the old king at the Battle of Bosworth. The boy was denied the title of Earl of Warwick, which had been promised him by Richard III, and simply kept in the Tower for the same reason as Richard had imprisoned the sons of his elder brother. Henry VII probably hesitated to kill the young Plantagenet outright. Therefore the king decided to keep him within arm's length.

Under Simon's tutelage, Lambert learned his lessons well and went along with the charade. Most of the kingdom knew well enough that the boy was in the Tower, so the priest told everyone around him that Edward had escaped his prison. When the rumor caught on, Simon took his student to Ireland and produced him for the appraisal of the large York contingent there. Lambert Simnel was immediately embraced by the Plantagenet supporters there, including the powerful Earl of Kildare, leader of the Irish government.

Once Simon had cultivated the support of the Irish, his plan to usurp the English crown via Lambert moved swiftly. Kildare vowed to send an army to defeat Henry VII and put Edward in his place. In celebration, the imposter was hoisted on someone's shoulders and paraded through the streets. On the 24th of May, 1487, the false Edward Plantagenet was crowned Edward VI, King of England and Ireland, at the Christchurch Cathedral in Dublin. While the Irish army was gathered, Margaret of York (daughter of Edward IV), and York relative John de la Pole gathered supporters in England and Germany. De la Pole went so far as to say he'd assisted the imprisoned Plantagenet in his escape.

Only two years into his hard-earned reign, Henry Tudor knew first-hand how simple it was for one faction to overthrow another. Forewarned about the upcoming challenge, he quickly gathered his own army and prepared to meet his foe in battle. It was the beginning of summer when John de la Pole returned to England with his gathered troops. The two armies met on the 16th of June near Newark, Henry at the head of 12,000 soldiers and de la Pole at the head of 8,000. The battle lasted about three hours, after which de la Pole and about half of his troops were dead.

It was the first time Henry was forced to defend his throne with military might, and he could not afford to lose. Though the king realized it was hardly the fault of Lambert Simnel, he punished the peers who had risen against him by stripping them of their lands and titles and removing their heirs from the peerage succession. The ambitious priest, Richard Simon, was sent to a bishop's prison for life. As for Lambert Simnel himself, after a brief turn in prison he was put to work in the castle kitchens. The real Edward Plantagenet was briefly removed from the Tower and shown to the public to prove he was still very much alive. Afterward, he was quickly returned to the Tower of London and remained there until 1499, where he met the next major challenger to King Henry VII: Perkin Warbeck.

It is impossible to accurately depict the early life of Perkin Warbeck, since there are two conflicting tales that he told about himself. The first and most controversial identity Warbeck gave himself was that of Richard of Shrewsbury, the youngest of King Edward IV's sons.

It seems most likely that Warbeck was born in a continental European country, then brought by his family to Ireland as a child. English may not even have been his first language.

In 1490, Perkin made his first official claim to the English throne while in Burgundy, a region of France ruled by the York family. He claimed that he had been in hiding since his brother, Edward V, was killed in the Tower of London, and that he had been spared from death because of his very young age. After making his royal claim, Warbeck traveled to Ireland to garner support for his cause. As with Lambert Simnel, the Irish were captivated by the teenager who claimed to be a Plantagenet heir to the English throne. In fact, Warbeck once claimed that it was the Irish who convinced him to act the part of Edward IV's lost son – though such a statement clashed with the boy's own timeline.

Though the Mayor of Cork was happy to lend support to Warbeck as Richard of Shrewsbury, Perkin's case didn't find the traction he was hoping for. The young man returned to Burgundy where the real Richard's aunt, Margaret of York, took him in and taught him the ways and manners of the English court. She unofficially gave him the title of Duke of York, a name by which he was known throughout Europe. Perkin met a great many nobles and members of royal houses while under the care of Margaret, some of whom went as far as to call him King Richard IV.

While the supposed Duke of York sheltered in Burgundy, King Henry VII kept tabs on his whereabouts and activities. Henry complained to the Duke of Burgundy, but his request to have the man extradited was ignored. In retribution, Henry imposed a trade embargo on the duchy and prohibited commerce between the two nations. Burgundian support of the supposed Duke continued.

Thanks to European support, by 1495 Perkin Warbeck had earned himself the attention of several English peers. These peers personally visited the Duke of York in Burgundy, then colluded to develop a plan of attack against Henry VII. The Tudor king was well forewarned, however, and as many as a dozen English Lords were found and arrested on his behalf. They were tried, found guilty of treason and ultimately sentenced to execution – however many had their sentence changed to imprisonment and fines afterward.

Warbeck and Margaret of York were still hopeful even after losing their English contingent. That same summer, the pretender to the throne sailed to Kent at his aunt's expense, in search of more support. Instead, the troops he brought with him were attacked by royalists upon landing. Before Warbeck even disembarked, he was forced to retreat to Ireland, where this time he was more popular than he had been upon his first visit. He used the momentum to invade Waterford, but failure there led him to quickly flee to Scotland.

King James IV of Scotland was just as welcoming to the alleged Duke of York as the nobility and rulers of France and the Holy Roman Empire had been. With Henry VII arranging a marriage between his son Arthur and the daughter of Spain's most powerful monarchs, James IV was eager for a friendlier English connection, especially one who was on good terms with France. Warbeck even married a member of the Scottish aristocracy, Catherine Gordon, before conspiring with the Scottish king to invade England.

Warbeck was clearly grateful for all the favors granted him by the Scottish king and his lords, as indicated by his overwhelming statements of gratitude. In a letter to his bride-to-be, he gushed about her beauty and charm.

After the marriage, the mutual invasion went forward. The Scottish troops attempt to enter England commenced in September of 1496, hinging on the assumption that the old Yorkist faction in northern England would rally behind Perkin Warbeck. Only a few days into the campaign, it became clear that no Warbeck troops would materialize. Lord Neville approached with a royal army from the south, and James was pushed back into his own territory. Finished with Perkin Warbeck, the Scottish king sent him back to Ireland. The so-called Duke of York fled back to mainland Europe after bungling another attempt at taking Waterford.

One year later, Warbeck returned to England, this time via the south at Cornwall. He tried to capitalize on their recent revolt against Henry VII's taxes, which were being raised to pay for a war with Scotland. Again employing the guise of Duke of York, Warbeck told the Cornish people that he had an excellent relationship with Scotland and that not only would he avoid war with James IV but he would remove the war tax. He had very good timing, since this was exactly what the Cornish wanted to hear. They hailed Warbeck as King Richard IV and sent him northward with 6000 troops.

At Taunton, Warbeck surrendered to the king's army and was arrested. King Henry put the pretender in the Tower of London until he confessed to being an imposter, at which point the king allowed him the luxury of attending court – still under domestic arrest in Henry's palace. Warbeck was separated from his wife, who was under the guardianship of Queen Elizabeth. After a year and a half under close watch, Warbeck escaped and was quickly recaptured. He went directly to the Tower, where he met a very interesting inmate: Edward Plantagenet, the true Earl of Warwick and false identity of Lambeth Simnel.

By this point, Edward had been living in the Tower of London for 14 years. Aged 24 when he met the false Richard Plantagenet, it is believed that Edward was suffering from a mental illness.

Both men knew they had little chance of gaining the king's favor at that point, so they conspired to make a getaway. They made their attempt in 1499, but failed, after which they were sentenced to be executed. Warbeck was hanged on November 23; Plantagenet was beheaded for treason on November 28.

The final Yorkist heir was born just five years before King Henry VII died: Richard de la Pole. Richard was brother to John de la Pole, named heir to Richard III who swore an oath of allegiance to Henry Tudor. Richard had some degree of respect in France and Scotland, with whom he planned to invade England in order to put himself on the throne in 1523. Though he gathered as many as 12,000 troops to fight against Henry VIII, the war never took place. Before he could organize ships and take advantage of good weather, Richard de la Pole was killed at the Battle of Pavia where he fought on behalf of Francis I of France.

The death of Richard de la Pole in 1525 ended the York hereditary line, since he had no sons and only one illegitimate daughter. It could be said that with his death, the Wars of the Roses were truly ended. Having fought off multiple challengers, both the first and second Henry Tudor ensured the succession of their own line.

Chapter 18 – The Sainthood and Cult of King Henry VI

The gentle goodness of King Henry VI was not forgotten after his death, even though he spent only 15 of his 49 years truly ruling the kingdom. After the Earl of Warwick, Prince Edward, and finally Henry VI were killed in the Wars of the Roses, people unwilling to support a York monarchy spoke often of the goodness of the old king.

Sympathy for Henry VI intensified following his funeral since attendees claimed the old king's body bled during the service. According to medieval superstition, this was a sign that Henry had been a victim of foul play, for it was believed that a murdered body would bleed anew to betray the violence it had endured. The people of England lamented the loss and apparent brutal end to the Plantagenet line of kings, and in King Henry VI found the ideal subject for their own religious obsession. Almost immediately, a niche portion of English society chose Henry as their lost savior and saint.

When Henry Tudor took the throne of England, he realized that people would love and accept him more readily if he showed his own heavy lament at the loss of Henry VI. The dead king had been, after all, Henry's own half-uncle, and both Henry and his mother knew how important it was to show respect and reverence for rulers of the past. Henry Tudor showed his respect for Henry VI by building a chapel at Windsor Abbey to hold the remains of the king who, by that time, people overwhelmingly believed to have been murdered. With both Edward IV and Richard III dead, however, there was no one to question on the subject: the true cause of Henry's demise remains unknown.

Henry VII capitalized on the growing cult of Henry VI by allowing the publication of a book of miracles attributed to the dead king, which included more than 300 miracles supposedly performed by the last Lancastrian on the throne. Such miracles began to be reported as soon as the old king was interred in his tomb.

The English public knew very well that their lost king had been incredibly devout, reportedly spending up to an hour in silent prayer whenever he entered a chapel. He had been generous, passive, humble—all the things a devout Catholic was supposed to be. When the idea started to circulate that Henry VI had been murdered and did not simply pass away from depression, his mourners began to believe he was a martyr. They pursued the creation of Henry VI as a saint by the Pope, a goal for which the book of miracles would be evidence.

The miracles of King Henry VI include his supposed curing of a young girl with badly infected lymph nodes. Another person claimed that the king's spirit had raised a girl from the dead after she'd been killed by the plague. Still another report claimed that a man was revived following a public hanging for a crime he did not commit: While his dead body was being carted away, he started to breathe again and escaped. The man said King Henry had protected his windpipe. The bulk of the miracles compiled for the book occurred posthumously.

For the manuscript commissioned by Henry VII, many wonderful stories were collected. One told the story of a boy who fell into the trough beneath a water wheel and became stuck under the water. Nobody present could reach him, nor could any adult fit safely under the wheel. At that point, the old king entered the tale.

The dead king's hat was placed in his chapel at Windsor Abbey so that Catholic pilgrims might touch it and put it on. The hat became a popular cure for people suffering from migraine headaches. It stayed at the chapel for nearly fifty years, until England's church was reformed by King Henry VIII.

Due to Henry Plantagenet's cult following, the chapel built by Henry Tudor received masses of visitors every year. King Henry VII sent multiple petitions to the Pope in Rome asking for his predecessor to be officially canonized and made a Catholic saint. The paperwork and research were undertaken, but so slowly that by the time a decision might have been reached, Henry VIII had broken with the Catholic Church altogether. Multiple attempts have been undertaken to promote the would-be saint's cause, but as yet none of these has achieved its goal.

In the 16th century, famous playwright William Shakespeare immortalized the events and characters of the three-decade struggle between the Lancasters and Yorks in eight plays that cover the early history of the Plantagenets: "Richard II," "Henry IV Part One," "Henry IV Part Two, "Henry VI Part One," "Henry VI Part Two," "Henry VI Part Three," "Edward V," and "Richard III."

Shakespeare wrote multiple plays about Henry VI that speculated a great deal about his role in the Wars of the Roses, and his ultimate fate. Shakespeare portrayed Richard Plantagenet, still Duke of Gloucester under the rule of his brother Edward IV, as the murderer of King Henry VI.

Chapter 19 – The Legacy of the Wars of the Roses

After being at war with itself for 30 years, England was full of scars, many of which remain to this day. The kingdom's noble houses had been dragged through battle after battle, forced to question their traditional loyalties and watch – often up close – as their family members died violently. Members of the feudal poor suffered in the same way, being constantly forced to fight in support of those who owned the land on which they toiled. The population of the country was negatively affected, as were its basic industries. With able-bodied men away fighting, gardens and crops suffered, harvests were small, and the economy was crippled.

The fact that so many different claims could be made on the crown – successful ones – revealed a fundamental flaw in the monarchical English system. Because the lords of the land had so many people available to fight for them, it was possible for a member of the nobility to raise an army that was larger than the king's. It was a strange reality that meant land workers owed their primary loyalty to the lord of the land, not the monarch. That was exactly why the York family, extensive landowners, could persevere for so long and eventually triumph over Henry VI. Once Henry Tudor took the crown, he actively lowered the number of peerages (lordships, earldoms, etc.) by appointing very few new people to the nobility. As the possessors of such titles grew old and passed away, Henry oversaw a decline in the power of the aristocracy.

The Tudor era represented a much more stable kingdom in which people were able to work their land, ply their trades, and grow the national economy. Increasing population and industry in England following the Wars of the Roses led to an eventual blossoming of art, early sciences, architectural design, and leisure, particularly during the reign of Queen Elizabeth I. Playwrights like William Shakespeare found almost endless inspiration from the wars of the Lancasters and Yorks, while tapestry weavers and painters attempted to depict the moments they considered most significant to history.

Apart from Shakespeare, there are countless writers, spanning centuries, who have brought the history of 15th century England to fascinated audiences in the form of books, historical research, movies, and television series. Characters from the Plantagenet and Tudor dynasties continue to fascinate audiences of Showtime's "The Tudors," BBC's "The White Queen," and readers of multiple novels by writers of historical fiction like Philippa Gregory. Historians, archaeologists, genealogists, and royalists continue to this day to debate the validity of that infamous flurry of claims to the throne, as well as to search for further evidence of what happened to the lost princes Edward and Richard York in the Tower of London.

The physical legacy of the wars persists to this day. In 2012, an archeological excavation of the area that was once the church of Greyfriars in Leicester began. Remarkably, a human body was recovered in exactly the area that had been believed to hold Richard III's remains, under the parking lot of Leicester City Council. The body was a man in his thirties with the same deformed spine that characterized England's last Plantagenet king. Just as telling were the severe head injuries shown on the skull. The team ran multiple tests and concluded that the body they'd discovered was indeed that of King Richard III. Intense debate followed regarding what to do with the king's remains, with a group of apparent Plantagenet descendants desiring to make the decision on behalf of their ancestor. Ultimately, a court made the ruling to keep the old king's body in Leicester.

In March 2015, the king was ceremoniously interred at Leicester Cathedral after being led via funeral procession through the site of the Battle of Bosworth. He reentered the city in a wooden coffin, draped in black velvet and pulled by four horses. Though Queen Elizabeth II did not attend the ceremony, she personally wrote a eulogy for her 14th great-grand uncle Richard and was represented at the funeral by her daughter-in-law Sophie, Countess of Wessex. Several other members of royalty were present, as well as descendants of the Plantagenets, who placed white roses on the coffin. The original site of Richard's burial has been converted into a memorial center in which visitors can view the empty grave through a specially-designed glass floor.

The discovery of Richard's body has opened up the possibility of a large genetics project focusing on the timeline of the many royal handovers during the 15th century. The research conducted so far relies on the collected DNA samples from descendants the House of Plantagenet, who were selected following very precise genealogical studies. Historian John Ashdown-Hill pinpointed one idea candidate: Joy Ibsen, a female descendent of Anne of York, Richard III's sister, living in Canada.

The importance of Joy's connection to the late king's sister was maternal since DNA scientists needed to trace the familial connection through a purely female line. Such a precise relationship to the ancient royal family would preserve the mitochondrial DNA in each successive generation until Joy was born. Though Joy died before the research could be carried out, her son Michael was happy to participate in the research performed by Leicester University. In this case, Joy would have passed her mitochondrial DNA to all children, so the fact that Michael is a male will not pose any problems.

The University sought out a second DNA match through an all-female line, a search that produced Wendy Duldig. Duldig's and Ibsen's genetic samples do indeed show a matching female ancestor. The search for an all-male succession line was more difficult, since Richard III himself left no living heirs. Starting with Richard and Edward's great-great-grandfather Edward III, researchers traced the male lineage up to Henry Somerset, the 5th Duke of Beaufort. Five heirs to the bloodline were located for testing which came up with some surprising results.

Four of the male-line descendants showed Y-chromosomes that matched Somerset, but one had a different type. This means that at some point between Edward III and the Duke of Beaufort, at least one male listed in the family tree was not the father of the children listed as his. Another break was found when comparing the Y-chromosome from a French heir to Edward III.

All this means that at some point in history, the Plantagenet line was falsely recorded at least once – a fact that could impact the accepted royal line of succession today. There is a possibility that the oldest Plantagenet, Geoffrey of Anjou, is in fact not an ancestor of Richard III, the Tudor monarchs or today's Windsors. The royal family's genealogy could be much more muddled than any of us – including the royals themselves – realize.

It's a very ironic ending to a story that began with such strict adherence to genetic lines. And yet, the history of the Plantagenets, the Tudors and their relatives – confirmed by DNA or otherwise – is the collective story of all England, all France and Scotland, all Ireland, and Wales at the end of the Middle Ages. The end of the Wars of the Roses signified the beginning of the Early Modern Age in England, a time when prosperity and civility began to blossom. The 30-year war ultimately strengthened the power of the crown and allowed for much more effective legislation throughout a kingdom that would soon become an unquestioned world power.

That legacy continues today with the House of Windsor.

If you enjoyed this individual book on the Wars of the Roses, can you please leave a review for it?

Thanks for your support!

Part 3: The Six Wives of Henry VIII

A Captivating Guide to Catherine of Aragon, Anne Boleyn, Jane Seymour, Anne of Cleves, Catherine Howard, and Katherine Parr

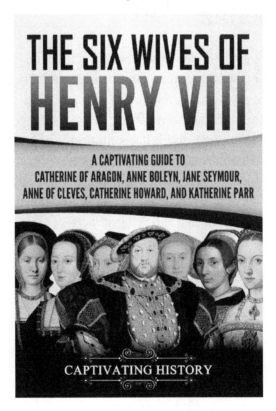

Introduction

Henry VIII, King of England and Ireland in the first half of the 16th century, is one of history's most famous monarchs for many reasons. He ruled ruthlessly, was quick to cry "treason!" and execute, and equally quick to fall in and out of love. Henry changed the religious fabric of England forever and left his mark on the wider world – but what of the six women he took as his queens? From the regal and capable Catherine of Aragon to the patient and generous Katherine Parr, Henry's wives represented a range of personalities, goals, beliefs, and influences on the king. Each of Henry's six wives represented a facet of the king himself, whether he liked to admit it or not; unfortunately, a Queen of England at the side of Henry VIII could never be sure of her husband's love – or her safety. These are the stories of three Catherines, two Annes and one Jane.

Chapter 1 – Henry Tudor

King Henry VIII was the second Tudor monarch on the throne of England and Ireland. Born in 1491, Henry inherited the crown from his father in 1509. He was a young, athletic, handsome, and ambitious man with plans for political expansion.

Perhaps Henry VIII assumed he would easily enjoy the sort of marriage his mother and father had. Henry VII was the first Tudor to rule England, Ireland, and France in the 15th century. He claimed his right to the crown after defeating King Richard III's armies in battle, then married Elizabeth of York to tie both sides of the royal Plantagenet line together. In fact, Elizabeth of York had full blood rights to rule England herself, but the concept of an independent queen was not yet accepted at the end of the Middle Ages.

Henry VII pledged himself to Elizabeth of York two full years before his army killed her uncle, Richard III. They were married in 1586, and though they were not particularly well known to one another, the couple is widely believed to have loved each other and been happy in their marriage. In addition to their child, Henry, the king and queen produced three more healthy children who survived infancy: Arthur, Mary, and Margaret.

To the man who would become King Henry VIII, his family must have seemed idyllic. They were rich, powerful, loving, and fruitful – every attribute of importance to a royal family. There was Arthur, the male heir, and Henry the second son, in case the first succumbed to illness or died before having any sons of his own. There were also two royal princesses to marry off to political allies throughout England and Europe. After his mother's death in 1503, young Henry Tudor saw his father grieve heavily, retreating from court. Every year of the anniversary of Elizabeth's passing, the old king had a Catholic requiem Mass sung, 100 candles lit and the bells of the palace rung.

When Henry VIII came to power in 1509, both his parents and his older brother, Arthur, were dead. In a few short months, the new king decided to marry the woman his father had originally chosen as Arthur's wife: Catherine of Aragon. He wanted to waste no time in creating his own generation of familial happiness, support, and political stability. The couple was married in June after Catherine received a papal annulment for her previous marriage to Henry's brother. It was clear to Henry that his father had greatly desired a connection to Iberia, so he believed this was the best move for himself and for his kingdom.

Sadly, lasting wedded bliss was not something for which King Henry VIII was destined. Time and time again, he found fault in Catherine, then with her various replacements over the years. The obvious reason was that none of the king's wives seemed capable of giving birth to the large family Henry desired. Though Catherine of Aragon gave the king his first daughter, Mary, her continued stillbirths and miscarriages frustrated the king and eventually led him to break the marital contract he had been so sure of as an eighteen-year-old monarch.

In his later years, Henry VIII became obese and chronically ill from ulcers in his legs – but in his youth, he was of decent health and was expected to father many children. The fact that as many as six potentially fertile women could produce no more than three heirs between them suggests that some medical issue plagued the king. Modern medical researchers have hypothesized that Henry VIII may have carried Kell-positive genes, which can cause blood group incompatibility issues and fetal mortality.

If this hypothesis were true, Henry and each of his queens would have had one chance to produce a healthy baby. That one successful pregnancy would leave the queen with an antibody that would attack fetuses during subsequent pregnancies. The queen's body would be unable to support the life of another Kell-positive fetus, resulting only in miscarriages and stillborn children.

If, after one pregnancy by Henry VIII, his wives could only support pregnancies of fetuses without his blood type, the likelihood of a healthy delivery was considerably less. The king's first child to reach adulthood, Catherine of Aragon's daughter Mary Tudor, may then have inherited only Henry's Kell-negative gene, instead of the dominant positive gene. She herself was never able to produce a child.

Whatever the true cause of Henry VIII's lifelong struggle to become father to many sons, it was undoubtedly the most important factor in his ultimate decision to remove Catherine of Aragon from his court and seek a new wife. Unfortunately for Henry and his many wives, each queen in succession struggled to produce not only a healthy boy, but a live child. By the time the king had produced three healthy children, he had segregated them and their mothers to the extent that the happy family unit he'd initially wanted was almost impossible.

It seems that Henry VIII's unaccepting nature toward a potentially infertile woman significantly lowered his chances at a happy and loving marriage. Though the king was certainly virile and capable of love, he was also capable of falling out of it rapidly if babies weren't quick to follow. It's likely that the infamous king's treatment of his very first wife solidified in his character a habit of discarding that which he perceived as an encumbrance - whether it was religious doctrine or an entire person.

In all, King Henry VIII married six times, rarely waiting more than a few days to remarry following the death or divorce of his previous wife. The longest period he spent in genuine mourning was two years, following the death of Jane Seymour.

Chapter 2 – Catherine of Aragon

During a time period in which the nation of Spain had yet to form from the alliances of Castile, Aragon, Valencia, Majorca, and other independent kingdoms, the Iberian Peninsula was a political patchwork. Two of these powerful Roman Catholic kingdoms were Aragon and Castile, famous for their heirs and rulers, Ferdinand and Isabella. Married in 1469, Isabella of Castile and Ferdinand II of Aragon ruled jointly and are credited with starting the process of total Spanish unification. They are also credited with the much more controversial creation of the Spanish Inquisition, in which between 3,000 and 5,000 people were executed for anti-Catholicism over the course of three centuries. Ferdinand and Isabella Trastámara became parents to their youngest surviving child, Catherine, on December 16, 1585.

Isabella and Ferdinand Trastámara were, in many ways, non-traditional monarchs. Not only was Isabella the full Queen of Castile without having to concede to her husband, but she was also considered Ferdinand's political and marital equal. Theirs was a family in which the female children were provided with an excellent education, right alongside the male children. Catherine, therefore, was extremely well-educated and considered very intelligent. She learned how to read and write in Latin, Aragonese, and Castilian, and to speak Greek and French. She was also very well-read in religious philosophy and was taught to hold very firmly to her Catholic faith by her devoted parents.

Princess Catherine's main tutor was Alessandro Geraldini, a dedicated educator who would later accompany his youngest royal charge to England before sailing to the New World. Geraldini taught Catherine math, history, genealogy, law, and a number of other subjects worthy of a future monarch. Her main interests were literature and theology.

The young princess and her five siblings were privy to an incredible wealth of information, not only through their tutors but through life alongside Isabella and Ferdinand of Spain. Catherine's parents, dubbed the Catholic Monarchs by Pope Alexander VI, were not idle royals. They were passionate about the creation of a purely Roman Catholic empire in which no members of other faiths resided. They employed military tactics to ethnically cleanse the Iberian Peninsula of Jews, Moors, Protestants, Atheists, and other people deemed heretics by the strict letters of Catholic law. In watching her mother and father pursue their enemies throughout the Old and New World, Catherine learned a great deal of administrative war-time skills.

Catherine and her siblings were heirs in line to the most powerful regime in Europe at the end of the 15th century. Her options in terms of a husband were not taken lightly by her parents or their respective kingdoms. A number of marriage partners for Catherine were considered before her parents decided on a match with Arthur Tudor. England was not Spain's first choice for an ally, but after having married their first four children to monarchs in Portugal and Austria, it was a timely decision on the part of Isabella and Ferdinand.

This was an extremely strategic partnership on the part of England's Henry VII because there were still factions throughout Europe who believed his conquest of England and Ireland was invalid due to his debatably illegitimate birth. Since Catherine of Aragon was also descended from King Edward III of England, just as were the Tudor heirs, Henry VII thought it best to consolidate that power into one marriage. Catherine was promised to Arthur Tudor before she was even four years old; she arrived in England with the promise of a 200,000-crown dowry.

Chapter 3 – Catherine and Arthur's Wedding

Catherine of Aragon and Arthur Tudor were married by proxy on May 14, 1499. Since they were still both underage, the couple remained apart until Catherine was 16 and Arthur was 15. Over the course of the next two years, they kept in touch via letters written in their common language of Latin. Those letters portray an impatient young prince and a very polite and elegant young princess, both eager to move forward with their lives and stop waiting for the future to arrive:

"I have read the most sweet letters of your highness most lately given to me, from which I have easily perceived your most entire love to me. Truly those your letters, traced by your own hand, have so delighted me, and have rendered me so cheerful and jocund, that I fancied I beheld your highness and conversed with and embraced my dearest wife. I cannot tell you what an earnest desire I feel to see your highness, and how vexatious to me is this procrastination about your coming."

In 1501, Ferdinand and Isabella promised Henry VII that Catherine would soon arrive in England. Throughout the first part of the year, weather delayed her departure several times. In May of the same year, the princess fell ill for a time before finally beginning her journey to the sea at the north of her country. This journey alone was quite arduous, as it stretched more than 500 miles from Grenada to Galicia. Crossing the country took nearly three months, after which Catherine finally boarded a ship to England on August 17. Even then, the journey was difficult – storms in the Bay of Biscay caused damage and forced the ship and its accompanying fleet to retreat to Spain soon after departure. On the 24th of September, the same fleet set sail a final time under the leadership of one of England's best sailors, Stephen Butt.

Once the refitted ships set out a second time, the voyage took less than six days. Catherine and her retinue arrived at Plymouth on the 2nd of October 1501. They were received by local nobles and directed to their prepared lodgings at Exeter, where King Henry sent a party to escort them to Lambeth Palace in London. The princess arrived in London on the 9th of November 1501, more than five months after her journey had begun from the south of Spain.

Catherine of Aragon had a pale complexion, blue eyes, and light auburn hair; she was considered a beautiful young lady by many who saw her. Said lawyer and philosopher Thomas More:

"Ah, but the lady! Take my word for it, she thrilled the hearts of everyone: she possesses all those qualities that make for beauty in a very charming girl. Everywhere she receives the highest of praises; but even that is inadequate."

The Spanish princess married Arthur Tudor on November 14, 1501, never having laid eyes on him before. The bride wore a thick veil during the ceremony, so she and Arthur only really saw each other after they had personally exchanged their marital vows at St. Paul's Cathedral. Catherine's future husband, Henry Tudor, escorted her down the aisle to meet her brother. Afterward, the couple was publicly shown to their bed.

Arthur's grandmother, Lady Margaret Beaufort, prepared the marriage bed for her grandson and his new wife. She sprinkled the bed with holy water before Catherine's ladies-in-waiting helped dress the new Princess of Wales in her night dress and left her in the bed when the Prince entered the room in his own nightgown. The marriage bed was blessed by the Bishop of London, then the newlyweds were finally left alone.

The morning after the wedding, Arthur boasted jocularly that he'd consummated his marriage with Catherine, which was of course expected of him by his parents and in-laws. Whether he was merely acting the part, however, or excitedly telling the truth, would become a hotly-debated point in history. After the wedding, Catherine and Arthur both moved to the Welsh border at Ludlow Castle to govern their piece of the kingdom. The couple both fell very ill in March, and though Catherine recovered, Arthur died only four months after the wedding. The princess insisted that she and Arthur had not consummated the marriage before her young husband's death.

It isn't clear just what illness the royal couple suffered from, though possibilities include the mysterious English sweating sickness or tuberculosis. Catherine took several months to recover from the illness, after which royal doctors sent by the king determined she was not pregnant and therefore not carrying a royal heir. Arthur's funeral was held on the 23rd of April, and his widow did not attend. Traditional forbade her appearance, though even if she'd wanted to see her husband buried, Catherine was still very sick.

The teenage widow was kept in England following the death of Arthur. Her fate was yet to be decided by Spanish ambassador Doctor de Puebla and Henry VII of England. Henry VII wanted to keep Catherine in the family and he certainly wanted to collect the second half of her dowry – the only logical solution was to remarry her to young Henry Tudor. Fortunately, Isabella and Ferdinand agreed, but the negotiations took over a year to reach completion. In June of 1503, Henry Tudor became formally engaged to his brother's widow. The couple was given permission for their arrangement by Pope Julius II the next year, on the basis of Catherine's statement that the former marriage had not been consummated. So, Catherine waited in earnest for the king's youngest son to come of age.

The years she spent in waiting were not particularly pleasant for the young Princess of Wales, as she was without an income and totally reliant on her father and King Henry – her mother Isabella having died in 1504. In a letter to Ferdinand II in 1505, Catherine was forced to ask for money to pay her lady in waiting:

"Most high and most puissant lord,

It is known to your highness how donna Maria de Salazar was lady to the queen my lady, who is in blessed glory, and how her highness sent her to come with me; and in addition to the service which she did to her highness, she has served me well, and in all this has done as a worthy woman. Wherefore I supplicate your highness that, as well on account of the one service as the other, you would command her to be paid, since I have nothing wherewith to pay her...

From Durham, the eighth of September.

The humble servant of your highness,

who kisses your hands,

The Princess of Wales."

Catherine also wrote to her father asking very politely for dowries to be provided for all the ladies he had sent with her to England. She was very aware of the fact that none of her ladies had been paid to follow her or provide their services and wanted them to find good marriages instead of continuing on in the same manner, unable to buy themselves clothing or necessities. Another letter from Catherine to her father in 1505 shows just how uncomfortable the princess had become away from Spain:

"Most high and most puissant lord,

Hitherto I have not wished to let your highness know the affairs here, that I might not give you annoyance, and also thinking that they would improve; but it appears that the contrary is the case, and that each day my troubles increase; and all this on account of the doctor de Puebla, to whom it has not sufficed that from the beginning he transacted a thousand falsities against the service of your highness, but now he has given me new trouble...

*Your highness shall know, as I have often written to you, that since I came into England I have not had a single maravedi [*type of Spanish coin*] except a certain sum which was given me for food, and this such a sum that it did not suffice without my having many debts in London; and that which troubles me more is to see my servants and maidens so at a loss, and that they have not wherewith to get clothes; and this I believe is all done by hand of the doctor, who, notwithstanding your highness has written, sending him word that he should have money from the king of England...*

...A few days ago donna Elvira de Manuel asked my leave to go to Flanders to get cured of a complaint which has come into her eyes...I begged the king of England, my lord, that until our donna Elvira should return his highness would command that I should have, as a companion, and old English lady, or that he would take me to his court. [The doctor] negotiated that the king should dismiss all my household, and take away my chamber and send to place it in a house of his own, so that I should not be in any way mistress of it.

Your highness will see what would serve you best, and with this I shall be most content.

The humble servant of your highness,

who kisses your hands,

The Princess of Wales. "

For his part, Ferdinand II deferred almost entirely to King Henry VII to provide his daughter with what he saw as proper. In 1507, after repeated entreaties by Catherine, The King of Aragon appointed her his ambassador in England. With a job and some income, the princess' status and confidence were much improved, and she took her role very seriously.

Chapter 4 – Catherine's Second Marriage

Early in 1509, King Henry VII died of tuberculosis, leaving his son Henry VIII to succeed him as King of England and Ireland. Impatient to begin his reign, the new king arranged to marry Catherine of Aragon just a few months after the death of his father. The two of them were married privately at Greenwich Palace on June 11, 1509. Catherine was 23 years old and Henry VIII was just shy of his eighteenth birthday.

The couple was crowned in a joint ceremony just weeks after the wedding, with much fanfare and celebration. The new king participated in the celebratory jousting competitions and performed with gusto. According to contemporary accounts, he seemed to all assembled the perfect specimen of a king:

"The King tilted against many, stoutly and valorously. According to their own observation and the report of others, King Henry was not only very expert in arms and of great valour, and most eminent for

his personal endowments, but so gifted and adorned with mental accomplishments, that they believed him to have few equals in the world. He spoke English, French, and Latin, understood Italian well, played on almost every instrument, sang and composed fairly, was prudent, sage, and free from every vice, and so good and affectionate a friend to the Signory, that no ultramontane sovereign ever surpassed him in that respect."

Catherine was also enamored of her new husband, and the new Queen of England became pregnant soon after her second wedding. In January of 1504, however, the baby girl she delivered was stillborn. It was a huge disappointment for Catherine, Henry, and their kingdom, who awaited the birth of a male Tudor heir. Nevertheless, miscarriages and pregnancy complications were a thing of normalcy in Tudor England, so the royal couple simply hoped for better results next time.

Catherine of Aragon is estimated to have had six to 10 pregnancies throughout her marriage to King Henry VIII, only two of which resulted in a live baby. The first was a boy named Henry; the second a daughter called Mary. Baby Henry died at two months of age, but Mary lived to adulthood and would be the future Queen of England, the first female to independently hold that position.

Despite the royal couple's troublesome fertility, Catherine and Henry were a loving and powerful couple. The king trusted his wife's judgment and spoke with her regularly about the business of running the country. In turn, Catherine confided in her father, and so the three monarchs became very closely-allied. Ferdinand II and his daughter were primarily concerned about the fate of Spain in ongoing wars with France, and in time Henry VIII decided to put his own armies on the continent to side with Spain. Furthermore, Henry VIII was determined to win back France for himself, as Henry V had done a century before. The timing was ideal for such a campaign.

While Henry headed to France to command his army, Queen Catherine became Regent of England at home. She would not be idle, for while her husband was away, King James IV of Scotland seized the moment and attacked England. A Scottish army of 80,000 crossed the English border on August 22, 1513. As a long-term ally of France, Scotland's monarch felt it was his duty to attack his southern neighbor in its weakened position. Catherine, however, summoned 40,000 reserve troops and enacted an impactful victory over the enemy at the Battle of Flodden in September. Not only was the Scottish army heavily weakened, but King James IV of Scotland himself had been killed.

Catherine proudly wrote to her husband in France to send him the news:

"Sir,

My lord Havard sent me a letter open to your grace within one of mine, by the which ye shall see at length the great victory that our Lord hath sent your subjects in your absence: and for this cause it is no need herein to trouble your grace with long writing; but to my thinking this battle hath been to your grace and all your realm the greatest honour that could be, and more than should you win all the crown of France: thanked be God of it, and I am sure your grace forgetteth not to do this, which shall be cause to send you many more such great victories, as I trust he shall do...

My husband, for hastiness with Rogecrosse, I could not send your grace the piece of the king of Scots' coat, which John Glyn now bringeth; in this your grace shall see, how I can keep my promise: sending you for your banners a king's coat...

Your humble wife and true servant

Katarine."

Catherine of Aragon proved herself a true disciple and daughter of Isabella and Ferdinand of Spain, who had managed armies side-by-side during her youth. Unfortunately, however, the queen had been pregnant during the military campaign and worried that the overwork required of her would harm the baby. Indeed, the next month, Catherine delivered a baby boy who died very soon after his birth.

King Henry VIII returned to England soon afterward, having been successful in taking Tournai from France. Ironically, at the death of King James IV, Henry's sister Margaret became Regent of Scotland. Except for the death of the newborn Prince of England, it was a time of pride and celebration at the Tudor court.

On February 18, 1516, Queen Catherine delivered a healthy baby girl named Mary. She wanted to provide the same opportunities to Mary that her own parents had given her, which meant a more comprehensive education than girls at that time received in England. Catherine began to visit educational facilities such as Oxford University and donate generously. Her belief that girls should be well-educated caught on throughout England and became the subject of literature and debate.

While Catherine devoted her time to Mary, Henry VIII took up with several mistresses. One of these, Elizabeth Blount, delivered a healthy baby boy in 1519. Though the boy was illegitimate, there was still talk that he could become the next King of England if his father chose to recognize him officially. Excited at the prospect of a healthy son, Henry VIII did indeed acknowledge that young Henry was his progeny and made sure that he was well-cared for. In fact, it was the king himself who named the boy Henry Fitzroy, literally "Henry Son of the King." Catherine was deeply hurt and embarrassed at the news. By 1519 she was 34 years old and not expected to produce any more royal children.

King Henry VIII began to pull away from Queen Catherine after the birth of Henry Fitzroy, and, embarrassed, she did little to fight for his attention. By 1525, the king had not only begun an affair with his wife's lady-in-waiting, Anne Boleyn, but he had fallen desperately in love with her. Anne, for her part, told the king that she would not engage in sexual intercourse with him unless they were to be married. Frustrated, Henry continued to send the young woman love letters and expensive gifts.

Catherine began dining alone, much to her personal regret, as Henry no longer joined her and their nine-year-old daughter Princess Mary had been sent to Ludlow Palace to establish her own court.

Chapter 5 – Mistress Elizabeth Blount

Known at court as Bessie Blount, Elizabeth was born to John Blount and Catherine Pershall in about the year 1500. As a young girl, she came to court as a lady-in-waiting to Queen Catherine of Aragon. Seven or eight years the king's junior, Bessie caught the eye of her sovereign and they embarked on a relationship that would be quite substantial – at least five years in length.

The young girl was pretty, engaging, and fifteen years younger than Queen Catherine. Blonde and blue-eyed, she enjoyed dancing, singing, and riding horses, a hobby she shared with the young king. Though Henry was still apparently satisfied with his marriage, at least in the theoretical and political sense, he had no problem seeking out the company of other women. In fact, seeking out lovers from among those who served his queen would become a lifelong habit.

The affair was quite hushed, especially compared to Henry's later amorous trysts, and it is possible that the queen was unaware of it.

Until, of course, the king's mistress became pregnant. Bessie discovered she was pregnant early in 1519 and was sent away from the royal palace to give birth in June. The baby was Henry Fitzroy.

For his part, Henry VIII was gentle concerning the birth and the unwed mother. He made sure that Bessie and the boy were safe and comfortable and went so far as to officially acknowledge his fatherhood of little Henry, giving him the title of Lord of Richmond. The love affair, however, had come to a necessary end since Bessie could no longer serve at court with an infant. King Henry set up an annual 200-pound income and property for Bessie Blount and set her up to marry Gilbert Tailboys, another aristocrat whose livelihood now depended on the goodness of the crown.

Before the marriage to Tailboys, however, Bessie gave birth to her second child, a girl named Elizabeth. Though Elizabeth would take Gilbert Tailboys' name after 1522, it seems very likely this child was also fathered by the King of England. Given Henry Tudor's indifference to female children, however, he never acknowledged Elizabeth publicly nor did he attempt to groom her for the throne.

It may seem cold-hearted of Henry not to have kept his mistress and children near, but the king did care enough to give Bessie, young Henry and Elizabeth a life no other unwed mother or illegitimate children could hope for at that time. She had a husband, an income and a place to live in safety with her little boy and girl. Bessie and Gilbert moved to Lincolnshire and had two more children, but Gilbert died in 1530. At that time, Fitzroy was becoming seriously ill and King Henry was personally focused on Anne Boleyn. Knowing it was futile to hope the king might marry her and legitimize their children, Bessie married Edward Fiennes de Clinton, twelve years her junior. They had another three children, making the king's former mistress a mother of seven.

King Henry made a point of becoming acquainted with his illegitimate son, which meant that he did continue to see his former lover for years following their prompt breakup. He brought gifts for the boy and bestowed more money on Bessie whenever he saw fit. The young Henry wrote to his royal father often, thanking him for the gifts and always asking for his blessings. The two kept in close contact, not through any manipulations of the mother but from the pure desire of Henry Tudor to know his boy and ensure he grew up well.

In addition to frivolous gifts, the king provided his child with professional tutors so that young Henry could learn to read and write in English, Latin, and French. The tutor chosen personally by King Henry was John Palsgrave, an Englishman who had been educated in London and Paris. In addition to a dedicated teacher, the boy was also appointed his own council – also handpicked by the king himself – as if Henry were being groomed to become the king's official heir.

King Henry was not content to pin all his hopes of the royal succession either on Mary or his illegitimate son, so he remarried in 1533 despite already having produced a potential male heir. Fitzroy struggled with poor health for several years but seemed strong enough to continue fighting the disease and rallying to health. In July of 1536, however, that fight ended and the king's only son died. It seems most likely that he died from tuberculosis, but some have theorized that the boy contracted a strain of the plague. He was interred at the Thetford Priory in Norfolk but following the Reformation his tomb found a permanent home at St. Michael's Church in Suffolk.

During the short tenure of Anne of Cleves as King Henry's wife, Bessie returned to the English court to serve the new queen. Her service was as brief as Anne's, unfortunately, because she no longer enjoyed good health. Only three years after the death of her firstborn, Elizabeth Blount died shortly after giving birth to her seventh child, Margaret Clinton. She was estimated to have been 42 years old and had lived to a very good age for the time. Much of the luxury and comfort she enjoyed throughout her life were due to her close and enduring friendship with King Henry VIII.

After having lived such a life, it is strange to find that there is no clear information about Bessie's funeral or her burial place. Most historians agree that these details have been lost to the centuries. However, St. Mary and All Saints Churchyard in South Kyme, Lincolnshire, claims to host the remains of one of King Henry VIII's most favored women, Elizabeth Blount Clinton, deceased on the 15th of June 1541.

Chapter 6 – Mistress Mary Boleyn

After the departure from court of Henry's long-time mistress Bessie Blount, the king began to take particular notice of the most attractive girls around him at court. The one he most favored was none other than the sister of his future Protestant Queen, Anne Boleyn. Mary, perhaps a year or two older than Anne, appeared first among the ladies of Queen Catherine of Aragon. Born in 1501, she was 10 years younger than Henry. Upon meeting, she was likely 19 years of age.

Mary Boleyn had had an excellent education that included history, languages, reading, writing, arithmetic, music, sewing and embroidery, dancing, singing, card games, hunting, riding, and falconry. Her first position was as lady-in-waiting to Mary Tudor, the king's sister, in Paris. Though the Tudor sister returned to England as soon as her husband, the French king, died, Mary was allowed to stay on at the French court. She may even have had an affair with the new king himself, Francis I, a rumor that the monarch wasn't bothered to negate.

Mary returned to the English court in 1519, the same year that Elizabeth Blount delivered Henry Fitzroy. She was a grown woman but still young, pretty, and remarkably interesting given her extensive education and time spent in France. The English king charmed his way into Mary's heart but was wary of becoming stuck with another unwed mother as a result of an affair. Perhaps for this reason, Henry pushed Mary Boleyn to marry one of his council members, William Carey. The marriage went through in early 1520 and Carey enjoyed several gifts of land and money from the king thereafter.

There are so few concrete details surrounding the life of Mary Boleyn that it is easy to overlook her, but historians all agree she did have an explicit affair with King Henry VIII at some point during the early 1520s. Whether this was before the wedding, after the wedding or both, is simply unknown. What researchers do know, however, is that theirs was not a long-lived affair, though the paternity of Mary's children – ostensibly named Catherine and Henry – has always been in question.

William Carey died of the English sweating sickness in 1528, leaving Mary free to remarry William Stafford in 1534. That marriage was not sanctioned by the king, a fact that Henry took very seriously. He angrily cut her off from her annual salary and banished her from court. Nevertheless, Mary believed in her second marriage, which was purely for love. The couple had debts and only a small income, however, so the former lover of the king wrote to Henry's most favored advisor, Thomas Cromwell, and beseeched him to speak on her behalf to Henry so that she would not end up destitute.

This letter is the weightiest piece of evidence Mary Boleyn left behind of her life:

"Master Secretary,

After my poor recommendations, which is smally to be regarded of me, that am a poor banished creature, this shall be to desire you to be good to my poor husband and to me. I am sure it is not unknown to you the high displeasure that both he and I have, both of the king's highness and the queen's grace, by reason of our marriage without their knowledge, wherein we both do yield ourselves faulty, and do acknowledge that we did not well to be so hasty nor so bold, without their knowledge. But one thing, good master secretary, consider, that he was young, and love overcame reason; and for my part I saw so much honesty in him, that I loved him as well as he did me, and was in bondage, and glad I was to be at liberty: so that, for my part, I saw that all the world did set so little by me, and he so much, that I thought I could take no better way but to take him and to forsake all other ways, and live a poor, honest life with him. And so I do put no doubts but we should, if we might once be so happy to recover the king's gracious favour and the queen's. For well I might have had a greater man of birth and a higher, but I assure you I could never have had one that should have loved me so well, nor a more honest man; and besides that, he is both come of an ancient stock, and again as meet (if it was his grace's pleasure) to do the king service, as any young gentleman in his court.

Therefore, good master secretary, this shall be my suit to you, that, for the love that well I know you do bear to all my blood, though, for my part, I have not deserved it but smally, by reason of my vile conditions, as to put my husband to the king's grace that he may do his duty as all other gentlemen do. And, good master secretary, sue for us to the king's highness, and beseech his highness, which ever was wont to take pity, to have pity on us; and that it will please his grace of his goodness to speak to the queen's grace for us; for, so far as I can perceive, her grace is so highly displeased with us both that, without the king be so good lord to us as to withdraw his rigour and sue for us, we are never like to recover her grace's favour: which is too heavy to bear. And seeing there is no remedy, for God's sake help us; for we have been now a quarter of a year married, I thank God, and too late now to call that again; wherefore it is the more almones [alms] to help. But if I were at my liberty and might choose, I ensure you, master secretary, for my little time, I have tried so much honesty to be in him, that I had rather beg my bread with him than to be the greatest queen in Christendom. And I believe verily he is in the same case with me; for I believe verily he would not forsake me to be a king.

Therefore, good master secretary, seeing we are so well together and does intend to live so honest a life, though it be but poor, show part of your goodness to us as well as you do to all the world besides; for I promise you, you have the name to help all them that hath need, and amongst all your suitors I dare be bold to say that you have no matter more to be pitied than ours; and therefore, for God's sake, be good to us, for in you is all our trust.

And I beseech you, good master secretary, pray my lord my father and my lady to be so good to us, and to let me have their blessings and my husband their good will; and I will never desire more of them. Also, I pray you, desire my lord of Norfolk and my lord my brother to be good to us. I dare not write to them, they are so cruel against us; but if, with any pain that I could take with my life, I might win their good wills, I promise you there is no child living would venture more than I. And so I pray you to report by me, and you shall find my writing true, and in all points which I may please them in I shall be ready to obey them nearest my husband, whom I am most bound to; to whom I most heartily beseech you to be good unto, which, for my sake, is a poor banished man for an honest and a godly cause. And seeing that I have read in old books that some, for as just causes, have by kings and queens been pardoned by the suit of good folks, I trust it shall be our chance, through your good help, to come to the same; as knoweth the (Lord) God, who send you health and heart's ease. Scribbled with her ill hand, who is your poor, humble suitor, always to command,

Mary Stafford.

To the right worshipful and my singular good friend, Master Secretary to the king's highness, this be delivered."

Mary Boleyn could not warm the heart of the king who once loved her, though Queen Anne Boleyn managed to send money and a golden cup to help with expenses. Mary would never return from the countryside and probably did not see her sister again.

Chapter 7 – Anne Boleyn

The object of King Henry VIII's affections was born into a noble and wealthy family around the year 1501. Since no church records were kept of her birth, scholars disagree on the exact year and date, and the range of Anne's estimated birth year stretches from 1501 to 1507. She had a slightly older sister named Mary and a younger brother called George. Her father, Thomas Boleyn, had been one of King Henry VII's favorite linguists and diplomats and enjoyed many positions and titles under Henry VIII.

With their family background, it was natural that young Anne and Mary would be offered places at the English court to serve the Queen of England – Catherine of Aragon. As it happened, Anne would first join the French court before serving her own queen. When King Henry VIII's sister, Mary Tudor, was sent to France to marry the King Louis XII, Anne was required by her father Thomas to attend her in Paris. Only three months after the royal wedding, the elderly French king died. Mary Tudor secretly married her brother's good friend, Charles Brandon, and returned to England. Anne

Boleyn did not accompany the royal party but stayed on at the French court in service to the teenaged Queen Claude.

In previous centuries it had been commonplace for queens and princesses to be accompanied by a staff of five to six noble ladies, but by the Tudor era that number had increased to at least a dozen. Noble girls like Mary and Anne would have been expected to join the court at the age of 12 or so, serving as junior maids before turning 16 and becoming a Maid of Honor. The term "lady-in-waiting" served as a generalization for the various jobs and titles of such servants. Their job was primarily to keep the queen company and make sure that she was never made to do anything resembling physical labor. The latter included dressing and undressing, using the lavatory by herself, bathing, and styling her hair. Ideally, a royal girl or woman would develop close friendships with her maids.

Anne had studied the usual subjects that a girl of her day was expected to study in England: Latin, singing, dancing, and music. Her education was considered good for a girl, but it expanded a great deal while she served for a year at the court of Margaret of Austria in a southern principality of the Netherlands. Margaret hired a tutor to help the young Anne Boleyn perfect her French skills, which served the girl well when she moved to Paris the next year. Margaret's court was very artistically-inclined, taking pleasure in fine paintings, music, and illustrated books. Anne was influenced greatly by her time in the Dutch principality, and she gained a love of art that would continue to grow in France. One of her favorite trends was the illuminated book. These books included the traditional blocks of text, surrounded by intricately drawn and colored borders, details, and illustrations on each page. Anne had her own books created in this style, as did many of her fellow courtiers.

In all, Anne Boleyn spent an estimated ten years in France. By the time she returned to the English court to serve Queen Catherine of Aragon in 1522, she was arguably more French than English. Anne's role at court was considered one of the greatest positions a noble lady could obtain. Though it was usually unpaid, ladies-in-waiting were given room and board. In particular, their presence at court gave Anne and Mary the chance to make friends with other upper-class ladies and meet potential husbands. Instead of finding bachelors, however, both girls became involved with the most ineligible man at the palace: the king.

Before he divorced Queen Catherine of Aragon, King Henry VIII had an affair with Mary Boleyn. Henry's love of flirtation and mistress-taking was well-known, and if a lady accepted his advances she could expect gifts and elevated ranking. Mary enjoyed the king's attention for some time before his wandering eye caught Anne, at which point he made up his mind to seduce the younger Boleyn girl.

As a young, attractive, and worldly noble girl, Anne became a popular member of the English court. She became engaged to her cousin James Butler at the will of her family, but the two rarely spoke although they were both at court. Anne fell in love with the Lord of Northumberland, Henry Percy, and the two of them decided to marry despite the wishes of Anne's family.

Noble marriages required the consent of the king, and when Henry VIII heard of Percy's intentions to wed Anne he refused outright. Soon afterward, the king began to pursue Anne for himself. For her part, Anne rejected – politely – the first advances of the king. She returned his gifts of jewelry and replied to his letters saying that she did not wish to be his mistress. Henry persevered for more than a year, writing letter after letter to the object of his affection while plotting to rid himself of Queen Catherine:

"MY MISTRESS & FRIEND,
my heart and I surrender our-
selves into your hands, beseeching
you to hold us commended to your
favour, and that by absence your
affection to us may not be lessened:
for it were a great pity to increase
our pain, of which absence produces

enough and more than I could ever
have thought could be felt, reminding us of a point in astronomy
which
is this: the longer the days are, the
more distant is the sun, and nevertheless the hotter; so is it with our
love, for by absence we are kept a
distance from one another, and yet
it retains its fervour, at least on my
side; I hope the like on yours, assuring you that on my part the pain
of absence is already too great for
me; and when I think of the increase
of that which I am forced to suffer,
it would be almost intolerable, but
for the firm hope I have of your un-
changeable affection for me: and to
remind you of this sometimes, and
seeing that I cannot be personally
present with you, I now send you the
nearest thing I can to that, namely,
my picture set in a bracelet, with the
whole of the device, which you al-
ready know, wishing myself in their
place, if it should please you. This is
from the hand of your loyal servant
and friend,

H.R. "

Eventually, Anne relented and gave Henry an opening: She told him that she could not become romantically involved with him while he still had a wife. At that point, the king must have realized he would have to choose between a foreign princess or Anne Boleyn as his next wife. There has been much speculation by contemporary peers and historians about whether Anne's father had anything to do with the change in Anne's stance towards the king.

The girls' father, Thomas Boleyn, had a shrewd political mind and could clearly see the benefit to his family if his daughter were able to become the king's long-term mistress. Or, better yet, the mother to another son. It is possible that Thomas even had inside information about Henry VIII's secret plot to denounce Catherine as queen and replace her with a younger, potentially more fertile woman. The little remaining evidence from that time, however, seems to suggest otherwise. In a letter from Eustace Chapuys, France's ambassador to England, to Charles V of France, the subject of Henry VIII's proposed marriage to Boleyn's daughter was touched upon:

"I must add that the said earl of Wiltshire has never declared himself up to this moment; on the contrary, he has hitherto, as the duke of Norfolk has frequently told me, tried to dissuade the King rather than otherwise from the marriage."

Though Anne Boleyn was loyal to her family, she was a relatively independent woman who made as many of her own decisions as possible. The most likely scenario is that Anne genuinely grew to love Henry Tudor as he loved her and agreed to marry him on her own terms.

Chapter 8 – The Reformation and Divorce

By the late 1520s, King Henry VIII had had enough of his marriage to Catherine of Aragon. He no longer consulted the queen for political or spiritual advice, nor did he visit her. He was cold and distant, focused only on his future with Anne Boleyn, whom he had decided to marry. Under the Catholic church, however, divorce or annulment could only be granted by the Pope. Henry set his team of lawyers and clergy to the task of convincing the sitting Pope that his marriage to Catherine had been unlawful, since Catholic doctrine stated that a man must not marry his brother's widow.

Of course, this issue had already been dealt with before Catherine and Henry were married. Catherine had sworn she and Arthur Tudor had not consummated their marriage and based on that statement she and Henry were granted a papal dispensation to go ahead with their own wedding. Now, Henry wanted to undo all of that.

Henry's decision was not taken as lightly as it may have seemed to Catherine; he had, in fact, come to believe that the lack of male heirs between him and his queen was due to the fact that he had unlawfully taken his brother's wife. This personal revelation changed the king's perception on his family and caused Catherine – and Mary – a great deal of pain. It was the first glimpse of a new piece of Henry VIII's character, one that would come to define him.

Henry and Anne waited six years to acquire permission to marry, while Catherine fought desperately to change her husband's mind. She wrote to Pope Clement to plead her case, which convinced the latter to keep the royal couple's marriage intact. She also wrote to Henry, who would not speak to her face-to-face, and asked desperately what she had done to offend him so greatly.

Henry replied largely through his messengers and advisors, politely telling Catherine of his belief that their marriage was unlawful and unholy. He wished her no harm or ill but would not continue on as her husband.

On November 15, 1529, members of the court witnessed a heated argument between Henry VIII and Catherine of Aragon. Henry mentioned that due to the queen's having consummated her relationship with his brother Arthur, they could never have truly been married:

"The Queen replied that he himself, without the help of doctors, knew perfectly well that the principal cause alleged for the divorce did not really exist, 'cart yl l'avoit trouvé pucelle,' [translation: 'you found me to be a virgin'] as he himself had owned upon more than one occasion. 'As to your almoner's opinion in this matter,' she continued, 'I care not a straw; he is not my judge in the present case; it is for the Pope, not for him, to decide. Respecting those of other doctors, whether Parisian or from other universities, you know very well that the principal and best lawyers in England have written in my favour. Indeed, if you give me permission to procure counsel's opinion in this matter I do not hesitate to say that for each doctor or

lawyer who might decide in your favour and against me, I shall find 1,000 to declare that the marriage is good and indissoluble.'"

Catherine was correct in her assumption that no lawyer or clergyman could find reason to annul her marriage to Henry. She was a much-loved and respected queen, and Henry's papal dispensation to remove her from his life would never come. In 1533, he stopped waiting for outside authority to vote in his favor and married Anne Boleyn anyway. She was rumored to be pregnant and did indeed give birth to a healthy girl only a few months after the wedding. The baby was named Elizabeth Tudor.

Catherine was moved from Hampton Court Palace to her own dwelling, allowed to visit neither Henry nor their daughter Mary. Mary Tudor was declared illegitimate and therefore not an heir to the throne of England. Henry VIII asked Mary to swear an oath that her mother was not the Queen of England, which she refused to do. Young Mary was eventually embraced back into her father's life, but she would never see her mother again.

The marriage of Henry VIII to Anne Boleyn caused more than just a break in the king's first marriage. It also caused a break between England itself and the Catholic realm. In divorcing Catherine and marrying a second time, Henry had directly disobeyed the Pope and struggled to have his second marriage accepted throughout Europe. The king was prideful and sure of himself, however, and instead of pandering to his neighboring Catholic nations, he had the English Parliament declare him Head of the Church of England. As such, all religious doctrine, law, dispensations, and rituals were in the king's hands within his own kingdom.

Catherine continued to sign letters "Catherine the Quene" and thought Henry's heretical marriage to Anne was nonsense. She wrote him often and seemed worried for the state of his soul. She prayed for him and advised him to do the same. As for herself, she prayed for the reinstitution of her daughter Mary into the line of succession so that her life would be filled with the comforts and rights befitting a Princess of England.

The deposed queen became very sick soon after she was turned away from the palace she shared with Henry. At Kimbolton Castle in Cambridgeshire, Catherine grew weak and isolated. She stopped receiving most visitors except for close friends who could exchange her and Mary's letters. Three years after being officially demoted to Dowager Princess of Wales, which had been her English title after the death of Arthur Tudor, Catherine of Aragon asked for early communion from the Bishop of Llandaff and prayed ceaselessly until her death on January 29, 1536. Surgical procedures performed during Catherine's embalming revealed a black mass attached to her heart that may have been indicative of advanced cancer.

She was buried in Peterborough Cathedral, her funeral not attended by Mary or Henry VIII. To the end, Catherine believed herself to be the rightful Queen of England:

"In this world I will confess myself to be the king's true wife, and in the next they will know how unreasonably I am afflicted."

Chapter 9 – The Marriage and Death of England's Protestant Queen

King Henry VIII is believed to have proposed to Anne Boleyn in 1527. He waited for papal dispensation for a full six years before taking matters into his own hands. In January of 1533, Anne and Henry were married in secret. After the wedding, Henry's Parliament had little choice but to validate the marriage and name the king Head of the Church of England. Henry and Anne's kingdom was henceforth separate from the Catholic church.

The king wanted his new queen to be beloved by all of England and respected throughout Europe. To this end, he arranged a lavish, three-day coronation at the Tower of London for Queen Anne that began on May 29, 1533.

On the first day, Anne was dressed richly and taken from Greenwich Palace to the Tower via the River Thames. King Henry received her there with an assembly of London's political officials. A thousand guns were fired in her honor from the Tower, then some of the accompanying ships in the river followed suit. She stayed at the Tower that night with Henry before embarking on a royal procession through the city of London the next day. Her chariot was covered in silver cloth and all her ladies wore matching scarlet gowns; they paraded through the city and met with the Mayor of London, who presented Anne with a beautiful purse on behalf of himself and the residents of London. The procession carried on to the Palace of Westminster and Anne stayed there for the second night.

On the third day of her celebrations, Anne was finally brought to St. Peter's Abbey. The church was filled with Westminster monks, Lords of the Parliament, bishops, abbots, and every noble from the English court and surrounding area. Before Anne herself entered the Abbey, her crown and scepters were carried in by the Duke of Suffolk and two appointed earls. Anne walked under a golden canopy, wearing a crimson dress with purple velvet and ermine. Her brown hair was dressed in a coronet with gold and pearls.

The ceremony was officiated by the Archbishop of Canterbury and the Archbishop of York, with Anne Boleyn seated on an elevated throne in front of the altar. The congregation said Mass, then moved into Westminster Hall where the new queen was crowned and given the two scepters of her royal office. When the ceremony was finished and she was the official Queen of England, Anne was led by her father, Lord Wiltshire, to the celebratory feast. She sat on a high dais in front of several richly-laded tables and was served by various members of the nobility.

The kingdom was not as overwhelmed by Anne's charms as the king hoped. Despite all the pomp and circumstance of her coronation, the people of England were still quite loyal to Catherine of Aragon. They did accept that Anne Boleyn was queen, however, which was more than could be said for the rest of Europe. In Spain, France, and the Holy Roman Empire, Catherine was still considered the official Queen of England, while Anne and King Henry were marked as heretics by a continent that was largely Catholic.

The new queen was considerably different than Catherine of Aragon had been. She was Protestant and supportive of the king's religious reformation; she was also younger and very interested in French arts and fashion. Anne's dresses featured pointed long sleeves and square necklines, and she preferred rounded French hoods to the sharply-angled English gable hoods. She made a point always to wear the color green and use pearls somewhere in her outfit, as they were her favorites. Many of her ladies-in-waiting began to use pearls as well as copy Anne's style of dress, which had been popular since she began to serve at court in 1522.

Fashion wasn't the only thing that changed at Henry's palace once Anne was formally installed there. She introduced French-style music and dancing at court and had many friends and courtiers join in with the new trend. Anne created dance steps of her own which she taught to her ladies and performed with them during parties.

Anne wasn't exactly warmly welcomed at home or abroad as the Queen of England, but she was confident in her marriage and acted the part splendidly. She was already pregnant when she married the king, and her first child was born on September 7, 1553. The royal couple's first baby was a healthy girl, called Elizabeth Tudor. Over the course of the next three years, Anne became pregnant at least two more times, but both pregnancies ended in miscarriage or stillbirth. The last of these is believed by many to have occurred on the very day of Catherine of Aragon's funeral: January 29, 1536. The date of the miscarriage may have been a few weeks later, but in any case, the stillbirth was that of a male baby.

Though King Henry VIII was notoriously impatient regarding male heirs, his marriage to Anne was only three years old at that point and there were few serious signs that Anne was in danger. Nevertheless, he had taken notice of Jane Seymour while visiting her family home on business in 1533 and was clearly aware of her presence at court the following year in the service of Queen Anne.

While the Queen of England rested and recuperated from her miscarriage, the king became strict and decisive; he stated that Anne had used trickery to seduce him and he was finished with her. With Anne in her sick bed, completely ignorant of these events, Henry placed Jane Seymour in the royal apartments. Not even four months later Anne would be executed at the desire of her beloved husband. Neither contemporary friends of Henry VIII nor world-class historians can interpret the king's exact reasons for having his queen's reputation ruined and her life ultimately ended, but there has been much speculation. The death of their unborn son is considered a primary factor behind Henry's treatment of the woman he changed England to wed, but so too is the meddling of Thomas Cromwell.

Thomas Cromwell had been a crucial figure in the plan to remove Catherine of Aragon from court and replace her with Anne Boleyn; he did not, however, remain loyal to his choice of queen. Cromwell and Anne were at odds when it came to the administrative rules of the new Church of England, mainly because Anne wanted church proceeds to be used for education and charity. Cromwell wanted to use the church money to grow the royal treasury – and of course, he wanted a percentage for himself. While the queen and Henry's closest advisor argued, the latter began plotting with the French ambassador, Eustace Chapuys, to rid the English court of Anne. It was hardly an unprecedented move on his part, though he did need Henry's approval to move swiftly.

In April, a musician named Mark Smeaton, employed by Anne Boleyn, was arrested on suspicion of having an affair with her. He denied the charge, however after having been imprisoned and tortured for some time, he confessed. A member of the nobility, Henry Norris, was arrested under the same charge, as were Sir Francis Weston, Sir Richard Page, and William Brereton. The most shocking arrest was that of George Boleyn, Anne's own brother. He was accused of incest and treason.

On May 2, 1536, Anne Boleyn herself was arrested and charged with treason against the king, though the charges were not explained to her. She was taken to the Tower of London via the River Thames, and once she was within the Tower she collapsed, immediately asking where her father and brother were, and what she was charged with.

A letter survives from the Tudor era that is said to be Anne's last message to Henry VIII, though its contemporary owner explained inaccuracies in the writing to the fact that it was copied by Cromwell:

"Sir, your Grace's displeasure, and my Imprisonment are Things so strange unto me, as what to Write, or what to Excuse, I am altogether ignorant; whereas you sent unto me (willing me to confess a Truth, and so obtain your Favour) by such a one, whom you know to be my ancient and professed Enemy; I no sooner received the Message by him, than I rightly conceived your Meaning; and if, as you say, confessing Truth indeed may procure my safety, I shall with all Willingness and Duty perform your Command.

But let not your Grace ever imagine that your poor Wife will ever be brought to acknowledge a Fault, where not so much as Thought thereof proceeded. And to speak a truth, never Prince had Wife more Loyal in all Duty, and in all true Affection, than you have found in Anne Boleyn, with which Name and Place could willingly have contented my self, as if God, and your Grace's Pleasure had been so pleased. Neither did I at any time so far forge my self in my Exaltation, or received Queenship, but that I always looked for such an Alteration as now I find; for the ground of my preferment being on no surer Foundation than your Grace's Fancy, the least Alteration, I knew, was fit and sufficient to draw that Fancy to some other subject.

You have chosen me, from a low Estate, to be your Queen and Companion, far beyond my Desert or Desire. If then you found me worthy of such Honour, Good your Grace, let not any light Fancy, or bad Counsel of mine Enemies, withdraw your Princely Favour from me; neither let that Stain, that unworthy Stain of a Disloyal

Heart towards your good Grace, ever cast so foul a Blot on your most Dutiful Wife, and the Infant Princess your Daughter:

Try me, good King, but let me have a Lawful Trial, and let not my sworn Enemies sit as my Accusers and Judges; yes, let me receive an open Trial, for my Truth shall fear no open shame; then shall you see, either mine Innocency cleared, your Suspicion and Conscience satisfied, the Ignominy and Slander of the World stopped, or my Guilt openly declared. So that whatsoever God or you may determine of me, your Grace may be freed from an open Censure; and mine Offence being so lawfully proved, your Grace is at liberty, both before God and Man, not only to execute worthy Punishment on me as an unlawful Wife, but to follow your Affection already settled on that party, for whose sake I am now as I am, whose Name I could some good while since have pointed unto: Your Grace being not ignorant of my Suspicion therein.

But if you have already determined of me, and that not only my Death, but an Infamous Slander must bring you the enjoying of your desired Happiness; then I desire of God, that he will pardon your great Sin therein, and likewise mine Enemies, the Instruments thereof; that he will not call you to a strict Account for your unprincely and cruel usage of me, at his General Judgement-Seat, where both you and my self must shortly appear, and in whose Judgement, I doubt not, (whatsoever the World may think of me) mine Innocence shall be openly known, and sufficiently cleared.

My last and only Request shall be, That my self may only bear the Burthen of your Grace's Displeasure, and that it may not touch the Innocent Souls of those poor Gentlemen, who (as I understand) are likewise in strait Imprisonment for my sake. If ever I have found favour in your Sight; if ever the Name of Anne Boleyn hath been pleasing to your Ears, then let me obtain this Request; and I will so leave to trouble your Grace any further, with mine earnest Prayers to the Trinity to have your Grace in his good keeping, and to direct you in all your Actions.

Your most Loyal and ever Faithful Wife, Anne Bullen From my doleful Prison the Tower, this 6th of May."

All of the accused were found guilty, including the queen and her brother, and sentenced to be executed. According to existing law, a queen found guilty of adultery was supposed to be burned alive. Henry asked that Anne be beheaded instead, and had a special executioner brought in from France to do the job with a sword instead of the traditional axe. The day before Anne's execution was scheduled to take place, Thomas Cranmer pronounced the marriage between her and Henry Tudor void.

Anne climbed the scaffold on 19 May, 1536, dressed like a queen. She wore a dark grey damask gown with a scarlet petticoat underneath. Wearing a splash of vibrant, defiant red while facing execution was something Mary Start, Queen of Scots, and Marie Antoinette, Queen of France, would both do as well. Red, though to symbolize martyrdom, was a subtle way to show one's innocence in the face of death. Her hood, usually French, was a stiff English garment. She removed her ermine cape and headdress, tucked her hair into a small cap and allowed one of her maids to tie a blindfold in place. She knelt, prayed, and was killed with one stroke of the Frenchman's sword.

Chapter 10 – Mistress Mary Shelton

Mary Shelton was the youngest daughter of John and Anne Shelton, and one of 10 children who lived with their parents at Sheldon Hall in Norfolk. Her mother, Anne, was governess to Princess Mary Tudor, the king's first child by Catherine of Aragon. It was a strained relationship, since Shelton was under strict instructions not to let the little girl call herself "Princess" following the Reformation. Advisors to King Henry VIII did not want Mary to grow up to consider herself a royal, privileged heir. Anne was encouraged to physically punish young Mary if she referred to herself as a princess.

Anne's employment within the royal family was beneficial to all of her children. When her daughters became old enough, they were easily placed as ladies-in-waiting at the royal court. Mary, born sometime between 1510 and 1520, entered Henry Tudor's court to serve Queen Anne, the Protestant queen, soon after her marriage to Henry VIII. The young lady was thought to be a beautiful, well-read, and talented girl by her friends and peers. First cousins of the queen, her family were supporters of the Reformist movement, meaning that Mary understood much of the doctrine of the new Church of England. This could well have endeared her to the king, though it was likely her good looks and popularity that did the most to catch Henry's eye.

There is much confusion regarding the identity of Mary – and Margaret – Shelton. She appears either to have had a similarly-named sister, Margaret, or to have also been called Madge. Most historians concur that there were two Shelton girls, though it is difficult to say with conviction which was closest to King Henry. The most current research concludes that the girl in question was indeed Mary Shelton, while Margaret or "Madge" Shelton was closer to Queen Anne.

Mary was not only an avid reader, but a writer of poetry. She delighted in romantic verse and even worked together with other girls to create a book of poems and letters called the Devonshire Manuscript. This book was a collection of classic romantic writing copied out in full or excerpt, but it also contained new works allegedly by Mary Shelton, Margaret Douglas, and Mary Fitzroy, all of whom waited on Queen Anne Boleyn.

The Devonshire Manuscript was a huge success among Henry's courtiers, who enjoyed reading the verses as well as guessing who may have written the anonymous entries. The vivacious and exciting text most definitely came to the king's attention, since Henry loved literature and above all, romance. Mary's involvement in the popular book probably endeared the king even more to the attractive lady-in-waiting.

Some theories have gone so far as to suggest Anne Boleyn herself persuaded Mary to engage in a sexual relationship with King Henry VIII, apparently in an attempt of Anne's to put a sympathetic friend near the king. This theory may have some truth to it. By the time Mary and Henry began their affair, the king and queen's relationship had soured due to Anne's multiple miscarriages and Henry's constant cheating. As a friend and family member, Anne may have believed that it was better to have someone she could control in Henry's bed rather than a stranger. If this was indeed her strategy, it failed. Just a few months after Mary and Henry are said to have connected romantically, Anne Boleyn was put to death.

The executions of that spring seem to have put an end to Henry and Mary's relationship. There are no records available to suggest why their tryst came to a halt, but it was certainly a tumultuous time for everyone close to the king. Mary's sister, Margaret, suffered a great deal from the allegations made against her queen, since they also involved her fiancé. Henry Norris, an avid sportsman and close friend of King Henry, was likely matched with Margaret Shelton by the king himself. And yet, when the king needed his wife's reputation ruined, Norris was accused of adultery. He insisted that he was innocent, as did she, but both were found guilty and executed for adultery and treason in the spring of 1536.

It must have been a terrifying time for Margaret, and for her sister Mary as well. Though virtually all courtiers were at the mercy of King Henry's whims, she must have wondered if it would be better for her to pull away from Henry or encourage his desire. Perhaps he chose to end the affair himself, either because of her closeness to the queen or simply because his mind was occupied with so many other matters. It seems most likely that the king had decided to choose another woman for his next wife and was busy putting that plan into action.

It is difficult to say just how the execution of a woman Henry had clearly once loved affected the king, particularly because his behavior went on very much as usual throughout the entire year of 1536. His affair with Mary was not a new situation for the king, nor was his frustration with a queen who had delivered a girl and then suffered multiple stillbirths and miscarriages. It was, however, the first time the king was so desperate to rid himself of a wife that he actually had her accused and executed. This, like his fascination with the ladies-in-waiting at court, would prove to be another lifelong tendency.

Mary Shelton escaped the wrath of the king and his advisors, whereas many other women and men were not so lucky. Henry's fascination turned from her to Jane Seymour, another lady at court, and Mary was left mercifully without charge. Ten years after the execution of Queen Anne Boleyn, Mary Shelton married Sir Anthony Heveningham and the couple had five children together. At least one of her daughters, Abigail Heveningham, waited on Queen Elizabeth I in 1588. Her husband predeceased her, and Mary married for a second time in 1557 to Philip Appleyard. She and Heveningham are considered direct ancestors of Diana, Princess of Wales.

Chapter 11 – The Wooing of Jane Seymour

It was no secret that Henry VIII's new infatuation was Jane Seymour. In fact, this was mentioned in Anne Boleyn's last letter to her husband before he had her executed for treason. Indeed, the king had been romancing Anne's Maid of Honor for some time by the day of Anne's death, and this was so well known that Londoners sang rude rhymes about Jane and Henry's relationship. The king worried that his mistress would be insulted and scandalized by such things and immediately wrote to her on the subject:

"My dear friend and mistress,
The bearer of these few lines from thy entirely devoted servant will deliver into thy fair hands a token of my true affection for thee, hoping you will keep it forever in your sincere love for me. Advertising you that there is a ballad made lately of great derision against us, which if it go much abroad and is seen by you, I pray you to pay no manner of regard to it. I am not at present informed who is the setter forth of this malignant writing, but if he is found out he shall be straitly punished for it. For the things ye lacked I have minded my lord to supply them to you as soon as he can buy them. Thus hoping shortly to receive you in these arms, I end for the

present your own loving servant and sovereign,
H. R. "

Jane Seymour's estimated year of birth was 1509; the same year in which King Henry VIII was crowned. Like much of the nobility, Jane was related to the king via their common ancestor, King Edward III. Henry and Jane were fifth cousins; the latter was also distantly related to both Catherine of Aragon and Anne Boleyn. The middle daughter of ten children, Jane received a traditional education for a woman of her time. She knew how to read and write her own name, but nothing more. Instead of literature and history, like Queen Catherine, or arts and fashion, like Queen Anne, Queen Jane's interests were in domestic arts like embroidery and household organization.

Jane was so different from Queen Anne Boleyn, in fact, that it was said she was chosen by Henry because of her stark contrast to the deposed queen. She was never described as a beautiful girl, like all the others Henry took up with, but rather as meek, mild, pale, and plain. She was not the vivacious, headstrong girl that Anne had been, but a subservient mistress inclined to do as she was expected. Some even remarked that she seemed rather dull and unintelligent, but given Henry's charm, education, and intellect it seems unlikely that he would choose someone less than intuitive and insightful for a companion.

It is not possible to know exactly what was Jane Seymour's character, or what went through her mind during the whirlwind betrothal and marriage in 1536, but she must have immediately known when Henry's interest was piqued. Perhaps she did not know whether he intended to make her his mistress or wed her, but in either case she knew the potential pitfalls. To become Henry's mistress probably meant gifts of land and money as well as a quick marriage to someone friendly with the king. Becoming his queen, on the other hand, meant becoming responsible for producing a male heir – and if she proved incapable of such responsibility, suffering the ultimate price.

Jane Seymour probably acted according to what she believed was necessary to survive. After all, she was raised as a member of the reformed church and had served two Tudor queens before catching Henry's eye for herself. She had seen the failure of Catherine of Aragon's marriage, as well as the rushing highs and deadly lows of the marriage of Anne Boleyn. Jane was likely perfectly aware of what was needed of her as Henry's consort, and what could become of her if she did not act accordingly.

Jane's family may have done its own fair share of pushing Jane into the king's arms. The Seymours were an important family that was close to the crown. Knowing that Anne had fallen out of favour with Henry, Jane's father and brother believed they could provide the king with a new and better-suited match. The family crest, featuring a proud peacock, was suddenly changed to feature a phoenix. Clearly, the Seymours did not want anything resembling pride or assertiveness reflected on their pure, servile Jane. Many historians consider the swift replacement of Anne with Jane a coup on the part of the Seymours – a successful one whose remunerations would continue to flow long after the death of Jane herself.

King Henry found that Jane Seymour would not submit to his gifts and caresses for the same reason Anne had not – she would not become a mistress, but only a wife. It was a method that had worked for Anne Boleyn, and it worked once more for Jane. Most likely, King Henry believed that Jane's modesty was her own doing, and indeed this may well have been the case. It may also have been the advice of Jane's family, which she knew all too well was a good strategy.

Henry believed he was wooing Jane, but her family was probably equally wooing him! Of course, Jane herself had done most of the work in presenting herself as a modest and chaste lady simply because that's who she was. She had reached the age of 25 without having married or becoming caught up in an affair. The king assumed she was a virgin, and he was probably correct. The only scandal concerning Jane was actually the fault of her father, who had

had an affair with his daughter-in-law. That scandal passed and if it did Jane any personal harm, it was not long-lasting.

When the king sent a gift of golden coins to his love interest, Jane is said to have knelt on her knees and begged the messenger to take them back. She told him that she was a virtuous maiden who could not accept gifts from a married man. She added that if the king wanted to make a gift of gold to her, it should perhaps be when she had attained an honorable marriage. Henry had heard that kind of talk before, and this time he didn't need to change the fundamental religious premise of his kingdom or wait for six years to follow through. The humility of his chosen lady was everything to him, just as it had been seven years before.

Once the reigning queen was thoroughly vanquished, Jane was at the mercy of King Henry's wishes, for good or ill.

Chapter 12 – Jane and the Prince

Jane Seymour and Henry VIII were married at the Palace of Whitehall, 11 days after Anne's execution. The ceremony took place in the Queen's Closet, which was actually a lush and well-appointed space among the official Queen's Rooms at the palace.

Henry gifted his new bride over a hundred properties but did not arrange for her coronation, allegedly due to the outbreak of plague in London. Gossip among courtiers insisted that Henry wouldn't bother to crown Jane until she provided him with a prince, and there may have been some truth to the rumor. It was also true that during the summer, the royals tended to leave England's capital city due to plague flare-ups, and thus it makes sense that the new queen should not spend time in the heat of the infected city. Despite not having an official coronation ceremony, Henry's third wife was formally pronounced queen on June 4, 1536.

Soon after the wedding, the king received disheartening news: his only son, Henry Fitzroy, had died from tuberculosis at the age of seventeen. Fitzroy and Henry were close; the king had been considering marriage arrangements for his illegitimate son since his birth. For many years, it appeared that young Fitzroy would be Henry's only male candidate for the succession – at least, the only illegitimate candidate whom the king condescended to recognize as his own. It was a difficult year for King Henry VIII, but the stresses the king suffered were surely compounded onto his new wife. Jane must have felt more responsibility than ever to give the king children as soon as possible.

Unlike her predecessor, Jane Seymour was not pregnant at the time of the marriage, nor did she become pregnant until the next year. Finally, an impending birth was announced in January 1537 and the baby was delivered safely on the 12th of October. It was a healthy boy and the instant heir to the throne of England. They named him Edward and named him Prince of Wales,

During those long first months of Jane and Henry's marriage, while they undoubtedly tried to conceive, Jane made an effort to reach out to the king's existing children. She was already very sympathetic to Mary and her mother Catherine of Aragon and wanted to find a way to reunite the girl and her sister, Elizabeth, with their father. Her timing was ideal, as far as Mary was concerned, because she was sick, weak, and worried that she might be next on the scaffold. At the end of June, Mary Tudor signed a court document stating that her mother was never the lawful Queen of England, and that she would follow the laws of her father, Henry VIII, to the letter. It was very difficult for Mary to sign any such statement, but by 1537 she had held out for nearly five years. At the age of 21, Mary Tudor needed the love of her father so that she could re-join the royal court, be married, and claim her allowance.

Jane wanted both Mary and Elizabeth to be reinstated as royal heirs to Henry's crown – after any of her own children, of course. While she did not succeed in convincing the king to recognize his daughters as potential heirs, she did convince him to welcome them into his home on several occasions. It was the beginning of a long-winded mending of a deep familial rift. This was especially important for Elizabeth Tudor, whose mother was killed by her father's order. It is possible that Jane was concerned for the safety of Anne's only child, which prompted her to soothe Henry's temper in reference to the young girl. Henry seemed satisfied to keep both daughters alive and well-cared for and he included them in more royal events. The two girls were present at their half-brother's christening and held the train of the baby's gown.

Unfortunately for Jane, delivering Prince Edward was a very painful and exhausting two-day process. She remained in bed while preparations were made for Edward's christening at the Chapel Royal on the 15th of October. King Henry organized an unforgettable event for his new son and had the christening font raised up so everyone in attendance could see the prince. The ceremony was performed by Archbishop Thomas Cranmer and at its end little Edward was pronounced Prince Edward, Duke of Cornwall and Earl of Chester.

Cranmer, Charles Brandon, and several other men highly-regarded by the king stood as Edward's Godfathers; the king's daughter Mary stood as his Godmother. There is some confusion as to whether or not Queen Jane actually participated in part of the christening ceremony, though most sources agree she did not venture from her bedroom and the boy was returned to her afterward.

Jane's physical state deteriorated, improved, then worsened again over the course of the next nine days. Modern doctors and historians can only guess what may have caused her illness, but many agree that Henry's third wife suffered from puerperal fever: a sickness related to childbirth in which the mother develops a severe uterine infection. Whatever the exact reason, Jane died on the 24th of October, not even two weeks after the birth of her son. Henry gave her a large funeral and buried her at St. George's Chapel in Windsor Castle, where he would later be interred.

Jane Seymour, Henry VIII's wife for just short of one year and six months, is the only one of the king's wives whom Henry actively mourned. The king was reportedly devastated at her death and wore black well into the next year. Henry's companions noted that he took up needlepoint after his wife's demise, which had been a great hobby of hers. It was a commemorative act that both memorialized Jane and connected Henry to her in his time of sorrow. Many of Jane's embroidered creations, including sleeve cuffs and pillows, were kept in the royal collection as long as a century after her death.

After Jane's death on October 24, 1537, the king only halfheartedly discussed other potential marriages. Henry wanted Jane to be remembered, cherished, and respected properly as the mother of the heir to England's throne, Prince Edward, and he made sure to keep her memory alive at court through paintings, embroidery and pointed references. The updated bird on the Seymour crest came to be particularly apt.

Her epitaph reads:

> *"Here lies Jane, a phoenix*
> *Who died in giving another phoenix birth.*
> *Let her be mourned, for birds like these*
> *Are rare indeed."*

Chapter 13 – Two Years a Widower

1537 was an emotional year for King Henry VIII. In January, he sustained a frightening concussion and leg injury which nearly killed him. His love of jousting was lost to him for the rest of his life, as was his formerly active lifestyle. He'd fallen out of love and instigated the downfall of a woman he once cherished so much that he broke with the very head of the Catholic Church. Reginald Pole had been sent from Rome to rally a war-cry against heretical England, and Henry Fitzroy, the king's illegitimate but well-loved son, was dead.

From October 1537 to January 1540, King Henry remained unmarried. It was the longest period of time in his adult life that he was without a wife. These particular years were also difficult because of the growing pains of the Church of England. Now that his personally-headed church had been established and its basic rules laid out, the world's first English-language Bibles had been written and distributed throughout the country. More people than ever before had different opinions about what the gospels truly meant, while priests and clergymen struggled to understand exactly what the king regarded as heretical. Henry had a lot on his plate, and perhaps with his son Prince Edward safely tucked away in the palace, he found the time in his bachelorhood to fully address other issues besides the succession.

Despite his genuine melancholy at the death of Jane, Henry knew that it was in his best interest to marry and ally himself with a powerful family or country. He was back on the marital market by 1538, mostly for political reasons, but did not marry until the beginning of 1540. He'd begun to put on a huge amount of weight due to his inactivity, the pain in his legs, and his constant eating, but this did not make the King of England any less attractive in the political sense. There were many available matches both at home and abroad, but no one in particular seemed fit to fill Jane's place by his side.

Henry spoke of marriage but did not focus on it for at least six months following the birth of Prince Edward. In fact, Henry turned his attention to the infant and made every effort to keep the tiny prince healthy and safe. He insisted that the boy's residence be kept impeccably clean so as to lessen the risk of disease and illness, asking that the servants in attendance wash the rooms and the prince's belongings according to instructions very strict for the time period. The little boy had everything a tiny child could want and much more, as his father installed him in his own formal household headed by members of the Seymour family. It was just as it had been for Henry Fitzroy, but much more fastidious in terms of security.

The same year that Jane Seymour died, Hans Holbein the Younger completed his iconic painting of King Henry VIII. The portrait is still the most well-known likeness of King Henry, depicting the overweight monarch as a stout and strong, broad-shouldered man of physical greatness. His posture, fists at his hips and feet planted firmly apart, shows intensity and confidence. The robes are finely-sewn, the codpiece large and the calf muscles the king was always so proud of were thick and well-defined. Though Henry may have been as large as 300 pounds by that time, the portrait seems to only hint at a broadness of the body with a well-placed coat and fur trim. It is a masterpiece in that Holbein managed to allude to Henry's great size without displeasing the subject. The painting, though lost in a 17th-century fire, was copied numerous times by other contemporary artists

Throughout 1538, the king was in discussions with German envoys and councils interested in writing out a treaty. At first uninterested, Henry decided to look into the matter further and invited his guests to take part in long, detailed forums about the finer points of his true religion. Talks continued into the next year, when Henry sent his own envoy to Cleves to seek the alliance of the Duchy's new ruler, William.

Thomas Cromwell, King Henry's most trusted advisor, remained very eager to transform England into a fully Protestant state. He had helped arrange Henry's marriage to Anne Boleyn on the premise that by doing so, England would enter a new religious age. Cromwell's continued push for reform had begun to irritate the king, but Henry's displeasure did nothing to dissuade the chief minister's scheming. Cromwell wanted to reconnect King Henry to the other European Protestant nations, which were few but not insignificant. To this end, he searched out potential brides from the continent.

The Duchy of Cleves, situated in the territory of the Holy Roman Empire, was a singularly Protestant region under the ultimate rule of a staunch Catholic ally. It was small but fierce and there were two girls within its lands who were noble enough to become Queens of England. When King Henry had had enough of bachelorhood, Cromwell pointed him in the direction of the Cleves family.

In the early part of 1540, King Henry enacted strict legislation against remaining Catholic monasteries in England and Ireland. Shap Abbey, Dunstable Priory, Bolton Abbey, Thetford Priory, and Waltham Abbey were all closed down due to the Dissolution of the Monasteries Act. It was huge progress for the Church of England but just as much of a loss for England's large population of traditional Catholics. The latter saw King Henry as a tyrant, while the former applauded his strong hand in shutting down and essentially looting the monasteries throughout the nation.

Despite this move, Henry remained unsure about just how far he wanted to go in terms of changing England's religious practices. He had been raised a devout Catholic and therefore hesitated to embrace full Protestantism, in spite of seeming to do so only seven years earlier. Instead, the king searched for a sort of medium-ground between the drastic reforms of Protestant Europe and the fully-Catholic traditions of his youth.

His choice of bride on January 6, 1540, was telling.

Chapter 14 – Anne of Cleves

Anne La Marck, better-known by her House name of Cleves, was 24 years Henry VIII's junior. She was born September 22, 1515, in the Duchy of Cleves which was inherited by her father, Johann III La Marck. She and her younger sister, Amalia, were both under serious consideration for the vacant position of Queen of England in 1539. For the king's fourth wife, Henry's Chief Minister was interested in a foreign queen; the Duchy of Cleves was an independent state of the Holy Roman Empire, now part of modern Germany.

Anne grew up in Schloss Burg, a beautiful castle near the city of Solingen, with three siblings: Amalia, Sybil, and Wilhelm. Upon the death of Johann III in 1558 (or 1559, depending which sources are correct), Wilhelm inherited the Duchy of Jülich-Cleves-Berg and conducted his property under many of the ideals of the European Reformation; he was a member of the Schmalkaldic League, a union of Protestant states against the Holy Roman Emperor.

Anne was not formally educated, but she knew how to read and write in German and was considered an attractive and gentle young woman by most nobles from nearby Duchies and neighboring nations. She enjoyed playing cards and made efforts to be an enjoyable conversationalist; she was also very skilled at contemporary domestic duties such as sewing and embroidery. Unlike most noble women in England, Anne of Cleves learned no foreign languages, nor was she taught to sing or play an instrument.

Like all members of European royal families, Anne of Cleves was subject to the whims of her parents when it came to marriage. At the young age of ten, she was engaged to Francis, heir to the Duchy of Lorraine, but this arrangement was canceled in 1535.

Six years after Henry VIII had reformed England's religion, Cromwell and some of his top Protestant advisors began to feel the king was less enthusiastic about Protestantism than he had been in past years. It also appeared that France and the Holy Roman Empire were conspiring to invade anti-Catholic England, which doubly prompted Thomas Cromwell to seek Henry's new wife from a fellow Protestant state. The youngest daughters of the Duchy of Cleves were selected as the most appropriate brides for King Henry VIII, so the king sent his court portraitist, Hans Holbein the Younger, to create likenesses of both girls.

Holbein created a beautiful portrait of Anne wearing the puffed, wide sleeves and high-waisted skirt of German style, as well as the isolated style of headdress traditional in her part of Europe. The young woman made a lovely portrait that showed off her symmetrical facial features, classically well-balanced figure and pleasant facial expression. Focused entirely on Anne's upper body, however, the portrait failed to show the lady's height and size. She was a tall and robust woman – still considered very attractive by many, but not within King Henry VIII's normal taste.

Holbein also created a rudimentary sketch of Anne's sister, Amalia, wearing very similar clothing and accessories. Amalia had a thinner, perhaps longer face than Anne. It was ultimately Anne of Cleves' portrait that won Henry VIII's admiration, so Wilhelm arranged a marriage contract with the King of England and sent his sister to Henry's court.

By the time Anne was ready to travel to England, the short-lived peace between the Holy Roman Empire and France was growing unreliable. It was not safe for Anne to travel through either of these nations, but there was no other way to reach England from Cleves. French King Francis I offered his support, while Charles V gave Anne a French passport that enabled her to travel through the Netherlands and depart the continent.

Ironically, the animosity between Francis I, Charles V, and England was a large part of the reason Henry VIII sought a Protestant alliance with the Duchy of Cleves in the first place; when the French and Holy Roman Empire decided to cooperate with Henry and Wilhelm, Henry lost his reason to wed Anne at all. The King of England was not unaware of this, but he'd agreed to marry the girl and he wanted to follow through on his promise. So, Anne of Cleves traveled westward in the heart of winter and arrived in England by New Year's Day of 1540.

As soon as his bride was within reach, Henry hurried to meet her – in costume, with eight of his privy councilors:

"On which day the kyng which sore desyred to see her Grace accompanyed with no more then viii. persons of his prevy chambre, & both he & they all apparelled in marble coates prevely came to Rochester, and sodainly came to her presence, which therwith was sumwhat astonied: but after he had spoken & welcomed her, she with most gracious & loving countenance and behaviour him received & welcomed on her knees, whom he gently toke up & kyssed: & all that after-noone commoned and devised with her, & that night supped with her, & the next day he departed to Grenewich , & she came to Dartford. [sic]"

Though Henry was every bit the gentleman during his impromptu meeting with his bride-to-be, his friends later stated that the king was in no way satisfied with the way Anne looked. This may have been true, but there is likely another reason why the king was not impressed by Anne. Appearing in disguise to the person you love was a tradition at court, whereby the person being visited is supposed to recognize their loved one or fall in love immediately.

Given the king's well-known ego, it's possible that he was insulted Anne didn't recognize him until he removed his disguise and his courtiers began to wait on him. Henry VIII was accustomed to his brides showing the utmost respect and attention to him; believing he was a servant of the king, Anne merely showed Henry politeness and then ignored him. After their meeting, rude rumors circulated concerning just what Henry had said about his bride-to-be. Nevertheless, the marriage went ahead on January 6, 1540, at the Palace of Placentia in Greenwich. The Archbishop Thomas Cranmer performed the ceremony.

Henry confessed to Thomas Cromwell the next day that he had not made love with his new wife and therefore the marriage was not yet official. Furthermore, the king could not say whether he would finalize the marriage at any point in the future. Anne, though 24 years of age, had never been married before and seemed not to understand this detail. She confessed to one of her Maids of Honor that the king bid her good morning and good night each day, kissing her hand sweetly; the latter assured the queen that much more was necessary to bring about a baby.

Anne of Cleves never consummated her marriage to King Henry VIII of England. After she was ordered to leave Henry's residence and go on her own to Richmond Palace, she discovered that her marriage was in trouble. She fainted, and when she recovered herself, Anne refused to agree to Henry's proposed annulment.

Chapter 15 – Annulment and Later Years

Anne of Cleves was hurt that she had displeased her husband so severely, so soon into their marriage, but once she had time to gather her thoughts, she knew better than to argue with someone with Henry VIII's reputation. Though at first, she insisted on knowing what she had done wrong, Anne soon realized it was best to agree to the annulment and make things easy on the king.

On the 9th of July, six months after their wedding, Henry and Anne of Cleves had their marriage annulled. Henry blamed the split on many things, including Anne's looks, his disbelief in her virginity, her canceled betrothal to Francis of Lorraine, and mostly, Thomas Cromwell. The latter was executed for treason mere weeks after Anne of Cleves was turned out of Henry's palace and given her own collection of English residences.

She wrote to him on July 11 and expressed her desire to do as he willed:

"Pleaseth your most excellent majesty to understand that, whereas, at sundry times heretofore, I have been informed and perceived, by

certain lords and others of your grace's council, of the doubts and questions which have been moved and found in our marriage; and how hath petition thereupon been made to your highness by our nobles and commons, that the same might be examined and determined by the holy clergy of this realm; to testify to your highness by my writing, that which I have before promised by word and will, that is to say, that the matter should be examined and determined by the said clergy; it may please your majesty to know that, thought this case must needs be most hard and sorrowful unto me, for the great love which I bear to your most noble person, yet, having more regard to God and his truth than to any worldly affection, as it beseemed me, at the beginning, to submit me to such examination and determination of the said clergy, whom I have and do accept for judges competent in that behalf. So now being ascertained how the same clergy hath therein given their judgment and sentence, I knowledge myself hereby to accept and approve the same, wholly and entirely putting myself, for my state and condition, to your highness' goodness and pleasure; most humbly beseeching your majesty that, though it be determined that the pretended matrimony between us is void and of none effect, whereby I neither can nor will repute myself for your grace's wife, considering this sentence (whereunto I stand) and your majesty's clean and pure living with me, yet it will please you to take me for one of your most humble servants, and so to determine of me, as I may sometimes have the fruition of your most noble presence; which as I shall esteem for a great benefit, so, my lords and others of your majesty's council, now being with me, have put me in comfort thereof; and that your highness will take me for your sister; for the which I most humbly thank you accordingly.

Thus, most gracious prince, I beseech our Lord God to send your majesty long life and good health, to God's glory, your own honour, and the wealth of this noble realm.

From Richmond, the 11th day of July, the 32nd year of your majesty's most noble reign.

Your majesty's most humble sister and servant,

ANNE, THE DAUGHTER OF CLEVES"

For accepting his offer of marital annulment, King Henry VIII rewarded Anne of Cleves richly. If she worried that her life was in danger, she needn't have concerned herself; Upon their annulment, Henry gave his fourth wife Richmond Palace, Bletchingley Manor, Chelsea Old Manor and Anne Boleyn's childhood home, Hever Castle. He also gave her a comfortable annual salary and let her keep all the jewels, clothing, furniture, and other small property she had amassed during her short time as his wife.

Most prestigiously, Anne was granted the right to be called "Sister of the King." Thereafter, she was officially treated as a member of the royal family. Without a doubt, Anne of Cleves was the luckiest of all Henry VIII's wives. She neither died in childbirth, nor at the executioner's block, nor in isolation and sickness as had Catherine of Aragon. Instead, she flourished under the influence of the king and his lavish gifts.

After the marriage was ended, Anne decided to continue living in England, but stayed mostly out of the public eye. She chose Hever Castle, in Kent, as her regular home, and received King Henry there on multiple occasions. The two grew to be true friends, so much so that it was eventually rumored Henry would marry Anne a second time. This was untrue, but as the King's sister, Anne was often invited to court and received happily by Henry.

Among Anne's regular guests at Hever Castle were the Princesses Elizabeth and Mary. Both girls developed a close relationship with their former stepmother, particularly the like-minded Elizabeth. The younger princess was a faithful Protestant, having grown up entirely in the era of the Church of England, and her religious beliefs were perfectly in line with Anne's own. Mary was not spiritually likeminded, as her loyalty had always secretly lain with her mother's Catholic faith. When she inherited the throne in 1553, Mary's bloody reign spared few people: Anne of Cleves would be one of that lucky minority.

It was likely Anne's intelligence and positive that not only saved her life but gave her more luxury than she could comprehend. After her death on July 16, 1557, Anne of Cleves was given a full royal funeral and burial at Westminster Abbey at the behest of Queen Mary I. She had outlived King Henry VIII and his five other wives and been an important example of kindness and pragmatism to young Elizabeth Tudor. Anne of Cleves lived to the age of 41 and died following a short illness that modern historians believe may have been cancer.

Chapter 16 – Catherine Howard

It should have surprised no one (except Anne of Cleves) that Henry VIII had another bride in mind when he decided to annul his marriage to Anne. True to form, Henry's choice was one of his wife's ladies-in-waiting: Catherine Howard.

It's difficult to tell what the teenaged girl looked like from her Hans Holbein the Younger portraits, because Henry's official court portraitist had a rather stiff and particular style. His painting of the young object of King Henry's desire makes Catherine appear much older and less charismatic than she truly was. Besides the girl's pale white skin and dark blonde hair, we know little of her true likeness.

The very young and vivacious Catherine Howard was only 15 or 16 years old when she married 49-year-old King Henry on July 28, 1540. Their wedding took place the same day Thomas Cromwell was beheaded, which had been a somewhat shocking development in the king's council. It marked a new beginning for the king, who likely felt the effects of aging more acutely than ever and wanted to embrace new blood in his personal life as well as in the Privy Council.

Catherine Howard grew up in the care of her father's stepmother, the Dowager Duchess of Norfolk. It was normal for the daughters of poor nobility to live with a distant relative, in this case in the company of other girls with the same background. The duchess was responsible for teaching the girls in her care how to conduct themselves in the company of other nobles, including royalty, so that they might make excellent marital matches when the time came.

Not every young ladies' home quite delivered on this promise, and Catherine Howard's most certainly did not. Young Catherine and many of her friends at the estate were in the habit of sneaking their male friends into the bedroom late at night and staying up until the early hours flirting, gossiping, and falling in love. In 16th-century England, such behavior was beyond taboo. If discovered, it could ruin a girl's reputation for the rest of her life, not only preventing her from getting married and finding a comfortable situation but potentially breaking up any future marriage she did acquire.

In the bloom of youth and political innocence, Catherine and her friends simply enjoyed themselves and thought little of the consequences. Catherine herself had a serious romantic relationship with the secretary of the household, Francis Dereham. The two of them saw each other on a daily basis, and while Francis was away from the estate he left Catherine in charge of his household, belongings, and money. Completely in secret, the young couple agreed to marry one another as soon as it became possible. Unfortunately, the Duchess found out about their arrangement and immediately fired Dereham.

As supposedly inappropriate as Catherine's relationship was with Francis, it had the merit of being consensual. The same cannot be said for other so-called romantic affairs she would eventually be blamed for – in particular, the sexual relationship with her music teacher, Henry Mannox. This took place while Catherine was in the care of the Duchess, but before Francis Dereham joined the household. Though Mannox presented a case in which his student flirted with him and enjoyed herself, the girl told a slightly different story. In Catherine's opinion, Mannox had imposed upon her when she was only a young girl and she let him do what he liked, knowing little better.

Dereham and Howard, for their part, lovingly referred to each other as husband and wife, but their agreement was betrayed by the Duchess. Francis departed for Ireland and probably never saw Catherine again.

In 1539, Catherine moved into her uncle's house close to London and met a cousin of her mother's, Thomas Culpeper. Culpeper was one of King Henry VIII's Privy Chamber Gentlemen, meaning that he had access to the king's personal rooms as a body servant. Thomas was young, handsome and relatively important, which immediately impressed Catherine. Soon after this meeting, Catherine was given her own position at court as a lady-in-waiting to Queen Anne of Cleves. Almost immediately upon her arrival, Catherine was noticed by the king. In less than a year, the two were married and the new queen was happily installed in her own royal apartments.

It was a joyous time for Queen Catherine Howard, who had little to do but buy beautiful French gowns bedecked with expensive jewels and adornments. The couple left London in the heat of August to avoid plague season, and Henry entertained himself by lavishing the young queen in luxury everywhere they traveled. She had all the dresses, jewelry, and beautiful things she wanted, plus the best food and drink, and the king's indulgence in her relatively childish behavior. Though the king was aging, overweight, and in a great deal of pain from the ulcers on his legs, he enjoyed watching the little queen play with her friends in the dirt or chasing each other about the various royal estates.

One of Catherine's great joys was to meet 7-year-old Elizabeth Tudor, since the two were cousins through the Boleyn family. The new queen made sure to have Elizabeth sitting across from her or beside her at every meal when they were in the same palace. Her admiration was requited, and Elizabeth very much enjoyed spending time with her third stepmother and receiving little gifts from her.

After the plague died down along with the heat, Henry continued his liberal spending, this time on the Palace of Whitehall and a memorable Christmas celebration at Hampton Court Palace that same year. Queen Catherine received diamonds, furs, and pearls from the king on one of his most treasured holy days. Though often moody from the pain he suffered, King Henry did everything in his power to make 1540 an especially enjoyable year for himself and his little bride. He went so far as to have a special gold crown coin minted in honor of his latest marriage.

In the first part of 1541, the courtiers began to look for signs of pregnancy in Queen Catherine. It was determined that once she was with child, she would have her official coronation celebration. Unfortunately, peers from the queen's past began to appear at the palace, asking favors from Catherine in return for their silence about her relationships with Dereham and Mannox. She had little choice but to do as they asked, and soon her position at King Henry's court was teetering on the precipice of disaster.

Chapter 17 – The Culpeper Affair

Catherine Howard had already fallen in love with Thomas Culpeper by the time King Henry gave her any notice, and this was not something that marrying the king could change. Where a more mature woman would have known to use the utmost discretion in her personal life after entering into a marriage with Henry VIII, Catherine Howard either didn't understand this importance or she simply could not help but follow her young heart.

Catherine and Thomas had exchanged letters and spent time together at court before the former became betrothed, and even considered marrying each other. It would have been a fine match; they were of a suitable age, members of the English nobility, and even came from the same family. Moreover, Thomas and Catherine had a mutual affinity for one another, which Catherine surely could not have had for the aged, obese, sickly King Henry. Nevertheless, one does not turn down a marriage proposal from a king, even if said king has murdered a previous wife.

At some point after the royal wedding, the new queen began receiving visits from Thomas Culpeper in her private rooms. One of her most trusted Maids of Honor, Jane Boleyn, would sit outside in the hall and make sure the couple wasn't discovered. For many months, Catherine's affair eluded the king and his councilors, but the situation became impossible to control once the queen's old peers began making demands of her.

By the autumn of 1541, many of these very extortionists had been appointed to positions in Catherine's employment so as to keep them satisfied and quiet. They were not particularly inclined to remain silent, however, and soon the queen's secrets became known to Thomas Cranmer. The Archbishop immediately took it upon himself to research the allegations against Catherine and soon presented the king with a warrant for her arrest and trial. Among many confessions, Cranmer had located a letter in the queen's handwriting in Culpeper's bedchamber:

"Master Culpeper,

I heartily recommend me unto you, praying you to send me word how that you do. It was showed me that you was sick, the which thing troubled me very much till such time that I hear from you praying you to send me word how that you do, for I never longed so much for a thing as I do to see you and to speak with you, the which I trust shall be shortly now.

That which doth comfortly me very much when I think of it, and when I think again that you shall depart from me again it makes my heart die to think what fortune I have that I cannot be always in your company.

Yet my trust is always in you that you will be as you have promised me, and in that hope I trust upon still, praying you that you will come when my Lady Rochford is here for then I shall be best at leisure to be at your commandment, thanking you for that you have promised me to be so good unto that poor fellow my man which is one of the griefs that I do feel to depart from him for then I do know no one that I dare trust to send to you, and therefore I pray you take him to be with you that I may sometime hear from you one thing.

I pray you to give me a horse for my man for I had much ado to get one and therefore I pray send me one by him and in so doing I am as I said afor, and thus I take my leave of you, trusting to see you shortly again and I would you was with me now that you might see what pain I take in writing to you.

Yours as long as life endures

Katheryn.

One thing I had forgotten and that is to instruct my man to tarry here with me still for he says whatsomever you bid him he will do it."

It was difficult to argue that the letter had been forged, since Catherine was not very skilled at writing and her hand was easy to identify. Catherine was arrested, as were Thomas Culpeper, Francis Dereham, and Henry Mannox. On the 24th of November, 1541, the queen was imprisoned at Syon Abbey, Middlesex. Cranmer told the king that upon questioning, Catherine was in a such a frenzied state of terror that he found it necessary to remove everything from her room that she may use to harm herself. She would not see Henry again.

The king was furious. Henry's great love for Catherine Howard had been largely based on his perception of her as a youthful virgin, untouched by other men or the harshness of life. He called her the perfection of womanhood and believed that she was pure innocence personified. If he'd thought that Catherine's very tender age made her immune to the emotions, desires, and hardships of a fully-grown woman, he was wrong.

Catherine Howard testified that she had never been engaged to Francis Dereham, saying instead that he had raped her. She also stated that Henry Mannox took advantage of her young age but did not deny having a relationship with Thomas Culpeper before marrying King Henry VIII. As her letter was undated, the only proof that her statement concerning Culpeper was false came from the testimony of Jane Boleyn, the widow of Anne Boleyn's brother George. Jane had seen her husband and sister-in-law struggle with the very same accusation of adultery and treason in 1536 and she knew how the investigation was likely to turn out. Probably in an attempt to avoid torture and ultimately save herself, the Boleyn widow cooperated immediately with Cranmer. She, too, was arrested for complicity in treason.

Catherine Howard languished at Syon House until February 11, 1542, when she was taken to the Tower of London via the River Thames. The next day, she was told to prepare for her execution. She took advantage of the warning and asked to borrow the executioner's block so that she might practice how best to lay her head.

Stripped of her royal title, Catherine Howard climbed the steps of the scaffold looking very weak and fragile. She could not manage many words, probably due to sickness and fright, but she did tell those assembled how she deserved her fate for her trespasses against the king. She was executed on or near the same spot as Anne Boleyn had been six years earlier. It was the 13th of February. Thomas Culpeper had already been killed by the executioner's axe, and Francis Dereham hung, drawn and quartered. Henry Mannox received no punishment.

Chapter 18 – Katherine Parr

Katherine Parr was born to a noble northern English family whose roots stretched back to King Edward III. Her exact birth date is unknown but thought to be within the year 1512. She had two younger siblings, a father who was very close to King Henry VIII, and a mother who was a close companion of Queen Catherine of Aragon. In fact, Henry's first queen had been young Katherine's godmother.

The eldest Parr daughter had a lot of life to live before becoming Henry VIII's sixth and final wife. She grew up in Westmorland, receiving a typical education that consisted of some literature, music, needlework, and languages. Young Katherine was an eager student who had a particular penchant for languages, learning how to speak and write English, Latin, Italian, and French. She spent her formative years in King Henry VIII's Protestant England, which her father and mother supported. Protestantism would be a defining feature of

Katherine's character, particularly after becoming acquainted with the king.

Katherine married at the age of 17 to a sickly man named Edward Burgh who was in his twenties. This first coupling would turn out to be a typical sort of marriage for Katherine, who married four times throughout her life. Not much is known about the unfortunate Edward Burgh, since he only lived another four years after the marriage and did not survive to inherit his father's title of Baron of Gainsborough. Katherine's duties in her first marriage were typical of a woman in her status: household management and the care of her chronically-ill husband.

Katherine's second marriage occurred in 1534, to John Neville, 3rd Baron Latimer. Though her husband was twice her age and had two children from previous marriages, Katherine was able to move into her own house with her new family and start fresh. Between husbands, she had been reliant on friends and family relations to offer housing and provisions for her. Such a predicament was quite usual for the Tudor era, if one was a woman. Like the vast majority of her female peers, Katherine needed a patron to keep her from abject poverty. John Neville would be her lifeline for nine years.

Life as a Latimer was not simple, though it was reasonably luxurious. The family lived at Snape Castle and was quite influential amongst English northerners, but that influence became a liability during the Lincolnshire Uprising in 1536. Though Lord Latimer himself was allied with King Henry – if not actually Protestant himself – his neighbors wanted to strong-arm Parliament into allowing them to keep their Catholic churches, customs, and laws. Outraged at the king's decision to marry Anne Boleyn and reform all of England under Protestantism, northern rebels forced Katherine's husband to join them in revolt or face the consequences. Latimer did so, leaving his wife and children at home alone.

Still quite a young woman, Katherine struggled to care for two step-children and herself while isolated at Snape Castle, wondering if her husband would be killed or bring the household into ruin. There was little hope of a good outcome during those tumultuous years. If the Pilgrimage of Grace, as the northern rebellion was called as it formed and moved south, was successful, northern England could be split from its southern half. If, on the other hand, the king took offense to the revolt, Latimer and all involved could be stripped of their titles and land, then tortured and killed by soldiers of the crown.

Katherine had been born in the south of England and her parents were in direct service of the crown, which meant that she had a better understanding of the Church of England than did older generations or those Catholic strongholds in the north. Latimer's chapel at Snape Castle was in the Catholic fashion, but the lady of the house was Protestant at heart. John Neville had no desire to call out King Henry on his religious reforms, and so in the guise of supporting the extremist faction that surrounded him, he acted as a diplomat between the protestors and the crown.

His wife must have been incredibly fearful during those long years without John, especially when Catholic rebels took her and the children hostage in exchange for John's return from London. The absent 3rd Baron Latimer returned and negotiated the release of his family. Hard-pressed by both sides of the rebellion, Latimer came under close scrutiny by Thomas Cromwell, King Henry VIII's foremost advisor. To the king and his council, it seemed likely that John Neville was just as much a rebellious conspirator as the rest of those involved in the Pilgrimage of Grace; to the rebels, Neville seemed to close to the king. It was a situation he barely escaped. When the charge of treason was given up, Latimer moved his family south.

Katherine's husband had dampened his reputation, and for this reason Thomas Cromwell was able to use him as a sort of errand boy over the next few years. When King Henry grew tired of Cromwell's presence and had him executed in 1540, life became easier for the Latimer family. John attended business at court in London from time to time, where Katherine visited her sister. By the time the reputation of the family had started to improve, John Neville became sick and had to rely on his wife to care for him as well as his children. She nursed him until his death in 1553.

Living in and near London those five or six years meant that Katherine had been introduced to many influential people at the king's court, including the king's daughter, Lady Mary. The two were close in age and they became fast friends, Katherine often visiting Mary at court. She also became introduced to Henry VIII's brother-in-law, Thomas Seymour. The two enjoyed one another's company to the extent that Katherine hoped they would marry. Before any such arrangement could be made, however, the thirty-year-old widow came to the attention of the king himself. Henry, never satisfied with or without a wife, decided Katherine was the perfect candidate to become his sixth queen. Like her predecessors, Katherine had little choice but to agree to the king's proposal. After all, Thomas Seymour would never pursue her while she had the king's eye, and Henry was nothing if not persistent.

By 1543, King Henry VIII was 52 years old and not at all healthy. His weight had ballooned to over 300 pounds, his legs were full of infection that leaked and stank; he spent as little time as possible on his feet. It's entirely possible that Henry had witnessed the kind ministrations of Lady Latimer to her ill and dying husband for several years, and now he wanted that patience and kindness for his own benefit. He married Katherine on July 12, 1543.

Having twice been a wife, and stepmother to two children, Katherine was a practiced hand at matrimony. She was careful, sweet, patient, and caring, all qualities that appealed to Henry in his senior years. Furthermore, the king's sixth wife was genuine in her adoration of the new faith, which had kept her safe in the south of England while Catholics terrorized her in the north. Henry and Katherine bonded over their shared religious beliefs, talking about the finer points of the Church of England privately for hours. In those years, Henry's church was not formally known as Protestant, as there were variants between his religious laws and the laws of other Protestant nations.

Though Katherine seemed a happily full-fledged Protestant, she had to defer to Henry's specifications concerning religious practices.

Unlike the women who came before her, Katherine Parr was neither expected to be virginal nor produce children. She was there to be a sweet and loving wife, a role at which she knew how to excel. She took care to have her stepdaughter, Margaret Neville, installed as one of her ladies-in-waiting, and did the same for her stepson's wife. As for her three new stepchildren, Katherine made haste to become better acquainted with them and see that they had the mothering and education they deserved.

Princess Mary and Katherine were already friends; however Princess Elizabeth and Prince Edward were only ten and six years old, respectively. Elizabeth had just lost yet another stepmother in Catherine Howard and was old enough to truly feel the succession of losses in this respect. Edward had just reached the age at which his formal education was to begin, which meant a great deal of household administration awaited Katherine upon moving into Hampton Court Palace.

For Henry, this last marriage functioned much like his first. He and his wife were friends, and he trusted her. They sat together regularly, she in his lap or he with his sore legs in hers while she massaged them. Henry listened to Katherine when she spoke about the goodness of his daughters and the importance of reinstating their names into the royal succession. Remembering the same advice from Jane Seymour, the wife he'd treasured since her delivery of Prince Edward, the king finally wrote Elizabeth and Mary back into his will as legitimate daughters.

Having helped Mary and Elizabeth achieve their legitimacy, Katherine turned to the work of educating little Edward. He was a smart boy with a head for finance and military tactics, and his stepmother made sure he learned all he could of Protestantism, history, and language. Even she continued her own education alongside Edward and Elizabeth, taking up Spanish as well as theology. The younger royal children bonded with Katherine as one of their main tutors; it was a time that both Elizabeth and Edward would remember for the rest of their lives.

In 1544, Henry VIII brought his armies to France in another attempt to take back England's lost property there. Upon leaving England, the king did something he hadn't done since Catherine of Aragon was alive: he made the queen regent in his place.

Katherine was admired by Thomas Cranmer, her own uncle, and well-liked by the other members of her Regency Council; the queen ruled easily and as she pleased during the three months Henry was abroad. Though the king returned without victory in France, Katherine knew she'd earned his continued trust and respect.

The queen's confidence in her position grew after the French campaign, and she began to publish her own books on theology, such as *Psalms or Prayers*. These were notably the very first books published in England that had been written by a woman – at least in her own name. Katherine's writing and philosophical prowess, coupled with her solid command of the regency, must have made a lasting impression on both Mary and Elizabeth, who would both become future Queens of England.

The queen's blatant love of continental Protestantism earned her some enemies in the Privy Council, which was still partially constructed of die-hard Catholics whom Henry nevertheless trusted. After the death of Thomas Cromwell, Henry himself appeared to soften on religious reform. Taking advantage of the situation, the Bishop of Winchester and Lord Wriothesley made a case against the queen as a heretic and took it to the king. Katherine found a copy of the warrant and ran to see Henry as soon as she was sufficiently calm. She humbled herself before the king and lamented that she had spoken too much on the subject of theology without his approval. She apologized profusely and stroked her husband's ego desperately. Henry sent her back to her rooms.

She was spared in spectacular fashion. Henry, having already forgiven his wife for any perceived transgressions against his dogmatic religious doctrine, sought to teach his councilors a lesson. Soon after his wife's apology, the king took Katherine outside to enjoy the palace gardens. They were interrupted by Lord Wriothesley, who, not having been informed of the king's desire to overlook the heresy charges, attempted to arrest the queen for treason. Henry VIII struck the Lord and his attendants forcefully, sending them away and stating for all in earshot that his queen was not to be questioned.

Queen Katherine remained at her husband's side and was rebuked no more by anyone on his council. She continued to foster a loving relationship with the king's children, and on New Year's Day, 1545, Katherine received a religious book from Princess Elizabeth that the latter had translated into English herself:

"TO OUR MOST NOBLE AND virtuous queen KATHERINE, Elizabeth her humble daughter wisheth perpetual felicity and everlasting joy.

NOT ONLY knowing the affectuous will and fervent zeal, the which your highness hath towards all godly learning, as also my duty towards you (most gracious and sovereign princess) but knowing also that pusillanimity and idleness are most repugnant unto a reasonable creature and that (as the philosopher sayeth) even as an instrument of iron or of other metal waxeth soon rusty unless it be continually occupied. Even so shall the wit of a man, or woman, wax dull and unapt to do or understand anything perfectly, unless it be always occupied upon some manner of study, which things considered hath moved so small a portion as God hath lent me to prove what I could do.

And therefore have I (as for essay beginning, following the right notable saying of the proverb aforesaid) translated this little book out of French rhyme into English prose, joining the sentences together as well as the capacity of my simple wit and small learning could extend themselves. The which book is entitled, or named, The Mirror or Glass, of the Sinful Soul, wherein is contained how she (beholding and contemplating what she is) doth perceive how, of herself, and of her own strength, she can do nothing that good is, or prevaileth for her salvation—unless it be through the grace of God, whose mother, daughter, sister, and wife, by the scriptures she proveth herself to be.

Praying God Almighty, the maker and creator of all things, to guarantee unto Your Highness the same New Year's Day, a lucky and a prosperous year with prosperous issue and continuance of many years in good health and continual joy and all to His honour, praise, and glory."

From Ashridge, the last day
of the year of our Lord God, 1544."

By Christmas of the same year, King Henry was thought near to death. Suffering with much pain, the king's court was closed for the holiday and only Katherine and Lady Mary were with him. He died just over a month later, on January 28, 1546. Prince Edward succeeded him under a Regency Council appointed by the late King Henry VIII, and Katherine moved to her manor house in Chelsea with a 7,000-pound income granted by Henry's will.

Having done her royal duty, Katherine wasted no time in marrying her true love, Thomas Seymour, the new king's uncle. The couple wed secretly in May of 1546 and did not inform King Edward or the Princesses Mary and Elizabeth until later in the year. The royal family was shocked and disappointed in Katherine for not offering their father a proper mourning period. Furthermore, the Seymours had placed themselves as potential usurpers of the young king's throne, a fact that could not have been missed by the clever Katherine. She married Thomas regardless of his political ambitions, and published *Lamentation of a Sinner* in 1547.

The next year, she invited Princess Elizabeth and young Lady Jane Grey to join her at Sudeley Castle, Gloucestershire, so they could continue their education under her tutelage. Though Elizabeth, then 14 years old, was still very close to her stepmother Katherine, the latter found her husband embracing the girl and had no choice but to send her from the estate.

Katherine became pregnant for the first time that same year but died soon after childbirth from the same sickness that had claimed Jane Seymour. Her daughter, Mary, seems to have died around the age of two. Thomas Seymour was executed the very next year for plotting against King Edward VI.

Chapter 19 – More Theories on Henry Tudor's Fertility

King Henry VIII accomplished a great deal during his 37-year reign, including the reformation of the English church, the creation of a viable English navy, and the renovation of Whitehall into a lavish palace. Still, it is Henry's six wives and his obsessive need for a male heir for which most people remember him. What we can probably never know is whether there was indeed some medical reason for all the problems Henry's wives had in delivering healthy children, male or female.

By no means was King Henry VIII infertile, since his first three wives conceived within the first year of marriage and his first two wives became pregnant multiple times. So, fertility aside, it does seem that potentially, there may have been something about Henry that made carrying a child to full term nearly impossible for his wives. From our modern perspective, the sheer volume of miscarriages, stillbirths, and infant or childhood deaths in the Tudor household seems nothing short of horrendous. Research on the subject abounds and yet we cannot know if an illness was at work or if the royal family simply had a very unfortunate infant mortality rate.

Tudor England was not an easy place for any child, royal or otherwise, with 25 percent of newborns dying within their first year of life and 50 percent dying before their tenth. If a total count is taken of all King Henry VIII's children, including miscarriages, there would have been eight to 10 potential royal children. Three of these survived into their teens, and two died as adults. Two long-lived children out of 10 is not an unusual statistic for those times, but it also isn't particularly good. Furthermore, though history tends to remember Henry as the king with no sons, one of those three surviving children was in fact a boy: Prince Edward. Henry also fathered Henry Fitzroy and potentially other illegitimate children as well.

Some medical historians theorize that there was a problem with the Tudor king's post-conception fertility, however, and that it might be linked to syphilis. Syphilis is a sexually-transmitted bacterial infection that can cause long-term symptoms like joint pain and dementia – both of which have been attributed to King Henry, especially in his later years. In pregnant women, active syphilis can cut the odds of delivering a healthy baby in half. This would explain the late-stage miscarriages suffered multiple times by Queen Catherine of Aragon and Queen Anne Boleyn, who would have contracted the illness from Henry himself.

Syphilis has been a popular theoretical diagnosis for King Henry VIII mostly because it not only could explain problems in the birthing chamber but also issues with the king's personality. Henry was not known by his contemporaries as a "Mad" king, but many historians do believe the king suffered a trauma in early adulthood that affected his brain and temper. Considering Henry an unpredictable tyrant, an idea that is not without some merit, these theories portray Henry as a calmer and more subdued king before his accident in January of 1536. Knocked unconscious by the thrust of his opponent's weapon, Henry suffered intensely and never participated in a jousting tournament again. Months later, he called for the trial and execution of a woman he'd moved political mountains for just three years earlier.

If the accident did permanently change the king's personality, which cannot be proven conclusively, it certainly did not damage his libido. He took up with mistresses and remarried, producing a healthy baby in 1537 with Jane Seymour. After Jane's death there were no more reported pregnancies by any of the king's wives, though the king insisted he was virile and still able to perform sexually. But, in spite of assertions to the contrary that the ever-macho king made to his physician after not consummating his marriage to Anne of Cleves, modern doctors agree that it was unlikely that Henry could perform sexually at that point of his life due to his ill health.

Indeed, the fact that there were no reported pregnancies with Henry's last two wives seems to support later-onset infertility that had not been part of his physiology as a younger man. By his late thirties, Henry was obese, struggling with sores in both legs, and probably medically unable to consummate his marriages to Catherine Howard or Katherine Parr. If he did have sex with his last two wives, it was unlikely a common occurrence. After his annulment to Anne of Cleves, King Henry no longer spoke of the need for more sons. By that time, of course, he already had a male heir in the family.

Stress is another factor that may well have come into play in the Tudor household, since Henry's wives were immensely pressured to produce sons. Queen Catherine of Aragon became pregnant very soon after she was married to the 18-year-old king but delivered a stillborn daughter in her seventh month of pregnancy. Aware that her duty as queen was primarily to give birth to healthy children, including at least one son, Catherine felt immense guilt. She was a very devout Catholic and may have believed she'd done something to offend God and was being punished by having her child taken from her.

After one more stillbirth and the arrival of a boy in 1511 that died soon after delivery, her concern could only have grown more and more unbearable. She fasted to try to purify her body in the hopes of having a healthy child, which sadly could only have lowered her chances even more. Queen Anne Boleyn, in her time, was under at least as much stress as her predecessor to bring a son to term. Princess Elizabeth was considered a joy in that Anne and Henry's match was fertile, but the succession of miscarriages following that first successful birth sickened the new queen and made her fear for her position by the king's side.

Both Catherine and Anne chided themselves horribly over their failure to breed boys for Henry. This level of stress, potentially combined with an illness on the part of the father, must have made for a very difficult time in carrying any child all the way to term. Inept medical procedures of the time only made the situation worse.

Whether syphilis, Kell-positive blood, unbearable stress, or a combination of factors were at work in the Tudor bedrooms will not likely ever be known. Nevertheless, the mystery has remained one of the main legacies of the great Tudor king.

Chapter 20 – The Illegitimate Children of Henry VIII

Henry Fitzroy may have been the only child born out of wedlock that Henry Tudor acknowledged, but given the king's well-known infidelities, Fitzroy is unlikely to have been the only son or daughter begat of an extramarital royal affair. Bessie Blount's second child, a daughter, has been attributed to Henry VIII, as well as at least six more from other mistresses. Each of these children were born healthy and lived into adulthood, which suggests that many others were stillborn or miscarried, as was so common at the time.

Clearly, King Henry had a soft spot for Elizabeth Blount, since he not only provided her with a very comfortable life after her departure from court, but also that her son was the only illegitimate child Henry ever claimed as his own. Of the many mistresses the king took up with throughout his time on the throne of England, only a small number have been remembered as such, and even these few were only known for the parts they played in the larger political intrigues of the day. A small number of Henry's lesser-known love affairs are remembered only by the progeny they produced, though he would never admit to any such thing. He may have been proud to note that several of those children attributed to him were very clever, successful, and rather artistic.

It is impossible to track the histories of every one of Henry VIII's children or alleged children, but for many descendants of these people that tenuous link to the Tudor family is precious. In addition to Henry Fitzroy, there were five other children with a somewhat credible claim to Henry Tudor's patronage. Their cases were made either by a public affair or a private expenditure on the part of the king.

Thomas Stukley

About one year after Henry Fitzroy was born, Jane Pollard gave birth to a son named Thomas Stukley. This was around the same time that Elizbeth Tailboys, Bessie Blount's second child, was born. Jane Pollard was the wife of Sir Hugh Stukley, and like the majority of Henry VIII's mistresses she was married very near the date she gave birth, which does give the boy's later claim of royal heredity more clout. It was neither Jane nor Hugh who spoke of young Thomas' secret connection with King Henry VIII, but Thomas himself when he grew older. A contemporary of Princesses Mary and Elizabeth and Prince Edward, he joyfully paraded himself as the son of the king with no repercussions from the royal family. It was said that the young man resembled his alleged father, a rumor Thomas reveled in.

The Stukleys lived in Devon, but when Thomas came of age he moved north to Exeter where he became a mentee of the Bishop of Exeter and King Henry's closest friend, Charles Brandon. Thomas became a talented soldier and fell in with Edward Seymour, a powerful member of King Edward VI's Regency Council after the death of King Henry. Seymour was unpopular and had designs on the throne, however, so after his arrest Thomas Stukley exiled himself in France. He also served in the French military for a time before returning to England with a letter of commendation from King Henry II of France.

Upon returning to England, Thomas Stukley tried to gain favor with Edward VI by revealing a supposed French plot to recapture Calais. Unfortunately, John Dudley was then the main regent behind the crown and he used Stukley's information to manipulate Henry II into an uneasy truce at Stukley's expense. Thomas was imprisoned in the Tower of London as the creator of the French plot.

Stukley was released but faced trouble with debts and was constantly involved on the fringes of potential treason plots. He fled England several more times during his life and once told Queen Elizabeth I, whom he referred to as "sister," that he believed he would be a prince one day. Ultimately, Stukley was killed at the Battle of Alcácer Quibir, part of an ongoing campaign to ally himself with Spain and Portugal against England. The year of his death was 1578.

Richard Edwardes

In 1525, Richard Edwardes was born to Agnes Blewitt Edwardes, wife of William Edwardes. Unlike Thomas Stukley, Richard and his family were very quiet about their connection to Henry VIII, if indeed it did exist. It is difficult to say how Agnes came into the presence or service of the king, because the Edwardes family was quite poor. Richard was the only member of the family who received his education at Oxford University's Corpus Christi College and went on to be named the head of the Chapel Royal at Windsor Palace. Richard's luxurious education is his descendants' main claim to support his link to a rich benefactor – namely, King Henry VIII.

Richard became a successful poet, playwright and musical composer. This was a special achievement, not only for a man from a poor family, but for any artist who lived during the golden age of England's theaters. It was under the reign of Queen Elizabeth I that England built its first theaters and embraced the non-musical performing arts. Richard Edwardes was a contemporary of William

Shakespeare, having had at least one of his plays performed to an audience that included the queen herself. The title of his work was *Palamon and Arcite*, a play whose story was based on that of Chaucer's famous *The Knight's Tale*. Unfortunately, during the show, the stage collapsed and three people died.

Richard's play *The Excellent Comedie of two the Moste Faithfullest Freendes: Damon and Pithius* was also performed for Queen Elizabeth I during her infamous Christmas festivities of the 1564-1565 season. This time his work was shown successfully. *Damon and Pithius* is the only remaining play in print from Richard Edwardes, but several of his musical compositions remain in print to this day, as does a collection of his poems entitled *A Paradise of Dainty Devices*.

Richard died October 31, 1566.

Catherine and Henry Carey

One of Henry VIII's most controversial mistresses was the Lady Mary Boleyn, sister to his most famous queen, Anne Boleyn. It is not known how long Mary and Henry were lovers but the affair was a badly-kept secret at the Tudor court. Around the time the king married his mistress off to a rich husband, as was his way, the two were involved romantically which led to theories that Mary's first two children, born in 1524 and 1526, were fathered by Henry Tudor.

Catherine was the eldest child, Henry the younger. Both were named Carey after their mother's husband, William Carey. William was an important servant of the King and served as a Gentleman of the Privy Chamber. His family was wealthy and privileged even before Mary's sister became the king's new wife in 1533.

Both Catherine and Henry Carey were brought under the wardship of their aunt Anne Boleyn, which kept them very close to King Henry and ensured they were properly prepared for a future at court. Though the children no longer lived with their mother after the death of William Carey in 1528, they kept in contact until Mary Boleyn was banished from court for marrying William Stafford in 1534.

As Catherine grew up it was remarked that she resembled King Henry, and indeed the portraits believed to be her likeness show that classic shade of Tudor red hair. Catherine married Sir Francis Knollys, a politician who served under Henry VIII, Edward VI, and Elizabeth I, in 1540. She served as a lady-in-waiting to Anne of Cleves and Catherine Howard before King Henry's death, and then went on to serve in the court of Elizabeth I. Queen Elizabeth never mentioned Catherine's rumored patronage but held her in the highest of positions among her ladies.

Catherine and Sir Francis had 14 children. Upon the lady's death in 1569, Catherine was buried at Westminster Abbey. The plaque there relates her to Henry VIII only through her aunt Anne Boleyn

As for Henry Carey, he received an excellent education at a monastic school, worked with private tutors, and went on to become a Member of Parliament representing Buckingham. Henry's cousin, Queen Elizabeth I, knighted him in 1558 and created him a Baron the next year. As the First Baron Hunsdon, Henry had an annual salary of 400 pounds and oversaw the production of lands in Kent and Hertfordshire as well as the manors of Hunsdon and Eastwick. One year after becoming Baron, Henry was made master of the queen's hunting hawks. The job earned him another 40 pounds per year.

Henry went on to become the Lieutenant General of the Queen's army during the northern rebellion of 1569-1570. His troops were victorious and his cousin very generous in her appreciation. In addition to military promotions, Elizabeth I made Henry the Keeper of Somerset House, the estate where she had lived as a deposed princess.

In his later years, Henry Carey patronized William Shakespeare's theater group and had an affair with the very young poet, Emilia Lanier. He lavished her with money, gifts and comfort for several years until she became pregnant. In full King Henry VIII-style, Carey married his mistress off to a cousin in 1592, gave her a large sum of money and stepped out of the picture. His illegitimate son, Henry Lanier, was born in 1593. Carey and his own wife, Anne Morgan, had 16 children.

In 1596, Henry Carey died a wealthy and successful man. He was buried at Westminster Abbey.

John Perrot

In 1528, John Perrot was born to Thomas Perrot and Mary Berkeley. Said to be the product of an affair between his mother and King Henry VIII, John actually did grow to strongly resemble the Tudor king. He had rich red hair and beard and was thought to have the confidence and temper of King Henry. Though Perrot's claim to royal patronage was largely posthumous thanks to his granddaughter's husband, his is a compelling story that comes with a rather telling portrait.

The Perrot family lived in Wales, but upon his coming of age John travelled to England to attempt to make the acquaintance of the man he hoped was his biological father. He had the good luck to become part of William Paulet's household in the 1540s which brought him into view of King Henry. Perrot's career was looking up until Henry's death in 1547, but his case was taken up by the Regency Council of Henry's heir, King Edward VI. Perrot was knighted on the very day of Edward's coronation.

John travelled to France with an English envoy intent on arranging the marriage of the realm's young king with the daughter of French King Henry II. The marriage never took place, but Henry II immediately liked John Perrot and offered him a position in his own court. Intent on making a name for himself in England, Perrot declined but accepted Henry II's offer to pay off his debts.

When Queen Mary I took the throne out from under her cousin Jane Grey, John Perrot found himself imprisoned on the charge of sheltering Protestant heretics at his property in Wales. Upon his release he kept his head down until Elizabeth I took power. Under the new queen, Perrot once again flourished. He was put in charge of the naval ships of South Wales, and given the new post of Lord President of Munster, Ireland.

The Presidency of Munster was arduous and required Perrot to battle against constant attacks by the Irish against the Queen's authority. During his time there, Perrot hung an estimated 800 people who fought against him. He hated the job and quit without the Queen's consent in 1573, but was forgiven upon meeting with the queen at her court. Afterward, John returned to Wales with the intention of living a quiet life. The plan was of no use, since Queen Elizabeth had ongoing need of her trusted naval servant. In the 1580s, Perrot was sent back to Ireland as Lord Deputy.

The appointment was as difficult as before. Perrot faced revolts by organized Irish clans and spent years forging diplomatic relations with the Irish. He was ruthless, creating enemies on all sides. When he returned to England and was elected Member of Parliament for Haverfordwest in 1589, enemies in Ireland accused him of treason against Elizabeth. They produced letters, apparently written by John Perrot to King Philip II of Spain, in which the author wished to ally with Spain against the English crown. On the basis of this evidence, in which John had referred to the queen as a "bastard" on several occasions, Perrot found himself imprisoned in the Tower of London. He died there in September of 1593.

Chapter 21 – The Legacy of Henry's Six Wives

It is interesting to note that King Henry VIII loved many women over the course of his life but was incredibly choosy about which of those might become his wife and queen. Though Elizabeth Blount was widowed by 1533 and could have provided Henry with the chance not only to take a new wife but to legitimize Henry Fitzroy, the king had no interest in such a plan. He was similarly uninterested in a formal union with Mary Boleyn, Mary Shelton, or any of his other mistresses.

Henry put a great deal of thought into his potential marital matches, right from his first wedding with Catherine of Aragon. He had a specific vision in mind each time he married, though that vision changed drastically from wife to wife. Henry sought out charismatic, talented, and popular girls of noble birth who he felt could bring something to the office of Queen of England. This forethought perhaps shows the emotional side of Henry VIII that was forever searching for the right woman with whom to make the kind of family his own mother and father had.

Above all, the six wives of King Henry VIII of England and Ireland were passionate and intelligent women. Regardless of their particular brand of education, the various Queens of England next to King Henry Tudor were clever, charming, and hungry for knowledge. They influenced the future Queen Mary I, Queen Elizabeth I and King Edward VI, as well as helping reshape the way England perceived female rulers, leaders, thinkers and philosophers.

Catherine of Aragon was a beacon of hope for intellectual women of her age. She commissioned a book from Juan Luis Vives that was intended for young Mary Tudor: *The EDUCATION of a Christian WOMAN*. IT WAS RADICALLY FEMINIST FOR THE TIME, EXACTLY WHAT CATHERINE INTENDED FOR HER ONLY CHILD AND THE PRESUMED HEIR TO ENGLAND:

"From meetings and conversation with men, love affairs arise. In the midst of pleasures, banquets, dances, laughter, and self-indulgence, Venus and her son Cupid reign supreme...Poor young girl, if you emerge from these encounters a captive prey! How much better it would have been to remain at home or to have broken a leg of the body rather than of the mind!"

Catherine of Aragon is buried at Peterborough Cathedral.

The first queen's belief in female education would not die with her. Henry VIII's last wife, Katherine Parr, though Protestant, was just as dedicated to education for her stepdaughters as had been their true mothers. Elizabeth benefitted the most from Queen Katherine's teachings, not only becoming a religious expert but forming a love of literature and history that would last her entire life. The last of Henry VIII's queens was buried at the Sudeley Castle Chapel. Her remains were moved to the tomb of Lord Chandos in the 19th century after Sudeley lay in ruins.

Though very young and perhaps undereducated, Catherine Howard left behind a legacy of a different sort: that of the equality of the female spirit to that of the male. She was everything the king wanted and yet nothing he believed her to be. Though Henry and other men of his stature were expected to take multiple lovers, noble women were guarded carefully and punished for the same behavior. Little Catherine, left to her own devices as a largely ignored young girl, found joy in the company of boys and men and did nothing to rein in her natural desires. If nothing else, she proved to a conservative kingdom that women are every bit the same creatures as their male counterparts. Her death did not change that fact. The body of the executed girl was buried, unmarked, at the Chapel of St. Peter ad Vincula at the Tower of London, after her ladies-in-waiting wrapped her in a black cloak.

Anne of Cleves, Queen of England for only a few short months, is unfortunately best-known as Henry VIII's ugly wife. Looking more closely at her story, however, it seems possible that instead of having been unattractive, Anne of Cleves stands as proof of King Henry's unstoppable ego. In truth, Hans Holbein the Younger had only a fraction of the talent of future portrait painters, and none of his subjects were very well-portrayed despite his popularity as an artist. No one but the king and future biographers made any negative note of the girl's physical features, and yet it is largely this that Henry used as an excuse to rid himself of yet another wife. He may well have been impotent at that point in his life, having failed to impregnate the two wives who came after Anne of Cleves. Perhaps it was embarrassment and a general lack of interest that dissolved the marriage before it had even begun. Perhaps he truly found her unappealing.

For whatever reason, Anne lived a life of luxury as a reward for her quick-thinking and refusal to acknowledge the hurtful rumors about herself. She is buried in Westminster Abbey and memorialized there as a Queen of England.

As for Jane Seymour, Henry VIII himself recognized her most enduring legacy the moment she delivered little Prince Edward. It was the son the king had waited for through his entire reign, the reason he divorced Catherine of Aragon and lost his passion for the Catholic faith. Poor Jane didn't live long enough to see to the upbringing of her boy, but her good luck in producing a child of the male sex made her untouchable in the heart of Henry VIII, who cherished her most of all his wives. She softened her husband's heart to his daughters and helped convince him – though posthumously – to reinstate their births as legitimate. Her likeness was repeatedly used in court portraits with Henry after her death, even when other queens were on the throne. Jane was buried in St. George's Chapel in Windsor Castle in a grave King Henry had specially prepared for her. Following his death in 1547, Henry joined her there.

Finally, there was Anne Boleyn. The woman for whom Henry Tudor discarded his faithful and loving wife, detached himself from the power of the Pope of the Catholic Church, and declared England his own religious domain. Her legacy is unending, having produced one of the most beloved monarchs in English history: Elizabeth Tudor. Elizabeth's and Anne's blood are still connected to the British crown in a land that has long since welcomed and adopted its own special form of Protestantism. For her, Catholic idols were smashed, religious lands appropriated and countless lives lost – including, ultimately, her own. From Queen Anne Boleyn we have the modern monarchy, the Reformation, and the Anglican Church.

Her passionate affair with the King of England proved fruitful enough to keep England stable for well over half a century after the death of Henry's other two children. The furious king, now renowned for his unfaithful heart, may have killed his once-beloved mistress and buried her body in an unmarked grave at St. Peter ad Vincula, but Anne's title as Queen of England was revived under the rule of her daughter Elizabeth. During the reign of Queen Victoria, Anne's body was identified and marked on the marble floor of the church. Queen Victoria also had the spot at Tower Green paved where Anne Boleyn, Catherine Howard, and several others lost their lives on the executioner's block.

A memorial stands on the spot now, created by Brian Catling. Shaped like a pillow onto which the severed heads of the executed would rest, the memorial reads:

"Gentle visitor pause awhile: where you stand death cut away the light of many days: here jewelled names were broken from the vivid thread of life: may they rest in peace while we walk the generations around their strife and courage: under these restless skies."

If you enjoyed this individual book on the six wives of Henry VIII, can you please leave a review for it?

Thanks for your support!

Part 4: Elizabeth I

A Captivating Guide to the Queen of England Who Was the Last of the Five Monarchs of the House of Tudor

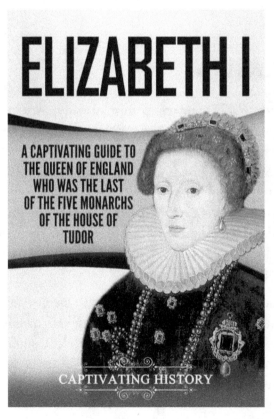

Introduction

The Royal House of Tudor was a formative dynasty in the history of England, Ireland, Scotland, and Wales. From the moment King Henry VII seized power from between the warring factions of York and Lancaster, to the last breath taken by Queen Elizabeth I, the Tudor monarchs fought hard to organize, structure, and strengthen their kingdom. Overpowered by France, Spain, and the Holy Roman Empire, England had come a long way from the chaotic days of the Plantagenet kings and queens to the economic powerhouse and cultural hub it was in the 17th century.

Elizabeth Tudor, daughter of the ill-fated Queen Anne Boleyn and temperamental King Henry VIII, was never meant to rule the country. Yet, when her time came, she didn't stumble under the weight of the English crown. Elizabeth was perhaps the most intelligent, forward-thinking monarch who ever sat on the throne before or since. Her reign is responsible for the strength of the Royal Navy, the cultivation of fine arts, the long-term stability and safety of her nation from foreign attacks, and the first steps toward international colonization.

Elizabeth's rule, while at times violent, was marked by fine art, literature, science, and theater that brought England finally into the Renaissance. Herself a highly-educated woman, Elizabeth inspired new generations of noble ladies to pursue education and become great thinkers. She also showed contemporary society that a queen had no need of a husband or king to be a perfectly capable ruler.

Under her rule, England and Ireland flourished, bounding out of the constricted era of the past and into a time of peace, prosperity, and enlightenment.

It is no wonder that Elizabeth's rule has been called the Golden Age.

Chapter 1 – The Birth of a Future Queen

Elizabeth Tudor's birth went smoothly enough, but the infant's very existence was cause for great controversy. As her mother, Anne Boleyn, went through labor and delivered her on September 7, 1533, Elizabeth was already many things to many people. To her mother and father, she was an accidental female who meant the wait for a son and heir to Henry VIII's throne would continue for at least another year. To millions of Catholics throughout England, little Elizabeth was the illegitimate love child of a king who'd gone mad with power. To the Protestants of the realm, she represented new hope for the future of English Reformation. Why so much fuss over an innocent baby? It had everything to do with her parents.

Elizabeth's mother, Anne Boleyn, was not the first wife of King Henry VIII. At the age of 17, Henry succeeded his father as king of England and Ireland, and a few months later, he married a Spanish princess, Catherine of Aragon. The couple struggled to produce a healthy child, and though Catherine eventually gave birth to Mary Tudor, the king stubbornly refused to accept a female heir. His desperation for a son led him to question the very legitimacy of his marriage to Catherine, calling on the Pope to declare their union null and void. The Pope refused, but Henry moved on anyway, publicly courting his queen's lady-in-waiting, the beautiful and charming Anne Boleyn.

Henry personally declared his marriage annulled, and he and Anne were married in January of 1533, Anne already pregnant with Elizabeth. Henry's new wife was crowned queen of England in July, heavily pregnant though she was, and the discarded Catherine of Aragon was moved to another estate and separated from her daughter Mary. Princess Mary was stripped of her title and forbidden to see her mother or father until she agreed to sign a document that recognized Anne as the true queen of England. She refused. As far as King Henry was concerned, Anne was his true wife, and she was fated to deliver his son and heir that very year.

Except, of course, Elizabeth was not a boy. She seemed to be a slap in the face to Henry, who had disconnected his entire kingdom from the papacy and Catholic Church, declaring himself head of the Church of England, all to marry his sweetheart and produce a son. Anne, who'd seen firsthand how her new husband had treated his long-time first wife in pursuit of an heir, must have been immediately anxious. All the same, Elizabeth was a princess of England, and she was treated with the utmost respect. Henry congratulated his wife on the safe delivery of their daughter and took heart that next time, surely, they would have a boy.

Elizabeth was the first royal baby born into the new Protestant England, though her parents had no idea she would come to rule it as an adult. Traditional bonfires were lit throughout the kingdom at the news that Henry had a new, healthy daughter, but in the minds of people like Catherine of Aragon and Elizabeth's half-sister Mary, neither Anne nor her offspring were legitimate members of the royal family. The Pope had never approved Henry's request for an annulment or divorce from his Spanish wife; therefore, all steadfast Catholics in Europe saw Queen Anne and Princess Elizabeth as nothing more than a celebrated mistress and love child of the English king.

Criticism aside, Anne and Henry went about their business, transforming both their court and the country in the first two years of Elizabeth's life. The new queen attired her ladies in the latest French fashions and held many grand parties in the palace. She swept away the remnants of Catholicism and conservatism left by the former queen and brought in modern décor, contemporary philosophers, and Protestant advisors. Elizabeth was given her own household of attendants to cater to her needs and introduce her to the new religion of England.

By the time she was two and a half years old, Elizabeth's future was in dire jeopardy. Anne Boleyn had miscarried a baby in January of 1536, after which the king appeared to lose his last vestiges of interest in the wife he'd worked so hard to win. By May of that same year, Anne had been charged and found guilty of treason against the king. She was executed at the Tower of London on May 19. Less than two weeks after Anne's death, King Henry was married a third time to Jane Seymour. She, like Anne, had been a lady-in-waiting to the previous queen.

Of course, this changed everything for the little Princess Elizabeth.

Chapter 2 – From Princess to Lady

Jane Seymour would prove to be the favorite wife of Elizabeth's father, though she died only one year and five months after her marriage to King Henry VIII. It was Jane's delivery of a healthy son in October of 1537 that solidified this position with Henry. For years after Jane's death, which was from a likely postnatal infection, the powerful Tudor king had court painters include her image in the family portraits. Their son, Edward, immediately became the focal point in the king's household, and young Elizabeth was put in his private household. Though still very young, Edward's older half-sister was expected to grow into her role as personal caretaker of the little prince.

Elizabeth herself was appointed a new governess in 1537: Catherine Ashley. Better known as Kat, the young girl's governess proved to be a lifelong friend and companion. She loved her charge and often remarked that Elizabeth was a good, gentle, and altogether intelligent girl. Kat taught her royal student various European languages, including Spanish, Flemish, French, and Latin. In the 16th century, Latin remained a silent language whose words only came to life on paper; nevertheless, it was an important common language shared by royals and aristocrats of almost all European countries. For Elizabeth and her siblings, Latin was an almost more integral part of their education than currently spoken foreign languages. She also learned a bit of Welsh from her beloved household member, Blanche Parry.

Though she was set up with servants, clothing, food, and education at Hatfield Palace in Hertfordshire, the former Princess Elizabeth suffered in title because of her mother's execution and her parents' marriage annulment. Now officially the illegitimate child that many English and European people had always considered her, the girl was now referred to only as Lady Elizabeth. She was removed from the royal line of succession (though King Henry VIII never intended her to succeed to the throne anyway), and was really only cared for because her father did not see her as a political threat. In a way, Edward's birth changed Elizabeth's life for the better, if only because the little prince was sent to be educated and cared for alongside his half-sister.

Both children received the best education. For Edward, this was to be expected, but Elizabeth's reduced station meant that her father's responsibilities toward her were much lower than they had been at her birth. The girl was incredibly lucky to remain in the royal household at all, let alone be tutored so well and in so many subjects. In Elizabeth's early youth, Kat Ashley was the primary source of her education.

Kat took it upon herself to ensure that the former princess was taught every bit as much as her brother and any European prince. Apart from languages, Kat taught her clever and eager student everything a girl of the 16th-century nobility should know to fit in with her social peers. Lady Elizabeth rarely saw her father, the king, and only saw Queen Jane once or twice before her death; still, she had to be prepared to be summoned to the royal court at a moment's notice. She learned to stand and walk gracefully, how to order her servants correctly, and how to greet other members of the nobility with propriety. She also learned how to sew, with particular attention to embroidery. For hundreds of years, Elizabeth's ancestors had spent endless hours embroidering, spinning, and weaving fibers into yarn and thread.

As a lady of a very wealthy kingdom, Elizabeth had little need to spend her personal hours spinning fiber and weaving clothing, but she was expected to excel at embroidery. This was the way contemporary noble women like her put their mark on the household. Elizabeth and her peers would have embroidered beautiful patterns or monograms on the cuffs of their sleeves, the hems of their dresses, the clothing of their husbands, and decorative fabrics around the house.

When Kat's pupil was around the age of six, the governess found that her own store of knowledge had been quite used up. It was time for a new wave of professional educators to step in—though Kat remained in the household as Elizabeth's primary caretaker. When Edward was old enough, he joined in his sister's lessons. Jean Belmain taught the siblings advanced French, while Richard Cox built their Latin skills and instructed them in current events. John Cheke taught the royal children scripture and Greek philosophy. She was described as "precocious" by at least one of her regular tutors, and Lady Elizabeth learned her lessons easily and had a good aptitude for each subject, including history, mathematics, theology, and music.

Elizabeth was by most accounts a star pupil, but her favorite subject was dancing. She excelled at her dancing lessons and would remain a fervent dancer throughout her life. At the time, dance routines for women and groups of men and women were being imported from Italy, Spain, and France to replace simpler English dances like the jig. Upper classes of the English population were expected to dance at any large gathering, particularly at court. It was a growing phenomenon that Elizabeth's own mother had embraced wholeheartedly, introducing many French musicians, artists, and dancing masters to England from the country in which she had lived half her life.

Three years after the death of Elizabeth's stepmother, Jane Seymour, her father remarried to a German princess by the name of Anne of Cleves. The relationship went no further than the wedding ceremony, however, and soon the royal pair's contractual marriage was annulled, and Elizabeth's foreign stepmother was dismissed from court. Later that same year, in 1540, on July 28, King Henry VIII remarried to a very young English girl. Catherine Howard, only about ten years older than Lady Elizabeth, became a favorite of the young royal daughter.

Chapter 3 – Elizabeth and the Royal Stepmothers

By 1540, England was no longer shocked by the marital antics of King Henry VIII, though keeping up on the news of his quick succession of wives that year was quite entertaining. Henry's choice of teenaged bride Catherine Howard was seemingly based entirely on his libido, plus his desire for a virgin wife. Though the young bride—probably only 15 or 16 years old at the time of the wedding—satisfied her royal husband in the bedchamber, her secret relationships of the past would be revealed in due time. Having no other mother figure in her life except Kat Ashley, seven-year-old Elizabeth developed a deep affection for her new stepmother.

Young Catherine delighted in the king's attention, accepting endless luxurious gifts of gems, gold, beautiful gowns, and even the lands that used to belong to Jane Seymour. By then, King Henry was not the handsome and desirable young king he once was. Catherine's husband may still have been king of England, but he was 49 years old, between 300 and 400 pounds, and extremely temperamental.

After suffering a nearly fatal jousting accident in 1536, the chronic pain and leg ulcers Henry dealt with turned him from a vivacious and sporting man into a sedentary man, quick to anger. The king was infamously unpredictable, except in his lust for young women.

Catherine Howard was actually a relative of her new stepdaughter, Lady Elizabeth, via the child's grandmother, Elizabeth Boleyn. As soon as she was established in the royal apartments, Catherine asked that Elizabeth be seated across from her at meal times so they could enjoy one another's company. The members of the royal family traveled frequently and so were often in different estates from each other. To remedy the time she missed with her little cousin while away, the queen arranged to meet frequently with Elizabeth. She doted on the girl and gave her many gifts including jewels and inscribed beads. To Elizabeth, still very young and mostly ignored by her royal father, the attention was life-changing.

For Catherine, her time as queen was short—but to a six-to-seven-year-old child like Elizabeth, those 16 months represented a formative period of life. After years of being ignored by the king, the former princess was invited into her father's home to dine with him and Catherine. It was the most parental attention she'd received since her birth. Six months after Catherine and Henry married, all the king's children joined them at Hampton Court Palace for Christmas and New Year's celebrations. For Elizabeth and Mary, it was a rare and touching family event that showed them they were indeed important to their royal father. Mary, having lost her mother four years earlier, was probably more desperate for a feeling of family connection than her younger sister.

Another member of the Christmas festivities was Anne of Cleves, the wife who had been passed over in favor of little Catherine. Now officially referred to as the sister of the king, Anne was extremely gracious to her ex-husband for his generosity toward her, and she fawned over the new queen and Henry's children. They all celebrated lavishly with food, drink, courtiers, and expensive gifts. Elizabeth and Mary, 17 years apart in age, had never been close before, but it was holidays such as this that cemented a certain sense of loyalty to one another. The relationship would prove tenuous, but intact.

By the next Christmas, Catherine Howard was in prison for treason, having almost certainly committed adultery with one of the king's grooms. She was executed early in 1543, and by July, Elizabeth and her siblings were introduced to their final stepmother: Katherine Parr. Unlike her predecessor, Katherine Parr was a mature widow who was not likely expected to produce more royal children. Instead, she was probably chosen by an aging, obese, and sick Henry for her experience nursing two former dying husbands. Though Elizabeth must have been bewildered by the sudden loss of her cousin and mentor Catherine Howard, she was immediately taken under the wing of her father's new wife.

The new royal wife had already raised stepchildren with her previous husband and showed a natural, motherly affection for Mary, Elizabeth, and Edward. A true reformist like Anne Boleyn, Katherine Parr was more of a Protestant than King Henry at that point, since the king had softened his stance on many remnants of Catholicism within his Church of England. The couple discussed theology regularly while Katherine massaged Henry's sore legs in her lap. In her, it seemed that finally the restless, libido-driven English king had learned how to appreciate an intelligent and empathetic woman.

As for Katherine's youngest stepchildren, she insisted on further guiding their ongoing education. As one of the most highly-educated women of Tudor England, the queen wished to pass on a great deal of knowledge to Edward, the heir to the throne, as well as his sisters. To help her youngest stepdaughter's progress, however, the queen had to smooth over an old rift between father and daughter: the removal of Elizabeth and Mary's names from the Tudor succession. By 1544, Katherine's gentle conversations with her husband produced their desired effect, and King Henry restored the title of "Princess" to both of his daughters.

The girls were extremely proud and happy at such a turn in their fortunes, and for Elizabeth, it meant a renewed vigor for study at the side of her stepmother. Katherine carefully selected tutors from Cambridge who instructed Elizabeth and Edward in advanced mathematics of the day, astronomy, written and spoken languages, music, philosophy, economics, and politics. Theirs was an education whose varied subject matter closely represented a modern syllabus. Interwoven in all lessons was the religious Protestant philosophy that Katherine found suitable for children of Reformed England. These spiritual teachings left a lifelong impression on both Elizabeth and Edward, though Mary remained a devout Catholic as had been her own mother.

On New Year's Day of 1544, 11-year-old Elizabeth presented her stepmother with a book that she had handwritten and translated from an original French book, *Le Miroir de* l'âme pécheresse by Marguerite of Navarre. The book, whose title translates to English as *The Mirror of a Sinful Soul*, showed every bit the devotion and belief Elizabeth held for the new religion, as well as the love and adoration she felt for the queen. In a letter to Katherine that accompanied the gift, Elizabeth asked her stepmother to forgive her mistakes and correct them as necessary. The cover of the book was heavily embroidered by the child herself, indicating the hours of work that went not only into the translation of the text but the physical presentation as well. The next year, Elizabeth made a similar gift to her father, this time translating Katherine's own work, *Prayers or Meditations*, into French, Italian, and Latin.

Elizabeth's intellect and work ethic were not something that her stepmother or her father found lacking. Katherine continued to supply the royal girl with the very best of tutors even after the traditional time passed at which girls stopped attending lessons. Personally speaking, Katherine was a strong role model for her stepdaughter at a time when females of all classes were, as a rule, oppressed. When King Henry traveled to France on a military campaign, he appointed Katherine Parr his regent—a role he hadn't given to any wife since Catherine of Aragon. Dutifully but proudly, Katherine kept council with her own advisors and met with those of Henry regularly, who were all men. She found intense distrust and dislike from the Catholics of the chamber but remained firm in her position. When Henry returned, she admitted it was a relief.

The king's health finally failed him by the end of 1546, and he uncharacteristically spent Christmas apart from his wife and children. Henry died on January 28, 1547, at the Palace of Whitehall, an immensely obese man who had to be carried in a chair by servants for many months. His crown fell, as he'd planned so carefully, to his only legitimate and royal son, the nine-year-old Edward Tudor. Princess Elizabeth and her cousins Katherine and Jane Grey went with the Dowager Queen Katherine to live, continuing their spiritual and practical educations.

Chapter 4 – The Teenaged Princess

The old king had prepared for the likelihood that he would die before his son reached an age appropriate to rule England and Ireland. Henry handpicked a Council of Executors of sixteen men, including his brothers-in-law Thomas and Edward Seymour, who would act in the young king's stead until he reached the age of eighteen. As for his widow and daughters, they would be provided for with extensive lands and annual pensions.

While Edward Seymour, brother of the late Queen Jane, wrested control of the council for himself and was declared Lord Protector of England, Thomas Seymour quickly proposed to the widowed dowager queen. After just a few months in mourning for King Henry VIII, Katherine Parr married for a fourth time to Thomas Seymour, uncle of the child king. It was a marriage unauthorized by the king or the council, and Princess Mary and King Edward were entirely unimpressed at their stepmother's lack of propriety. Mary even asked her younger sister to stop seeing Katherine altogether.

In fact, over a month prior to the marriage, Seymour had written a letter to thirteen-year-old Elizabeth asking her to marry him. When

Elizabeth rejected him in her reply, he made plans to marry the dowager queen, with whom he'd had a romantic relationship before she came to the attention of King Henry. Like his brother, who had a firm hand on Edward's crown, Thomas was power-hungry. He also may have had a true sexual attraction to Elizabeth, who was 25 years his junior.

According to recorded depositions from Kat Ashley, who accompanied her young mistress to Sudeley Castle in Gloucestershire, Katherine's new husband was entirely inappropriate with Elizabeth from the moment the girl moved into their home. Kat claimed that Seymour entered Elizabeth's bedchamber almost every morning, early enough to find her still in bed. Some mornings he would climb into bed with her, or play-act as if he was going to chase her around in her nightclothes while he wore a short nightshirt that exposed his bare legs.

Katherine clearly was unaware of the extent of her husband's behavior, for she joined him once or twice in the girl's bedroom and happily laughed while they both tickled her. The dowager queen may have believed—perhaps correctly—that Elizabeth actually had a crush on Seymour, despite having rejected his marriage proposal and claiming she was too young for such a relationship. Eventually, she asked the girl's governess to watch for signs that Elizabeth was involved with a man; Ashley saw no such thing but admitted the girl had a confused fondness for Seymour. The governess repeatedly reproached the master of the house for entering a maiden's chamber, but he only insisted he meant no harm and kept on visiting in the early mornings.

If Elizabeth had a crush on her stepmother's husband or not, she did have a strong sense of decency and propriety. She began to rise earlier in the mornings in an attempt to be out of bed and fully dressed by the time Seymour visited. In the summer of 1548, Katherine herself walked into a room to find her husband in a full embrace with the girl, at which point she made up her mind about the situation. The next day, Elizabeth left the Seymour home and went to live with Kat Ashley's family in Hertfordshire.

Despite the strange circumstances, Elizabeth continued to write pleasant, heartfelt letters to Katherine. The dowager queen, pregnant with her first child at the age of 35, wrote loving letters back to her favorite stepchild until giving birth that September to Thomas Seymour's child. A few days after Mary Seymour was born, Katherine Parr died from probable infection. Elizabeth, Mary, and Edward were left without a father, a mother, or a loving stepparent.

With the death of Katherine Parr, Elizabeth not only lost her beloved mother figure and mentor, but she lost the one person who had kept her safely out of the way of Thomas Seymour. Once his wife was gone, Seymour began once more to pursue Elizabeth's hand in marriage, which she again rejected. Unconvinced, Seymour forged ahead with a plot to wrest control of the kingdom from his brother, the Lord Protector. He wanted to kidnap King Edward and force his young nephew into marriage with his cousin, Jane Grey. He would then marry Elizabeth himself, thus somehow cementing himself within the inner circle of the royal family ahead of his brother. The plan failed early on, as Thomas was caught trying to break into the king's apartments in the middle of the night. He was arrested and put immediately on trial.

Unfortunately for fifteen-year-old Elizabeth, everyone closely involved with Thomas Seymour was also called to court to be questioned thoroughly by King Edward's official council. Councilors were aware that Elizabeth had spent time living in Thomas' household and they believed she was a willing party to his treasonous plan. At first, Elizabeth's concern was mainly for Thomas—a man she undoubtedly had conflicting emotions toward—but when she realized he had sealed his own fate, she focused on protecting herself and her governess. Both Elizabeth and Kat Ashley told the council about Seymour's continual behavior toward the princess and made it clear that there had never been any marriage agreement in place.

After several weeks of questioning, the council was not fully convinced of Elizabeth's story, but her consistency in answering questions forced them to move on. Thomas Seymour, however, was found guilty of treason and executed.

The effect of Seymour's death on Elizabeth was just as heavy as the death of Katherine Parr. She returned to her home without Kat Ashley, who was held in the Tower of London for several months before being let free. Elizabeth was sick with digestive distress for the entirety of her separation from Kat, and even after the governess came home, the princess was unwelcomed at her brother's court in London. For the next two years, Elizabeth stayed mostly out of sight of courtiers and tried to heal from the loss of her adoptive family. At the age of seventeen, however, it was time for her official coming out reception in London.

For her return to court, Princess Elizabeth was highly aware of the scandal she'd been involved in just a few short years earlier with the infamously traitorous Thomas Seymour. After the execution, Seymour's brother was replaced as Lord Protector by John Dudley, father of Elizabeth's childhood friend Robert. When she returned to the halls of the palace, Elizabeth wanted everyone—including the Dudleys—to see that she was a moral, chaste, and proper Princess of England. She put great thought into her wardrobe and chose modest dresses of plain black or white with no adornments. Just as she wanted, courtiers remarked on her modesty and piety. The simple garments were in stark contrast to the lavish, flamboyantly bejeweled gowns she would wear just a few years later.

Chapter 5 – A Flurry of Successions

Edward Tudor may have been the only one of King Henry's legitimate sons to survive his infancy, but he was not an exceptionally healthy child. He contracted several illnesses throughout his young life, the worst of which was tuberculosis early in 1553. The king began coughing in January and soon became fatigued, weak, and overcome by shortness of breath. With rising fever, Edward's legs soon swelled so large that he could no longer stand. He lay in bed in intense pain, hardly able to breathe until he finally died on July 6 at the Palace of Placentia. An autopsy revealed ulcers in his lungs.

King Edward VI was only fifteen years old when he died, which meant that he was unmarried and without an heir. King Henry, having written his daughters back into his will, had placed Mary next in line after Edward. Edward, however, had amended his own will very shortly before his death with his own intentions regarding the next monarch. The document was scribbled on with very messy and weak writing, accompanied by his signature. A very important—and apparently last-minute—change had been made in regard to his cousin Jane Grey. Where the text of the document had originally indicated that Jane's male offspring were part of the line of succession, a line and two words had been added to change the meaning. Instead of the crown potentially passing to "Jane's sons," it could now pass to "Jane and her sons."

For Elizabeth, there was not much opportunity lost, since her half-sister Mary would always be ahead of her in the line of succession. For Mary herself, that last-minute change to the succession affected her whole future. It was the same for 17-year-old Jane Grey, cousin to King Henry's children through Henry's sister, Mary.

There has been speculation that Jane's name was added to Edward's will by the manipulative hand of his Lord Protector, John Dudley. Even before she was named the king's successor, Jane had been pressed into an arranged marriage with the eldest of Dudley's sons, Guildford. Knowing the king was perhaps soon to die, Dudley had his son marry Jane that very May in an attempt to have the couple produce a son and heir. At that point, since there were literally no Tudor males available, a son from any of King Henry's daughters or their cousins would have been the first choice for the throne. Neither Jane nor her sisters, also pressed into advantageous marriages with aristocratic men, became pregnant by the time their cousin, the king, died.

Jane Grey, therefore, was Edward's first choice to take his crown. It was a slap in the face to his half-sister Mary, who had not only been close to him in his youth but had been the old king's choice after him. In retrospect, Edward had been raised Protestant while his eldest sister was a firm Catholic. Both Edward VI and his father had dedicated themselves to the new religion and the Church of England, an institution that had cost many lives and alliances. The young king was very dedicated to the religion in which he had been educated and second-guessed Mary's ability to work within the structure their father had laid out for them. Jane, on the other hand, had been educated alongside him and could be trusted to follow Edward's plans to the letter.

Sadly, for Elizabeth Tudor, herself a Protestant and a recorded part of her father's succession, Edward overlooked her along with Mary. In terms of religion and policy, Elizabeth would have been a fine replacement for her younger brother. So why did he pass her over for Jane? Perhaps it was as simple as needing a firm reason for rejecting Mary so it didn't seem like a personal decision. If, therefore, Mary was unsuitable as a candidate for the throne because she was still considered an illegitimate child of Henry VIII, so too would be the case for Elizabeth. So, both daughters of the old king were rejected by their brother.

Swiftly, to the terror and consternation of the girl herself, Jane Grey was declared queen of England on July 10 of 1553 by John Dudley and a collection of his political allies. At first, Jane protested, knowing full well that Mary Tudor had been the heir presumptive for Edward's entire reign. Dudley persisted, however, and the young girl eventually gave in to the wishes of her powerful father-in-law and his friends. She went to the Tower of London, as was traditional for a new monarch, and installed herself in her cousin's royal apartments.

Mary Tudor was not immediately told of her brother's death, but once the news finally reached her, she set off to London with a flock of supporters and her sister Elizabeth at her side. Their progress was so popular that by the time she reached the Tower of London, Jane's own privy council had already switched their allegiance. Mary was sworn in as the queen of England, while Jane, her husband, and John Dudley himself were arrested. Jane had only reigned for nine days. All were tried, found guilty of high treason, and executed on the order of Mary herself.

Elizabeth's older sister had waited to avenge her mother for years; once she gained control of the throne, she was determined to keep it. Jane Grey was no longer a threat, but her sister Katherine was   .

Therefore, the latter was imprisoned indefinitely. That only left Elizabeth as a potential rival, and Mary kept her sister very close. In 1554, Mary received an offer she couldn't refuse when Prince Philip of Spain proposed marriage. It was everything the oft-ignored daughter of a princess of Spain had ever wanted; she agreed wholeheartedly to the marriage, and soon moved forward with her plan to reunite England and Ireland with the Catholic Church.

The persecution of Protestantism in the kingdom was very unpopular, and before Mary's wedding to Philip of Spain, there were mass protests and rioting. When the rebellions were brought under control by Queen Mary, her advisors pointed their fingers at Elizabeth. She was convinced that Elizabeth must have had something to do with the rioting. On March 18 of 1554, Elizabeth was imprisoned in the Tower of London. Despite advice to have her sister executed, Mary sent Elizabeth to Woodstock, Oxfordshire, for house arrest in May. A year later, during what was probably a false pregnancy on the part of Mary, Elizabeth was released. She returned to her childhood home, Hatfield.

Chapter 6 – Queen Elizabeth I

Elizabeth Tudor spent her early twenties much as she had spent her young teen years after the scandal with Thomas Seymour: staying out of sight. Once more, it behooved the young woman to act and dress modestly, not only to convince naysayers of her innocence concerning the anti-Catholic riots but also to show plainly that she was not attempting to consort with her brother-in-law, Philip. His attentions were plain, especially when Mary herself, eleven years his senior, became terminally ill in 1558.

As the king of Spain, Naples, and Sicily, Philip was extremely interested in expanding his family's empire to include the British Isles. The marriage to Mary had been purely political on his side, though the English queen was very emotionally attached to her husband. Philip knew that if his queen died, he needed to quickly remarry either to Elizabeth, Katherine Grey, or Mary Stuart to retain his influence on the region. Elizabeth was his preferred choice.

For her part, Elizabeth was completely uninterested in the Spanish monarch. He, like her sister, was a staunch Catholic who wanted nothing more than to put England under the wider administrative powers of Spain. When Mary died on November 17, 1558, Elizabeth was her unquestioned successor—and Philip was out of luck. Elizabeth left Hatfield for London as an unmarried woman determined to restore the kingdom to its former state within the Church of England.

It was January 14, 1559, when Elizabeth and her entourage paraded through London on the eve of her official coronation as queen of England. She spoke kindly to the citizens who gathered on either side of the streets to welcome her, gaining their affection and trust. As had her mother, Anne Boleyn, on the night before her own coronation, Elizabeth stayed at the Tower of London. The next day, she was dressed in a lavish, golden gown with matching robes. The fabric was patterned with modified Tudor roses, the symbol of her family since King Henry VII united the houses of Lancaster and York in 1485. Her hair was long and red like that of her father, a man she would try to emulate from that point forward. The daughter of Anne Boleyn, the woman for whom King Henry VIII had reorganized an entire kingdom, was crowned queen of England and Ireland on January 15. The date was chosen by her astrologer, John Dee.

Though Elizabeth had probably come to terms with the fact that she would almost certainly become queen once her sister suffered multiple false pregnancies, she'd spent her childhood and early adulthood believing the opposite. At only 25 years old, she suddenly had the weight of an entire kingdom and family legacy on her shoulders. There were two immediate problems to face: the threat from Catholics within and without England, and the fact that she was unmarried.

The first problem could potentially be solved by addressing the second problem; Queen Elizabeth's choice of husband would either align a Protestant or Catholic nation with her own. Philip, for example, would provide Elizabeth with a strong Catholic army with which to continue to suppress England's displaced Protestants. A king or prince from Protestant Germany, on the other hand, would provide support in her plan to reinstate the Church of England.

There was an underlying issue that caused Elizabeth great anxiety, however, when it came to marriage. As much as she admired her powerful father, the young queen had seen him use an almost endless number of women to get what he wanted from them before moving on to the next. Her own mother was a victim of his wrath, followed not long after by Catherine Howard. Every wife of the great Henry VIII had suffered, from Catherine of Aragon to Katherine Parr, trying to give the king what he'd wanted. And none of those women had been given even a quarter of the power that Henry himself wielded. After a childhood and upbringing such as hers, how could Queen Elizabeth feel secure in any marriage?

To make her outlook on marriage even worse, Elizabeth had seen her own sister excitedly marry a man who'd harbored no love for her at all. Philip had insisted he be titled king of England and allowed to put Mary's kingdom under the heel of his own homeland. No matter how she looked at it, Elizabeth could find no clear answer. She knew very well that a contractual alliance with any man could at best strip her of her power and at worst rob her of her life. The queen was expected to choose a husband, however, and so Elizabeth adeptly appeared to play the game. Her first serious consideration was her lifelong friend, Robert Dudley.

It wasn't a great choice, because although the Dudleys were an ancient and noble family, they had no direct kinship to England's monarchy. Robert's father John had been executed when Mary I took the throne, and Robert himself was condemned to death but released from prison in 1554. Furthermore, Robert Dudley was already married to a woman named Amy Robsart.

Amy and Robert had married in 1550, and while Robert was imprisoned under Mary I at the Tower of London, his wife visited him. When he was released, they lived together on a small income. After Queen Mary's death, the Dudleys' fortunes changed for the better when Queen Elizabeth I made Robert her Master of the Horse. Restored to a position of importance, Robert spent the bulk of his time at court with the queen and her courtiers, while Amy kept her own house elsewhere. The couple saw each other rarely.

When Amy became sick with breast cancer and was found dead at the bottom of the stairs at her home, fingers immediately pointed to Robert. It was clear to everyone in London that Dudley wanted a real chance to become the queen's husband, but with a wife elsewhere in the country, that could never happen. It seemed to many at court that perhaps Elizabeth and Robert had grown tired of waiting for the ill Amy to die and arranged for someone to end her life much more abruptly. It's a theory that has been impossible to prove one way or another. Still, more contemporaries and historians posit that Amy, in a great amount of pain, committed suicide.

Whatever the true circumstances were around Amy Robsart's death, it tainted Robert's reputation and made it socially impossible for Elizabeth to marry him. Still, Dudley remained unmarried, probably in the hopes that the scandal would die down and Elizabeth would eventually feel it was the right time to marry. He waited, still at court, but no announcements were made. Their romance cooled slightly in the following years.

Meanwhile, the queen had other matters to attend to. She was determined to keep a close eye on the administration of the Church of England and make sure her religious will was being implemented properly. She demanded that every citizen of her kingdom attend church services each Sunday and that they use the Book of Common Prayer, which had been published under the rule of her brother. Though her expectations may seem very strict from a modern perspective, Elizabeth took a relatively soft hand on religious activity when compared with her sister. She repealed Mary's heresy laws and removed capital punishment from the equation.

The next big hurdle for the young queen came in 1562 when she contracted smallpox. It was a rampant disease at the time that either killed its victims or left them terribly scarred. Seven days into what was at first thought to be a bad cold, Queen Elizabeth was considered close to death. Delirious with fever, she told her advisors to make Robert Dudley protector of the kingdom in the event of her death, swearing that nothing inappropriate had ever passed between them. It was an order that never had to be carried out since Elizabeth made a full recovery. Only a few scars marked her face, and afterward, the queen took to wearing full white lead makeup.

Chapter 7 – Sir Francis Drake and the Elizabethan Settlements

Queen Elizabeth's denial of King Philip of Spain's marriage proposal, coupled with her re-installment of the Protestant Church of England, made for very poor relations between England and Spain. Each monarch wanted to prove theirs was the better religion and better kingdom, which created a sort of cold war between the nations. Meanwhile, King Philip had colonized vast tracts of land in the New World which sent unprecedented measures of gold and silver back to Spain. Queen Elizabeth and her predecessors had been very slow to act on the discovery of new land west of the British Isles, and without so much as a toehold in North or South America, England was completely behind the times. Thanks to the furtive and passionate efforts of a few skillful British explorers, the queen was finally convinced to invest in Western exploration.

Francis Drake was Elizabeth's most prized sailor and explorer. He sailed multiple times of his own accord to the Spanish colonies of the Caribbean and South America, excited by all the possibilities of the mostly unknown continent. For Drake, the Atlantic was full of opportunity in the form of Spanish and Portuguese ships packed full of gold, silver, and slaves. He pirated whatever he could and often sold the goods and imprisoned people back to Spanish colonists themselves. Pocketing the precious metals and presenting some of the haul to the queen when it suited him, Drake made a name for himself throughout Europe: The Dragon. Officially, Queen Elizabeth could have nothing to do with pirated goods belonging to King Philip, but she secretly gave her favor and support to Drake and his crews.

In 1577, Elizabeth met with Drake to propose a secret mission: The ruin of Spanish ships along the Pacific Coast of America and the pillaging of all valuable goods. No English subject had ever sailed the Pacific at that point, but Drake had been dreaming of it since he'd spotted the western ocean from high in a Panamanian treetop, years earlier. The sailor happily accepted the commission and set off at the end of that same year. His voyage took three years in total and took him around the entire span of the globe—another first for England.

During his journey, Drake claimed what is now California in the name of England. He also raided the Spanish ships en route as ordered and came home rich in gold, silver, and spices. Half was taxed by the crown, and it was enough to surpass the rest of Elizabeth's annual income for that year. Of the five ships and 164 men who left on the mission, one ship and 59 men returned to England.

For Drake's service to the crown, Elizabeth knighted him on April 4, 1581, aboard his ship the *Golden Hind*. Perfectly aware of the fact that her support of Drake's outright piracy against Spanish ships and camps could be viewed as means for war, Queen Elizabeth opted not to perform the knighthood ceremony herself. Instead, she graciously asked a visiting French diplomat if he would do the honors. Monsieur de Marchaumont was happy to do as the queen requested. Marchaumont had been sent to England to convince Elizabeth to marry the Duke of Anjou, brother to the King of France—therefore, he was very eager to please. In performing the knighting by proxy, the queen cleverly implied that France itself condoned hers—and Drake's—behavior against their Spanish neighbor.

While Francis Drake was happily raiding Spanish ships and causing trouble abroad, another naval expert, Humphrey Gilbert, had a different idea about how to use his skills. Gilbert was determined to establish an English colony in the New World, and he swore to the queen he would find a way to make it happen. In 1583, Gilbert sailed to what would become Newfoundland, Canada, and claimed it for the queen. Finding unclaimed land was a keystone of his plan, not only for the obvious reason that he needed a physical space for his settlers, but because he'd presold lots of land before so much as setting sail.

Gilbert sailed grandly into the bay and crashed into the rocks of Newfoundland. Fishermen from Spain, Portugal, and France towed the ship out and looked on in bemusement as Gilbert set up a tent and stuck a proclamation into the ground, claiming the land for Queen Elizabeth of England and Ireland. Unfortunately, it wasn't long before the over 200 pilgrims from Elizabeth's kingdom grew disenchanted with the cold, rocky coast they'd claimed. Soon after settling, they sailed southward in search of milder weather and were caught in a terrible storm. Gilbert was forced to regroup and return to England, only to be killed at sea during a violent storm while en route.

Queen Elizabeth passed the reigns onto Gilbert's half-brother, Walter Raleigh. Raleigh was a renowned charmer and handsome man who grew quite close to the queen. Also a writer, poet, soldier, and a member of England's land-rich aristocracy, Raleigh was a very popular figure at court. Elizabeth, always one to enjoy the company of a witty and intelligent man, took a strong liking to her loyal adventurer and rewarded him for his services by giving him a monopoly on wine trading. Elizabeth, still quite a young queen in her 30s, listened intently to the explorer's stories of exotic tribes, damp jungles, and a legend of a South American city of gold. It was, in fact, the legend of El Dorado that pulled Walter Raleigh back to the New World again and again.

Elizabeth loved the poetry and fantasy of her naval officer's stories, but she was still a pragmatic queen. She charged Raleigh with the job of starting an English colony that was well-positioned so that it might be self-sustaining. She hoped that the new establishment would be close enough to the gold-rich lands of New Spain to provide her own kingdom with regular income. Instead, while Raleigh headed off once more to explore South America in 1585, he ordered a select group of colonists northward—where he himself had never set foot—to establish a colony at Roanoke.

Roanoke was settled by Raleigh's colonists just off the coast of modern-day North Carolina in the Atlantic Ocean. It was incredibly important to Raleigh and his rich friends that Roanoke become a success because Queen Elizabeth refused to invest outright in the venture. Though she regularly invested in merchant ships and even the pirate fleets of Francis Drake, Elizabeth realized that there would be no immediate payoffs for the creation of a colony. It was a long-term project for which she provided royal decrees and permissions, not funds. Of course, she knew that Raleigh's earnings from England's wine imports and exports were going a long way to funding the project.

Roanoke, unfortunately, was a terrific failure. The first round of settlers abandoned the island, which Raleigh had named Virginia in honor of England's so-called Virgin Queen. A second round of settlers moved into the island in 1587, but by the time they reached their new home, it was too late in the year to plant crops. The governor, John White, was forced to sail back to England to gather more food and supplies. Upon his return to England, White found himself in the midst of a war between England and Spain.

The cold war had come to a violent end.

Chapter 8 – Mary, Queen of Scots and War with Spain

With every ship and able sailor needed for the war effort, White's and Raleigh's Elizabethan colony was forced to fend for itself. No supplies could be sent to the suffering colony at Roanoke until the fighting came to a halt. Furthermore, Elizabeth needed her best naval minds at home to keep the island safe from Spain's massive army of warships. She recalled Raleigh, Drake, and their counterparts and gave them vital roles within the English navy.

Robert Dudley had his part in the conflict as well. Through the 1580s, Dudley frequently spent time in the Netherlands to create an alliance with the Dutch against their colonial rulers, the Spanish. There was another reason that Catholic Europe was up in arms against England: the execution of Mary Stuart, cousin of Queen Elizabeth and deposed Queen of Scotland. Mary, a direct heir to the Scottish crown, had been raised in France with a strict Catholic upbringing. Briefly the reigning queen of France, Mary returned to

Scotland in 1561 to claim her throne after the death of her husband, King Francis II.

Mary's experience on the Scottish throne was not what she must have expected. She was constantly under threat from the many Protestant members of her council and kingdom, the most dangerous among those being her own half-brother, James Stewart, and husband, Henry Stuart. Henry conspired to have his wife murdered so he could take the crown for himself, but before the plot could be carried out, Henry himself was murdered. Soon afterward, Queen Mary's brother kidnapped her son and blackmailed Mary into abdicating in favor of the infant James VI. James Stewart declared himself regent over the boy, taking control of the country. Mary raised several armies to retake her throne but ultimately was forced to escape to England.

By 1585, Elizabeth had been host to her royal cousin for seventeen years. Though there had been animosity between England and Scotland for centuries, the royal families were closely related. Mary Stuart was a granddaughter to Margaret Tudor who was Elizabeth Tudor's aunt.

Queen Elizabeth wasn't at all sure what to do with Queen Mary, though the Scottish queen believed Elizabeth should support her cause. England's queen was not about to send an army northward to fight for someone she had viewed as a political rival since ascending the throne. While she considered the situation, Elizabeth provided Mary with clothing and basic supplies and housed Mary and a few of her ladies-in-waiting at Bolton Castle. It was treatment that seemed very hospitable on the surface, but Elizabeth was a careful queen who was ever vigilant over those who could potentially cause her trouble. Bolton Castle and other such estates became prisons for Mary Stuart, until intercepted letters between the Scottish queen and ally Thomas Babington revealed details of a plot to murder Elizabeth and replace her with Mary. Found guilty of treason, Mary of Scots was put to death in 1587—though the sentence was carried out before Queen Elizabeth herself gave the order.

The execution of a fellow Catholic monarch was the final straw for Spanish King Philip, who readied his armada to wreak revenge on Queen Elizabeth. Neither nation officially declared war, but both Elizabeth and Philip knew the time for subverted attacks was over. Francis Drake sailed to Spain's port of Cadiz and burned 37 ships, setting back the naval attack for another year. While Philip built new ships and gathered an army of thousands, he also reached out to Pope Sixtus V for support in his anti-British campaign. Sixtus not only spoke out against Queen Elizabeth but went so far as to grant King Philip the authority of the Catholic Church to remove her from the throne of England and replace her with someone of his own choosing. If Philip's army succeeded, he would have full control of England and Ireland.

In May 1588, 130 warships set out from Spain with 18,000 sailors and 8,000 soldiers. Their first stop was Spanish-controlled Netherlands, where they intended to pick up more soldiers. To reach the tiny coastal country, the armada had to sail northwards up the English Channel, where it was vigorously intercepted by Queen Elizabeth's own navy. The English fleet was fully prepared for the clash, with both Francis Drake and naval heavyweight Charles Howard, Lord High Admiral, ready to attack. The armada was pushed violently backward and finally forced to land in the French port of Calais.

On the English coast, Queen Elizabeth rode out to meet her troops in full battle armor as her father had done so many times before. Though she did not intend to join the fight personally, she realized there was great motivational potential in her mere appearance on the prepared battlefield. As was so like her, Elizabeth put great thought into her appearance and chose a suit of armor to make her appear large, strong, and kingly. The costume was a huge success with the English soldiers, and they gathered around by the thousands to hear her speak.

> And therefore I am come amongst you at this time, not as for
> my recreation or sport, but being resolved, in the midst and

heat of the battle, to live or die amongst you all; to lay down, for my God, and for my kingdom, and for my people, my honor and my blood, even the dust. I know I have but the body of a weak and feeble woman; but I have the heart of a king, and of a king of England, too.

Elizabeth had the advantage of ruling over an island kingdom that could only be reached by sea, and as strong and fearsome as the Spanish Armada was, even it could not influence the weather. The English navy attacked again when the Spanish tried to cross the Channel westward, this time forcing the armada north along the Scottish coast. Enduring heavy storms, the Spanish ships traveled up and over Scotland to come back around on the Irish coast. Many warships were wrecked in the insistent storm, while the sailors succumbed to sickness. The remainder sailed back home for refitting.

The Queen's military had been hugely successful in their defense of the kingdom, but the war dragged on for another decade in constant attempts from Philip II to capture England. For her part, Elizabeth desired to capture a few ports of Spain and Portugal but only managed to cause mischief with the same plundering as her captains had always done in South America. The death of the Spanish king and the succession of his son, Philip III, heralded the end of an expensive war that was, for Spain, completely unsuccessful.

By the time Philip III inherited the Spanish crown, Queen Elizabeth of England had retained her entire kingdom, seized innumerable goods from Spain, and gained the lasting trust and support of a large portion of the Netherlands. Unwilling to continue such a useless campaign, the new King Philip signed a peace treaty with his powerful neighbor. Peace negotiations between the nations took more than five years.

Chapter 9 – Arts and Culture in Elizabethan England

The first defeat of the Spanish Armada marked the beginning of the final chapter for Queen Elizabeth I. She was 55 years old, and any hopes the court and the country had held for a marriage between the monarch and a suitable man were long gone. Even Robert Dudley had remarried in secret in 1578, and the last serious courtier for the queen's hand—Francis, youngest son of French King Henry II—had died four years earlier, in 1544. Elizabeth was a determined spinster, "married to England" as she liked to say, and her youthful beauty had all but faded in the previous decade. Yet, perhaps still quite emotional over her first love, when the queen realized Dudley had a new wife, she banished both he and the woman from court.

As an aging queen, Elizabeth's goals for her kingdom became broader than they had been when she was a young adult. She had invested heavily in the military and protected her borders; her country was indebted 5 million pounds from the war effort, and the royal income was only 300,000 pounds annually. Nevertheless, the realm was considered secure and safe, which meant Elizabeth finally felt able to look toward the further cultivation of contemporary English culture.

The arts flourished during Elizabeth's reign, both for her own amusement at court and in the upper and middle classes of England. Miniature paintings, most commonly portraits, reached their height of popularity during Elizabeth's reign, as did the composition of lute and organ music that is now classified as Elizabethan in style.

A lover of art, dancing, and music from childhood, it was probably a great joy to the queen to turn her eye to the brand-new art form that had been imported from Europe: theater. James Burbage built The Theatre in 1576, and it was the very first formal venue in which English playwrights, actors, and spectators could come together. Burbage's own son was an actor by trade, and friend to scriptwriter William Shakespeare. The latter, of course, would go on to write dozens of plays that are still performed for live audiences, television programs, and movies today.

Queen Elizabeth herself was delighted with Shakespeare's work, commissioning him and his troupe to perform at court three times in 1595 alone. As was the custom in the rest of Europe, the queen did not deign to lower herself to the status of a mere citizen by appearing at the playhouse for a show. Instead, she would invite acting troupes to perform at one of her royal estates. Theater became such a joy to the queen that she ordered the formation of her own acting troupe called Queen Elizabeth's Men.

The Queen's Men were handpicked by Sir Francis Walsingham, one of Elizabeth's main secretaries. Walsingham selected those he considered the most talented and popular from existing acting companies, effectively poaching the best for the queen. Those who formed the final troupe were responsible for the bulk of entertainment in the royal houses, though the selection of their scripts was clearly the domain of the secretary himself. Queen Elizabeth's Men were granted salaries and uniforms from the queen herself; however, they were only allowed to perform in venues she thought appropriate, and act in plays that were politically innocuous. In other words, Elizabeth's acting troupe was expected to fully represent the crown, both in the ideals of its performances and the perceived nobility of the theaters they frequented. For the actors themselves, the salary probably outweighed the disappointment of artistic restriction.

Elizabeth herself was by no means restricted, of course. In fact, she invited William Shakespeare and his own acting company to court where she personally attended the very first showing of *A Midsummer Night's Dream*.

The queen's dreams of continental domination, however, were never realized. Having failed to conquer any lands on the European mainland, Elizabeth began to consider more untraditional methods of expanding her tiny kingdom into an international empire. The settlement at Roanoke in North America had failed, John White having returned to find every single colonist gone in 1590. The area in which Elizabeth's explorers had been mapping and attempting settlements, however, was still considered English land, named Virginia in honor of the Virgin (unmarried) queen herself. With American colonial efforts continuing slowly, Elizabeth turned her attention to the east.

Though Dutch and Spanish traders had been frequenting the Indian Ocean for decades already, bringing home exotic fabrics, spices, tea, opium, and other goods from as far away as China, English merchants were rare in the area. Seeking to remedy this fact, Queen Elizabeth issued a royal charter to the newborn East India Company in 1600, granting them the sole license to trade with Asia. Her decision changed England—and India—forever.

The East India Company's first years were very successful, focusing on classic trade goods. They brought tea into England by the shipload, transforming the tastes and cuisine of the once isolated, tiny kingdom. Elizabeth was probably 67 years old by the time she was presented with a cup of hot black tea for the first time, but she undoubtedly tried it just as she had previously tried smoking tobacco and eating potatoes brought to her from intrepid world explorers. Did she like it? Her opinion has been lost to the ages, but one thing is for sure: tea would become an integral part of English culture in just a few centuries. Future queens Victoria and Elizabeth II, both direct descendants of the Tudor monarch, would greet visiting dignitaries with a hot cup of tea and sweets. Today, even the word "tea" is synonymous with the British midday meal.

The trading company's influence went further than the spice trade, however. In the 17th and 18th centuries, the East India Company switched its focus from shipping goods to investing in Indian lands, a move that positioned British monarchs to colonize much of India by the 19th century. Though India is free of its colonial rulers today, the connection between the two countries has proved long-lasting. Workers, students, and travelers, and their home-style recipes and spices, transformed a land that under Queen Elizabeth I had been significantly white, almost completely Anglican, and used to a cuisine that was heavy in herbs but void of spice.

Elizabeth couldn't have known how exactly her queenly decisions would affect England centuries in the future, but surely she would have been proud to know she pointed her kingdom in the right direction to become a colonial empire, and a nation whose currency has remained one of the most valuable in the world. Personally, Elizabeth enjoyed her golden years to the fullest, smoking tobacco from the New World, eating endless sugary sweets, and enjoying a luxurious wardrobe so vast that she could only hope to wear each gown once. In her sixties, Elizabeth relied on her ladies-in-waiting to cover her face in thick white makeup to cover the scars of smallpox and the wrinkles of age, as well as to affix a lovely wig of red curls over her own very thin, probably balding locks.

Two years of the new century marched onward, marked most significantly by the treachery of a once-beloved courtier of Queen Elizabeth: Robert Devereux. Devereux came to Elizabeth's attention for his military prowess and was invited to stay close to the queen thanks to his charming personality. Courtiers remarked how the aged queen enjoyed the compliments and fawning of a handsome, accomplished young man—and this may well have been true. After all, Elizabeth was no longer pursued by suitors, and she knew very well she was no longer young and attractive. Devereux's desire for power couldn't be contained, however, and after an unsuccessful coup against the queen, he was executed on Tower Green.

Queen Elizabeth became quiet and depressed after the death of Devereux and several older friends, eventually moving into Richmond Palace at the beginning of 1603. She told friends it was the most comfortable residence for her old age.

Sick and lonely, Elizabeth had yet to name her successor.

Chapter 10 – The End of the Tudor Dynasty

To safeguard her position as queen of England, Elizabeth Tudor had spent her youth targeting cousins and relatives with potential claims to her throne. She was well-schooled in the history of the Wars of the Roses and knew how many years England had suffered before her grandfather, King Henry VII, had seized the throne and began the Tudor Dynasty.

At Elizabeth's coronation, there had been two Grey sisters left alive after the execution of Jane Grey, the Nine Days Queen: Katherine and Mary. Since Mary, the younger girl, suffered from dwarfism and was assumed to be infertile, only Katherine was considered a threat to the reigning queen. Both sisters were summoned to court to wait on Elizabeth, a privilege that would have been expected of family members.

When both Queen Elizabeth and her cousin were young ladies in their 20s, it seems likely that the former spent a great deal of time considering whether Katherine would make an appropriate heir. After all, there were no other obvious options, and it is possible Elizabeth had always planned never to marry nor to give birth herself. Katherine was allowed to stand directly behind Elizabeth in the royal procession—that is, once her mother had passed away—which signified her status as a lady of royal blood.

In 1560, however, Katherine fell in love with Edward Seymour and married him secretly without the queen's permission. By the time Elizabeth found out, Katherine was clearly pregnant and Edward was away in Europe at the order of the queen. Elizabeth had her cousin taken to the Tower of London, well aware that if Katherine delivered a legitimate boy, it could mean the end of her reign. The baby was a boy, followed by another boy after Edward returned, and in a rage, Elizabeth left the family imprisoned together for years before removing the children and Katherine for house arrest separately. The queen's cousin died in 1568, probably of tuberculosis, but her sons were eventually released.

With Katherine gone, and Mary, Queen of Scots executed decades earlier, there were few sensible options left for Elizabeth. Ostensibly it seemed that Mary of Scots' son, James Stuart VI, must inherit the English and Irish crown because of his connection to the Tudor family. Still, as she grew sicker and sicker in the early months of 1603, Elizabeth Tudor could not bring herself to say the words. When her close friend and lady-in-waiting, the ironically named Catherine Howard, died suddenly in January of 1603, the queen's remaining strength began to drain from her. The coronation ring which she had not removed since receiving it as a 25-year-old was filed off her swollen finger, perhaps having already caused blood poisoning.

In March of 1603, one month before Elizabeth's 70th birthday, the queen became acutely ill after weeks of undereating and dehydration. She refused to let the doctor examine her and stood for hours upon end, perhaps trying to maintain a sense of authority over those around her. She was visited by close courtiers and secretaries, one of whom remarked that Elizabeth suffered from visions of ghosts of people she had known. According to Sir Robert Carey, the death of Queen Mary of Scotland gave her the most pain, with Elizabeth crying out that she had never consented to the execution of her queenly cousin. Visions of Katherine Grey plagued her as well, the poor beautiful cousin whom Elizabeth had deprived of her freedom and future at such a young age.

The delirium, sickness, and emaciation of the great Elizabeth, Virgin Queen of England and Ireland, made it clear to those in her presence that death was coming soon. She continued to stand and refused to go to bed, probably knowing full well that once she lay down there would be no more standing up. Insisting that she rest, her ladies covered the floor of her chamber in cushions and convinced her to relax on them if not on her own bed. Eventually, Elizabeth could take no more and collapsed onto the cushions.

She lay there, immobile and mostly mute, for four days before being placed into bed, unable to argue. Her ladies played soft music to soothe her, while various family members and councilors paid their last respects to their monarch of 44 years. Her main advisor, Robert Cecil, asked her pointedly whether she chose James VI as her successor, and unable to speak, Elizabeth put a feeble hand to her head.

Elizabeth had never been particularly fond of James VI, though he seemed not to hold any particular ill will toward the English queen for her part in his mother's death. Her distrust of the Scottish king was softened in the first years of the 17th century, thanks to the wily diplomacy of Robert Cecil. Cecil knew that his queen was in her final years, but Elizabeth's refusal to broach the subject of the succession was something the kingdom could no longer deal with patiently. Corresponding personally with James VI, Cecil advised him in how to speak with the English queen so that he would be seen favorably.

Ultimately, Cecil interpreted the dying queen's motion as an affirmation and left her to rest. She spoke no more and died at some point between 2 and 3 a.m. on March 24, which was New Year's Eve of 1602, according to the contemporary calendar. In the modern calendar style, her death is recorded as having taken place on March 24, 1603.

After she passed away, Elizabeth was placed into a coffin, which was set with a statue of her likeness upon a barge in the Thames. The barge was covered in lit torches that brightened the queen's statue in the night. The coffin was placed at Whitehall Palace for three weeks before Elizabeth's body was interred at Westminster Abbey next to her half-sister, Queen Mary. The funeral procession in the streets of London saw the queen's body drawn by four gray horses, all adorned in black velvet. The coffin was covered in purple. According to John Stow, historian and contemporary of Queen Elizabeth I, the sight of the queen's final procession resulted in overwhelming emotions throughout London.

> Westminster was surcharged with multitudes of all sorts of people in their streets, houses, windows, leads and gutters, that came out to see the obsequy, and when they beheld her statue lying upon the coffin, there was such a general sighing, groaning and weeping as the like hath not been seen or known in the memory of man.

King James I of England had a monument built over her tomb, engraved into a likeness that wears an immense Tudor-style ruffled collar, a crown of gold, and a long gown. The queen lies on two tasseled stone pillows as if merely resting on her beautiful bed of fine marble. Four lions guard the corners of the bed while Queen Elizabeth I forever holds the orb and scepter of her office.

Epilogue

King James I of England was the first monarch to hold dual control over all the British Isles, a feat his ancestors would have envied greatly. Having survived an assassination plot that involved none other than Sir Walter Raleigh, James' welcome to the English throne was largely celebratory. Many courtiers and politicians of the time were excited for the change and eager to see what the new king had planned for their realm.

In truth, however, James had already arranged with Robert Cecil to keep Elizabeth's old advisors in place and bring in limited companions from Scotland. It was a promise he adhered to, which meant that there was no real sense of shift between Elizabeth's reign and James', except in one matter: the new king sought to unite the two kingdoms under one parliament and one monarch, permanently.

In 1605, King James VI, his family, and the entire English Parliament survived the attempted Gunpowder Plot of the anti-Protestant Guy Fawkes. His survival was heralded by the English and Scottish alike, endearing all Protestant subjects to him. Popular enough but never as well-loved as his predecessor, it was the succession of James Stuart following Queen Elizabeth's death that led to the Commonwealth of England, and eventually to the formation of the United Kingdom of Great Britain and Northern Ireland.

Elizabeth Tudor's decision to remain unmarried, to produce no heirs of her own, and to allow for what she surely knew would be the succession of her Scottish cousin to the throne of England, solidified the future of the United Kingdom. King James knew this and happily played his part in her masterpiece.

Read more Captivating History Books

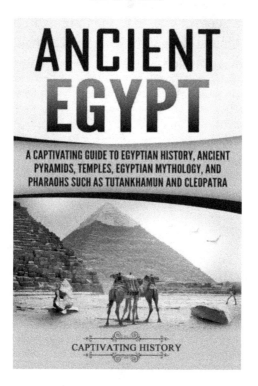

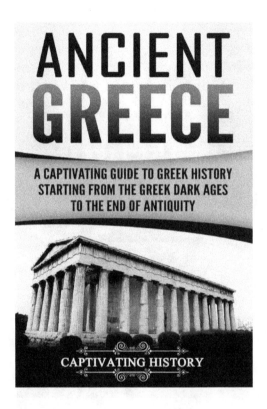

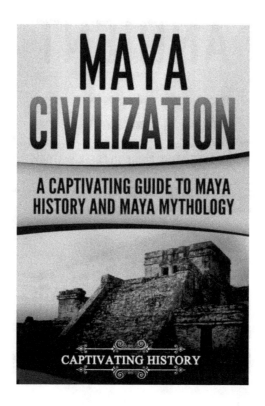

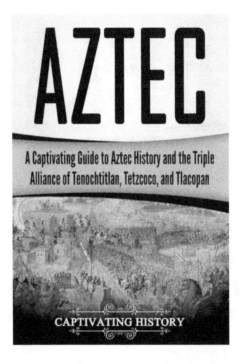

AZTEC

A Captivating Guide to Aztec History and the Triple Alliance of Tenochtitlan, Tetzcoco, and Tlacopan

CAPTIVATING HISTORY

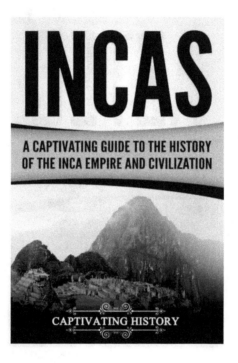

References

Brady, Ciaran (ed.) *A Viceroy's Vindication? Sir Henry Sidney's Memoir of Service in Ireland, 1556-78.*

Brigden, Susan (2000). *New Worlds, Lost Worlds: The Rule of the Tudors, 1485–1603.* London: Allen Lane/Penguin.

Cheetham, Anthony (1995). *The Life and Times of Richard III.* Head of Zeus.

Chrimes, Bertram Henry (1972). *Henry VII.* University of California Press.

Gairdner, James (1876). *The Historical Collections of a Citizen of London in the Fifteenth Century.* Camden Society.

HANSON, MARILEE. "QUEEN CATHERINE HOWARD TO MASTER THOMAS CULPEPER," *https://englishhistory.net/tudor/letter/queen-catherine-howard-master-thomas-culpeper/*, FEBRUARY 4, 2015

Harrison, G. B., (ed.) (1968). THE LETTERS OF QUEEN ELIZABETH I. New York: Funk & Wagnalls.

Loach, Jennifer (1999). *Edward VI. New Haven, CT: Yale University Press.*

Michael K. Jones and Malcolm G. Underwood, "Beaufort, Margaret, Countess of Richmond and Derby (1443–1509)", Oxford Dictionary of National Biography, Oxford University Press, 2004

Nichols, John Gough (1850). The chronicle of Queen Jane, and of two years of Queen Mary, and especially of the rebellion of Sir Thomas Wyat. London: J. B. Nichols.

Porter, Linda (2010). *Mary Tudor: The First Queen.*

Prescott, H. F. M. (2012). *Mary Tudor.* Hatchette UK.

Stone, Jane Mary (1901). *The History of Mary I: Queen of England.* Sands & Co.

Skidmore, Chris (2007). Edward VI: The Lost King of England. London: Weidenfeld & Nicolson.

Mumby, Frank Arthur; "The Youth of Henry VIII – A Narrative in Contemporary Letters

Letters and Papers, Foreign and Domestic, Henry VIII, Volume 17, 1542. Originally published by Her Majesty's Stationery Office, London, 1900.

Watkins, Sarah-Beth (2017) *Margaret Tudor, Queen of Scots.* John Hunt Publishing.

ARMSTRONG, C. A. J. (TRANSLATOR.) THE USURPATION OF RICHARD THE THIRD: DOMINIONS MANCINUS AD ANGELUM CATONEM DE OCCUPATIONE REGNI ANGLIE PER RICCARDUM TER CIUM LIBELLUS. New York: Oxford University Press. 1936.

Bergenroth, G. A. (ed). 'Spain: December 1495', in CALENDAR OF STATE PAPERS, SPAIN, VOLUME 1, 1485-1509, London; 1862.

Blakman, John. Translated by M. R. James. "Henry the Sixth. A Reprint of Blacman's Memoir with Translation and Notes." 1732.

Cheetham, A. The Wars of the Roses. University of California Press. 2000.

CUP Archive, (1923). *The Miracles of King Henry VI: Being an account and translation of twenty-three miracles…with introductions by Father Ronald Knox and Shane Leslie.*

ELLIS, H. (ED.) ORIGINAL LETTERS ILLUSTRATIVE OF ENGLISH HISTORY, series 1, vol. 1.

Gairdner, James (1880). *Three Fifteen-century Chronicles, with Historical Memoranda by John Stowe,* Camden Society, New Series, Vol. 28.

Hughes, P.L. and J. P. Larkin (eds.) ROYAL PROCLAMATIONS, Vol. I. The Early Tudors (1485-1553.) New Haven, 1964.

Kekewich, Richmond, Sutton, Visser-Fuchs & Watts (eds.) THE POLITICS OF FIFTEENTH-CENTURY ENGLAND: JOHN VALE'S BOOK. Allan Sutton, 1995.

Multiple authors. *Paston letters: original letters written during the reigns of Henry vi., Edward iv., and Richard iii.*

Recorder of London. *Historie of the Arrivall of Edward IV. in England: And the Finall Recouerye of His Kingdomes from Henry VI.* 1471.

Shakespeare, William. *Henry VI Part Three*, Scene 5 Act 6.

Stevenson, Joseph (ed.) *Letters and papers illustrative of the wars of the English in France during the reign of Henry the Sixth, king of England.* Pub. by the authority of the lords commissioners of Her Majesty's treasury, under the direction of the master of the Rolls.

Burnet, Gilbert (editor). Letter from Katharine of Aragon to her husband, King Henry VIII 16 September 1513. THE HISTORY OF THE REFORMATION OF THE CHURCH OF ENGLAND, Volume VI.

Calendar of State Papers Relating to English Affairs in the Archives of Venice, Volume 2, 614

Calendar of State Papers, Spain, Volume 4 Part 1: Henry VIII, 1529-1530, pp. 337-363, note 224, Letter from Eustace Chapuys to the Emperor, 6 December 1529.

Elizabeth I. "Letter to Katherine Parr, 1544." Transcribed by Anniina Jokinen. *Luminarium*. 10 Sept 2006. [accessed July 10, 2018]

Green, Mary Anne Everett (1846). Letters of royal and illustrious ladies of Great Britain, from the commencement of the twelfth century to the close of the reign of Queen Mary.

Hall, Edward. HALL'S CHRONICLE: CONTAINING THE HISTORY OF ENGLAND, DURING THE REIGN OF HENRY THE FOURTH, AND THE SUCCEEDING MONARCHS, TO THE END OF THE REIGN OF HENRY THE EIGHTH, IN WHICH ARE PARTICULARLY DESCRIBED THE MANNERS AND CUSTOMS OF THOSE PERIODS. CAREFULLY COLLATED WITH THE EDITIONS OF 1548 AND 1550, Printed for J. Johnson, 1809, p. 833.

Juan Luis Vives (1523). *The Education of a Christian Woman.*

Letters of Royal and Illustrious Ladies of Great Britain: From the Commencement of the Twelfth Century to the Close of the Reign of Queen Mary, Volume 1

Orchard, James. Letters of the Kings of England, Volume 1, 353. Halliwell-Phillipps.

Pascual de Gayangos (Editor) (1882). 'Spain: February 1533, 1-28', in CALENDAR OF STATE PAPERS, SPAIN, VOLUME 4 PART 2, 1531-1533, pp. 587-607. BRITISH HISTORY ONLINE http://www.british-history.ac.uk/cal-state-papers/spain/vol4/no2/pp587-607 [accessed 9 July 2018].

Rogers, E.F. (editor). Thomas More Selected Letters, 2-3, quoted in Henry Virtuous Prince, David Starkey, p143.

Wood, Mary Anne Everett (ed.) (1846). *Letters of royal and illustrious ladies of Great Britain, from the commencement of the twelfth century to the close of the reign of Queen Mary*, Volume II, Henry Colburn, p.193-197.

Armitage, Jill. *Arbella Stuart: The Uncrowned Queen.* Amberley Publishing Limited: 2017.

The History Place. "Great Speeches."
http://www.historyplace.com/speeches/elizabeth.htm